ST/ESA/251

DEPARTMENT FOR ECONOMIC AND SOCIAL INFORMATION
AND POLICY ANALYSIS

SUSTAINING SOCIAL SECURITY

UNITED NATIONS • NEW YORK, 1997

NOTE

Symbols of United Nations documents are composed of capital letters combined with figures.

The designations employed and the presentation of the material in this publication do not imply the expression of any opinion whatsoever on the part of the Secretariat of the United Nations concerning the legal status of any country, territory, city or area or of its authorities, or concerning the delimitation of its frontiers or boundaries.

The term "country" as used in the text of this report also refers, as appropriate, to territories or areas.

The views expressed in signed papers are those of the individual authors and do not imply the expression of any opinion on the part of the United Nations Secretariat.

Papers have been edited and consolidated in accordance with United Nations practice and requirements.

ST/ESA/251

UNITED NATIONS PUBLICATION
Sales No. E.97.IV.3
ISBN 92-1-130185-8

PREFACE

Social security questions have gained a new urgency around the world. In part, this is because personal economic insecurity has increased, or has been perceived to increase, in most societies.

The decline in the prospects for assured long-term gainful employment is at the heart of this heightened concern. In many countries, this fear has been validated by an increase in the magnitude and persistence of unemployment. At the same time, because of longer life expectancy, there has been an increase in the proportion of those who are beyond working age and who therefore have no current earnings to sustain themselves.

Most societies accept some responsibility for those members without gainful employment or otherwise unable to meet their own immediate needs. However, the resources to meet the enlarged responsibilities in this sphere have come under increasing stress.

In many societies, informal social structures, notably the family, have traditionally assumed responsibility for those who had no means of livelihood. However, these structures have themselves changed and are no longer so effective as safety nets. Of particular importance, families are smaller and have fewer members of working age to support those who are not working.

The social security provided by Governments as a complement to these informal structures varies greatly in nature and magnitude from country to country. Almost universally, however, government systems are or soon will be facing severe resource constraints.

The need for change and reform is clear. Governments considering how they can best meet the needs of their citizens must do so in the light of an increasingly competitive and integrated international economic environment.

Some countries have already embarked on reform of their State social security arrangements. They have shown that there is no universal solution to the challenges; the road to sustainability has to be attuned to each country's own economic and social circumstances.

The present volume presents specific experiences of a few of these countries and examines some of the common issues they faced in the hope that such a sharing of both practice and analysis will enable others to improve the effectiveness of their response to the needs of the disadvantaged within their societies.

Jean-Claude Milleron
Under-Secretary-General
for Economic and Social Information
and Policy Analysis

FOREWORD

In April 1995, the Department for Economic and Social Information and Policy Analysis of the United Nations Secretariat and the Universidade Nova de Lisboa agreed to hold a joint seminar on central problems in social security policies. The University kindly offered to host the seminar, which was financed in part by a grant from the Government of France.

The concept of social security is interpreted in a wide variety of ways, depending in large measure on the nature of the society that is being considered. For the purposes of the seminar, social security was defined as those public programmes that both support the members of society with inadequate earning capacity and compensate individuals in the event of either an unavoidable reduction or loss of income or additional unexpected but essential expenditures. The contingencies considered, therefore, included those arising from childhood, old age, injury at work, disability, sickness, health care, maternity, unemployment and death.

Seven papers were commissioned for the Lisbon seminar, addressing different aspects of this wide range of issues. Three of them dealt with central policy matters and four with different country situations. Each of the papers was reviewed by one designated commentator at the seminar and discussed by the participants. The present publication reflects the outcome of the fruitful discussions and exchange of ideas that took place at the Lisbon seminar.

All the authors participated in their personal capacity, and the Department wishes to thank them for the professionalism and enthusiasm with which they undertook their assignments.

Professor Jorge Braga de Macedo of the Universidade Nova de Lisboa kindly agreed to serve as the guest editor of the present publication, which would not have been possible without his extensive knowledge of the subject matter and his diligence in consolidating and editing the papers. The Department also wishes to thank its Portuguese hosts for their generous hospitality and support. It is particularly grateful to Mr. Falcão e Cunha, then Minister of Employment and Social Security; Mr. José Braz, then head of the Insurance Supervisory Authority of Portugal, who addressed the seminar; and Ms. Conceição Santos, who served as Secretary. The Department also wishes to acknowledge the very active participation of Mr. Colin Gillion of the International Labour Office and his gracious offer to contribute a chapter.

Mr. Geedreck Uswatte-Aratchi initially and Ms. Ana Cortez, in the later phases, were responsible for organizing and managing the seminar and producing the present publication. They wish to thank those who contributed by assisting the authors in preparing their papers. Ms. Atsede Mengesha was responsible for preparing the consolidated manuscript.

The reform of social security is an important and topical issue around the world today. The Department hopes that the present publication will contribute to that debate.

CONTENTS

Page

Part One
SYSTEM DESIGN AND GOVERNANCE

ix

TABLES

FIGURES

ANNEX

Chapter I

INTRODUCTION: CONVERGENCE AND DIVERGENCE IN SOCIAL SECURITY POLICIES

Jorge Braga de Macedo*

The present publication consists of nine papers contributed by a number of the participants at a seminar on sustaining social security held in Lisbon from 26 to 28 April 1995. Sustaining social security in today's interdependent national economies raises so many issues that any selection—including the one underlying the nine chapters of the present publication—is likely to be controversial. Social security reform has become a burning political issue in two of the countries for which case studies were presented at the seminar, while efforts in Italy and the United States have been closely followed internationally.[1] International economic interdependence notwithstanding, major policy issues differ from country to country. The process of economic and social development also brings changes to social security systems, which tend to require increasing government expenditures. The pressure for greater public spending may stem from too limited or from excessive coverage, from inherited inequities, from an ageing population or from long-term unemployment. Factors associated with developing and developed countries may also be present simultaneously, as they are in economies in transition.

The challenges that confront developing, developed and transition economies are very different in nature; accordingly, the present publication offers a number of case studies in an attempt to justify conceptually the need for social insurance. The need being established, it seems clear that social security cannot be sustained given the

*Professor, Faculty of Economics, Nova University, Lisbon, Portugal, former Minister of Finance and Chairman of the Ecofin Council. Comments from Ana Cortez and Jean-Claude Milleron on a longer version of this paper—which appeared as *Nova Economics Working Paper*, No. 275 (May 1996)—are gratefully acknowledged, but the editor remains responsible for the text. He also wishes to thank the authors of chapters V and IX for allowing him to significantly shorten their original contributions to the present publication.

[1]The front-page headline of the *International Herald Tribune* of 2 August 1996 read "America moves away from the welfare state", with two subtitles: "In a fundamental shift of social policy, US legislation stresses self-sufficiency" and "Europe, challenged by an explosive issue, follows debate but seeks other solutions".

1

combination of saving habits, growth prospects, employment creation, and fiscal discipline and demographic factors that prevail in many developing, developed and transition economies.

Because of the controversy over this question, however, the present introduction will not attempt to reflect all the views expressed at the Lisbon seminar. An alternative perspective on the reform of social security was presented at the seminar; it appears in chapter II below. In addition, the opening address by the President of the Insurance Supervisory Authority of Portugal stressed policy convergence within the European Union (EU), rather than the global approach emphasized here.

The costs of State ownership and planning, together with the costs of national economic autarchy, have been felt by resident populations at every stage of economic and social development worldwide. Redistributive taxation has proved to be less effective in market economies than was anticipated.[2] Citizens have become more sensitive to threats of increasing taxes to pay for allegedly universal benefits. Attempts to improve social protection may in fact stall due to the added uncertainty about who bears the costs of adjustment.

Indeed, calls for reform are currently being heard in most States, but there have been relatively few instances of regime change in this area. This reflects poor understanding of the benefits of reform and the costs of inertia. Once in place, a sustainable regime of social protection contributes to making citizens more secure of their property rights and their ability to benefit from the international exchange of goods, services and assets. In spite of several instances of popular resistance to social security reform, fiscal policies have been subject to closer scrutiny over the last few years, hopefully bringing about a more stable international economic and financial environment. Social security reform may therefore enhance long-run efficiency without sacrificing equity objectives within and among countries, least in countries in which downsizing the welfare state succeeds in improving its operation.

Since inflation is a major threat to a sustainable system, the same value of financial freedom applies to social security reform as it does to a regime change designed to acquire international policy credibility by moving to full currency convertibility.[3] There are, in addition, specific constraints on regime changes capable of sustaining social security reform. In fact, the constraints emerge from both the history of past policies and the expectation of future taxes. Even if all public expenditure were to provide social insurance—which remains no more

---

[2]This is suggested by Sinn (1995) and Kotlikoff (1995 and 1996), for example.
[3]Instances of a regime change as a signal of future policies can be found in monetary history going back to the gold standard; also Macedo et al. (1996).

than a convenient assumption in the literature—policies that cannot be sustained without tax increases elicit negative reactions everywhere. In open societies, reactions are more easily observable when they come from voters and financial markets (not necessarily in that order). The sustainability of policies without tax increases is thus required for their credibility in electoral as well as in financial terms. The reward for sustainable and credible policies at the national level is the ability to carry out enduring reforms. In other words, the signal that markets look for when unsustainable policies are spotted is the willingness and ability to start reforming so as to avoid more taxes today and tomorrow.

Conversely, a comprehensive and effective multi-annual fiscal adjustment strategy is the vehicle for social security reform and ultimately the convergence of living standards worldwide. If the fiscal adjustment strategy implies such short-term costs that the medium-term benefits pale in comparison, reforms may well be delayed and undermine national policy credibility still further. Global policy convergence is therefore far from being achieved and the standard is not universally practiced, but such reform is rarely challenged as a credible signal of sustained social security policies.

This basic perspective is illustrated in the present publication by presenting, alongside the introduction, an overview from the International Labour Office; the remaining chapters are organized into two parts. Papers dealing with system design and governance, with an emphasis on conceptual issues of social protection and the need to reform the pay-as-you-go systems found in most market democracies, are included in part one, in which management constraints on reform are also discussed. Part two presents policy analyses selected from diverse national experiences; each of the four case studies is intended to illustrate a specific instance of sustainability.

The Chilean reform of the pension system is assessed and seen to be easier to sustain than the traditional pay-as-you-go systems. The difficulties of gestation and retirement financing in Hungary suggest that reform may be even more urgent in countries seeking to complete the transition to mature market democracies. As these are newcomers to global policy convergence, uncertainty about who gains and loses is even greater. The narrow coverage and the variety of arrangements in Togo and in China are described and its costs suggested.

The cost of sustaining social security can be illustrated by a comparison of the two major systems of insurance against old age, the pay-as-you-go and the fully funded systems. The basic proposition is this. If the ratio of pensioners to workers matches the ratio of retirement years to that of working years, and if the rate of growth of wages equals the rate of interest, the two systems require the same contribution rate. If the number of workers rises, the required contribution

3

under pay-as-you-go systems, call it C^g, will be lower than the alternative, say C^f, unless a rise in the interest rate restores equality, or $C^g=C^f$.

A fully funded system may be a step towards privatizing social security, to the extent that—as Kotlikoff (1996) illustrates—it may increase efficiency and reduce the excess burden of taxation. Indeed, as the incentives of each system on savings and growth prospects differ, policy convergence at the global level may be reinforced by shifting away from pay-as-you-go systems. Moreover, when successful, privatization attempts tend to be imitated. Yet, in spite of the pressure for policy convergence, the way in which particular institutions develop varies greatly from country to country. Even if the existence of mechanisms of institutionalized peer pressure among States helps bring about the reform effort and make it enduring, tax decisions will continue to be taken at the national, regional and local—rather than global—levels.

The papers contained in parts one and two are reviewed below, with an emphasis on the issues of tax and social security reform. Section 1 makes the case for social protection; section 2 deals with managing social security systems; and section 3 highlights lessons from the various national policies reviewed in part two. After assessing the implications of the topics covered in chapters III through IX, section 4 concludes by analysing the prospects for global policy convergence.

1. THE CASE FOR SOCIAL PROTECTION

In chapter III, Söderström defines social protection as any attempt to solve the basic problem of consumption by a person whose working capability is reduced or non-existing because of childhood, old age, illness or unemployment. Even in a context of full certainty, any social solution will involve some form of pooling of resources within the family or any other group of people, including those with access to the relevant market institutions. Social security means that the State is involved in the process. While State involvement is pervasive, the family remains the primary pooling organization.

A four-period life-cycle model in which transfers among generations belonging to the same family take the form of gifts is used to underline when the best interest of all members is served by the arrangement. The result is compared with the one obtained through the market, in which a system of loans that crosses generation borders is implemented. It is not possible to say in general which system is preferable from the perspective, say, of the savings generated. But it can be shown that selfish individuals will prefer the family to the market the higher the rate of population and productivity growth and

4

the lower the rate of interest. Conversely, higher interest rates may tilt the balance in favor of the market.

The contrast with the State, in which the power to tax is introduced to facilitate risk-pooling across generations, is that the required transfers tend to be more expensive. There are two reasons for this. First, effort is discouraged when taxation is high. Second, uniform benefits cost more. Most actual experiences of the welfare state base the entitlement to their benefits on citizenship and not on merit, and provide these benefits in kind, equally distributed and financed by progressive taxation. As mentioned above, confidence in the redistributive ability of progressive taxation has largely subsided. To minimize the cost disadvantage, a significant role is left to the family and to the market. Introducing the State widens the choice of pooling arrangements but also raises the issue of public choice, in which different approaches to the role of the State can provide different answers to the problem of choosing pooling arrangements that are appropriate for the case at hand. Even the answer under majority voting requires additional assumptions about individual values.

Social choice ambiguities aside, the equivalence condition cited above included two strong conditions, under which, roughly speaking, population growth favoured pay-as-you-go systems, but this could be offset by higher interest rates. The precise conditions for $C^g=C^f$ in the notation above can be presented as follows.[4] If the target benefit rate fixed as a proportion of the average wage is denoted by B, then the contribution rate, also as a proportion of wages, necessary to balance a pay-as-you-go system is $C^g=BD$, where D denotes the dependency ratio or beneficiaries per contributing workers.

The fully funded contribution rate is instead determined by the accumulation of contributions $C^f w$, where w is the initial wage, growing at rate g over n working years, with a discount i to yield $C^f W$ Sum b^n, where $b=(1+i)/(1+g)$ is the ratio of discount and wage factors summed over the working years n, and W is the wage at retirement or the initial wage times the n period growth factor. These accumulated contributions then become pensions indexed to wages at a benefit rate B over the m retirement years, discounted back to the year of retirement, or BW Sum b^m. If the discount rate equals the rate of wage growth ($i=g$), one of the conditions for equivalence mentioned earlier ($b=1$), then capital accumulation at retirement is given by $C^f Wn$ and it equals the present value of the stream of pension payments after retirement, given by BWm. The required contribution rate is then given by the condition $C^f Wn=BWm$, or $C^f=B(m/n)$, where m/n represents the passivity ratio (number of retirement years over number of working years).

---

[4]World Bank (1994).

Clearly, another condition for $C^g = C^f$ is $D = m/n$. If wages grow at less than the discount rate used and $g < i$, this implies that $C^g > C^f$. The same result holds if $D > m/n$, the dependency ratio is greater than the passivity ratio. On the contrary, $C^g < C^f$ when the effects of inflation are such that wages grow faster than the discount rate ($b < 1$) and the dependency ratio is less than the passivity ratio ($D < m/n$). Shorter retirement years m and lower wage inflation g, longer working years n, more pensioners per workers D and higher interest rate i favour a fully funded system relative to a pay-as-you-go system, by increasing its required contribution rate C^g.

Even if this is the case and even if the market arrangement dominates the family, a shift to a pay-as-you-go system can be supported by a majority vote if the current generation is large enough and old enough. The reason is that the shift gives rise to a windfall gain for the current generation, and the older the voter the greater the windfall. This implies that there will be forced savings from the point of view of the youngest generation: the pay-as-you-go system will tend to be overdimensioned. Like the family system, it provides weaker incentives to save. As a result, it may be associated with lower growth prospects, thereby narrowing the limits in which redistribution can be implemented without threatening efficiency.

Adding uncertainty brings in two additional risks: a longer life and an early death. Both of these risks can of course be insured against, but an insurance market need not develop spontaneously.[5] Indeed, even if it does exist, the insurance market will introduce new costs as a result of unfavourable changes in behaviour, in particular moral hazard. Empirical evidence of health care in the United States suggests that patient charges succeed in lowering costs from 16 per cent of average annual income to about 10 per cent.

Compensation for permanent loss of income may involve a disability pension or, in the case of injuries from traffic accidents, car insurance. Temporary loss of income, on the other hand, is especially well handled by the family, particularly if the amounts are small relative to life-cycle income. Alternatives are loans from friendly societies, which complementary insurance is provided with limited potential for abuse of the system. As in the case of health care, coinsurance with a deductible or reduced premium bonus in the future limits both abuse and moral hazard. In the case of unemployment compensation, the incentive to return to work is weak throughout the EU, a topic examined in chapter IV.

Chapter IV begins by examining efficiency issues. Since alternative social security arrangements affect incentives to save and work,

---

[5]Sinn (1995) discusses this point; see also note 8 below.

and solve problems of asymmetric information in insurance markets, they affect economic efficiency. Indeed, these effects are as relevant as effects on equity, but they are less frequently stressed. The same can be said about macroeconomic stability and other conditions for sustained growth of interdependent national economies worldwide. They may be helped or hindered by alternative arrangements for social protection to the extent that they make domestic firms more or less competitive in world markets. Alternative arrangements, reflecting prevailing redistribution objectives, may also either promote or threaten social cohesion and enduring reforms. Mechanisms for multilateral surveillance may also be in place, and may help initiate and sustain fiscal adjustment and social security reform. While these mechanisms have been in place since the Maastricht Treaty on European Union entered into force, the cost of labour has remained excessive and unemployment high in most European States.

An efficiency analysis of old-age pensions and unemployment benefits confirms their desirability and the importance of the specific arrangements in force to protect against variations in earning ability due to either the life cycle or states of nature. There is a need for income-smoothing in both cases. For life-cycle income-smoothing, voluntary schemes are likely to cause the least distortions as long as there is adequate tax treatment of long-term savings. Although redistribution objectives often motivate pension schemes, they should be restricted to cases of life-cycle poverty. This implies, by definition, that no amount of individual savings can solve the problem. In that case, it should be concentrated on the old-age period, when the incentive to work is not affected. Nevertheless, it may be the case that retirees are richer than families with young children.

If the need for income-smoothing over the life-cycle and across states of nature cannot be neglected, the same applies to savings promotion. When the savings rate is too low, some forced savings may be desirable. Otherwise, investment and the growth rate will be lower. But this does not imply that the system should be publicly run, either as a fully funded or pay-as-you-go system. Indeed, it is debatable whether the method of financing makes a difference or not. Take the pay-as-you-go system. On the one hand, the windfall gain on the first generations of pensioners would lead them to reduce savings in life-cycle terms. On the other hand, if the savings rate of the young is too low, a mandatory payroll tax may reduce consumption. Retirement behaviour will also be affected, and the final result may well be a reduction in national savings. Conversely, if people would save less without a mandatory level set by the Government, then a fully funded system would have the opposite effect. But whether or not savings translate into higher investment and growth depends crucially on the

7

management of the funds: if the funds are mismanaged, additional private savings will be offset by public dissaving.

Independently of the funding method, insufficient savings may also be the result of moral hazard, so that people above the life-cycle poverty level may choose to become a burden on society—so-called "learned helplessness". Insurance against this problem should be financed by general taxation. Everybody—not just workers—should contribute, but only for a minimum pension.

The existence of market failures is clearly established in connection with insurance against these variations in earnings ability, but the same is true of government failures. Estimates of the value to American consumers of stabilizing aggregate consumption are less than one per cent of gross national product, whereas the cost of individual consumption instability has been estimated to be 10 times larger in the United States institutional setting. A major risk is unanticipated inflation: the only remedy against it is macroeconomic stability. Uncertainty about the time of death—already examined in chapter III—can be addressed by an annuity scheme, but again, it would not be possible for private markets to hedge against inflation.

The effects on the labour market are likely to be most negative when the link between benefits and contributions is perceived to be vague, as it would under general taxation or even a payroll tax.[6] In a system designed to minimize the excess burden of taxation, there is no reason to finance pensions through a payroll tax. The suggestion of replacing it by a higher value added tax may or may not be appropriate, depending on the incidence of taxation in very open economies, taking into account the incentives for tax evasion. The effect of old-age pensions on labour supply is also debatable; it is perhaps more likely to be negative.

The mobility of the labour force also has a bearing on the vesting periods and the portability of rights, a point discussed by Braz (1995) in the EU context. In general, if a basic scheme exists and firms induce a longer relationship with their workers by offering a complementary occupational plan, then the effect is likely to be positive. In any event, retirement rules that ignore a large amount of information about the past history of each person may penalize a gradual phasing-out from the labour market and be more prone to strategic behavior.

As for smoothing income across states of nature, this has considerable economic value for risk-averse individuals. Like inflation, unemployment has a macroeconomic dimension. If it can hit anybody in the economy, it is not amenable to pooling and the solution can be provided only by general taxation. Unlike inflation, however, adverse

---

[6]Kotlikoff (1995 and 1996) states that, in conjunction with a progressive income tax, an unlinked social security payroll tax is highly distortionary.

selection is very relevant in designing unemployment benefits. Some people are simply worse risks than others, and it may not be possible for private firms to monitor the relevant information. The availability of a past record on employment might alleviate this problem. But some groups are red-lined and will not obtain insurance at any price.[7] Making insurance mandatory, as in car accidents, would make a pooling equilibrium possible. And again, a last-resort public scheme would be needed to insure those that no company will accept.

Since some workers may well decide to be unemployed, moral hazard becomes a more difficult problem to solve. This is why a general unemployment insurance scheme cannot be run by private markets, especially with a replacement rate close to one. The only way to avoid this poverty trap is to offer only partial insurance, a low replacement rate and well defined eligibility conditions, possibly defined as a function of the individual's past history. Compensation may thus decrease with the length of the unemployment period and benefits be smaller the shorter the last unemployment spell. When combining both schemes, some of the negative properties may be avoided by providing access to liquidity schemes for pensions combined with partial unemployment insurance.

2. MANAGING SOCIAL SECURITY SYSTEMS

In chapter IV problems of governance motivate social security reform. Such problems too are specific to institutional set-ups and management procedures, but there are certain broad principles that apply to most mature market democracies: a universal, compulsory public system, financed through a payroll tax and general tax revenue on a pay-as-you-go basis. Among EU countries, in addition, multilateral surveillance procedures have been implemented to facilitate progress towards a medium-term orientation of macroeconomic policy. Price stability and sound finances reinforce the medium-term strategy contained in the 1993 *White Paper on Growth, Competitiveness and Employment*, and facilitate the reform of social security systems, together with a better functioning of labour and capital markets.[8]

In this regard, the importance of appropriate budgetary procedures cannot be overlooked, especially because these continue to be the responsibility of member States or of their local authorities.

---

[7]Based on OECD cross-section evidence, Sinn (1995) claims that 85 per cent of social insurance covers risks for which no private insurance would have been available. He interprets all public expenditure as providing social insurance.

[8]This point is developed in the chapter by the author contained in Macedo et al. (1996), which also draws on the Portuguese contribution to the *White Paper* submitted by the Ministry of Finance and reproduced in Commission of the European Communities (1993).

Among these procedures, a multi-annual fiscal adjustment strategy may be the most effective commitment technology.[9] By signaling the credibility of policy to national voters and social partners and to international financial markets, it may help to ensure that the authority that represents the collective interest in the efficiency of the public sector is able to dominate. This translates into a precondition for sustaining social security to the extent that contributions, even if earmarked, are part of the tax burden faced by present and future taxpayers.

Accounting procedures consistent with intertemporal balance have been presented in the United States Federal Budget for a number of years, and have been developed for several countries at different stages of economic development.[10] Generational accounts are based on the constraint that the present value of taxes paid net of transfers received equals government spending plus debt, since government capital is valued at the present value of its imputed rent. By distinguishing net taxes paid by each generation, it is possible to compare their respective lifetime net tax burdens.

Available estimates for the United States and other developed countries show a clear bias against future generations, largely due to the increase in social security and health-care annuities paid to the elderly. The decline in savings that has been observed in the United States is also explained in this way.[11] Expressing the taxes of future generations as a percentage of those of newborns, Kotlikoff (1996) produces figures of about 200 per cent for the United States and 300 per cent for Italy. The lowest figure is about 130 per cent for Germany. The bias against future generations remains when the public debt is set to zero, but the extra burden falls to 182 per cent, 164 per cent and 102 per cent in the United States, Italy and Germany, respectively.

The existence of taxation biases among generations as well as within each life cycle suggests that the present and future fiscal stance needs monitoring by the financial community, especially when budgetary procedures do not favour the existence of a fiscal adjustment strategy, let alone its implementation. Estimates of the debt implicit in unfunded pension liabilities in Europe show that it may be as large as the explicit debt.[12] And this is not the only case in which the

---

[9]The approach of von Hagen and Harden (1994) is used in section 4 below.
[10]The method due to Kotlikoff is briefly acknowledged in World Bank (1994), p. 135.
[11]The international comparisons are from Kotlikoff (1996). Gokhale, Kotlikoff and Sabelhaus (1995) conclude their extensive simulations by tracing the decline to two factors: government redistribution from current young and future generations to current older ones and a sharp increase in the propensity of older Americans to consume out of their remaining lifetime resources.
[12]The estimates of the hidden public debt contained in the influential 1993 report of Crédit Suisse First Boston are discussed in chapter IV below.

distinction between private and public sectors may become blurred. There are many others, especially in the countries in transition from State planning. Monitoring efforts become all the more demanding since normal multilateral surveillance procedures, including the structural adjustment programmes of the International Monetary Fund and the World Bank, concentrate on external balance. With respect to internal balance, there is the excessive deficit procedure included in the Maastricht Treaty, which is required for member States and highly recommended for those wishing to join.[13]

In chapter V, Pak and others discuss four major concerns in the management of social security systems: cost, access, funds and regulation. With respect to cost, it varies with the number of social risks that the system seeks to cover. Less developed countries ought to avoid too ambitious a coverage, since the trend towards in-kind benefits and preventive measures puts a strong upward pressure on costs. Given coverage, however, protecting the purchasing power of future payments becomes crucial in managing social security funds, since general tax and insurance premiums both contribute to financing. Although these objectives also vary with the level of development, avoiding their depletion is essential for sustaining social security.

Universal coverage requires cost-efficient, equitable and sustainable systems, and those are not easy to find in practice. The implications for access are clear-cut. Improvements in regulation involving combinations of private and public methods are called for, to the extent that they improve the management of the system. Indeed, privatization can increase equality rather than reduce it, and regulation that is too strong can be damaging.

Policy rules supported by institutions able to protect the interests of current and future taxpayers are thus required for good governance. Awareness of the sustainability of fiscal policies (including social security policies) is in turn centred around the Government's intertemporal budget constraint. If health care is provided by the Government to the public on a pay-as-you-go basis by a proportional payroll tax levied on all earnings, for example, the four fundamental elements of fiscal policy are present:

(a) Level and composition of government spending: purchases of health-care services from health-care providers;

(b) The distribution of the fiscal burden across and within generations: to those who are retired at the time the programme is initiated away from generations coming behind, and from high to low earners within generations who are in their working years (assuming the usage of medical services at a given age is independent of earnings);

---

[13]The argument is developed in Branson and Macedo (1995).

11

(c) The structure of economic incentives: the incentive to work is reduced since paying additional payroll taxes leads to no additional health-care benefits;

(d) The Government's pooling of economic risks: in this case across the population, in a way that differs from the private health insurance market (where smokers are not pooled with non-smokers).[14]

Because institutions may well obfuscate the fiscal fundamentals, especially the sustainability of given policies, monitoring by voters and international organizations helps to raise social awareness about future taxes.[15] Such institutional checks on budget illusion apply to the budget as the focal point of conflict resolution. They encompass the United States health-care reform, replacing the prevailing single-pillar public pension scheme with three pillars, the second of which is private but mandatory and the third of which is voluntary, as proposed by the World Bank (1994). But budgetary institutions oriented to the avoidance of excessive future taxation will not take hold unless current voters appreciate the unsustainability of current policies. The convergence criteria included in the Maastricht Treaty can be seen in this light, even though the debt sustainability condition from which they emerge does not capture the effects on fiscal policy within and among generations.

3. LESSONS FROM DIVERSE NATIONAL POLICIES

Part two begins with an assessment of Chilean social security by Cortázar.[16] The reform of the pension system in 1981 has been widely discussed, and its lessons for other countries are sometimes seen as the driving force behind World Bank (1994).[17] In that vein, some authors take pains to explain how difficult it would be to apply the lessons to, say, the United States because of the different political, institutional and even financial traditions of the two countries.[18] The case-study method followed in chapters VI through IX should not lead to any misunderstanding, since none of the selected cases is presented as a model for other countries to follow or avoid. Rather, they are simply specific instances of achieved or required reform.

---

[14]This example and the previous point about privatization are elaborated in Kotlikoff (1995 and 1996).

[15]Ignoring the intertemporal government budget constraint is only one manifestation of the "deficit illusion" identified by Branson and Macedo (1995); see also reference in note 9 above.

[16]Robert Myers and Peter Diamond in Diamond et al. (1996), as well as Kotlikoff (1995 and 1996), begin with a review of the Chilean case.

[17]See paper by Estelle James, the main author of World Bank (1994), in Diamond et al. (1996).

18See the comment by Dalmer Hoskins on Estelle James, and also a comment by Alicia Munnell in Diamond et al. (1996).

The change was from a pay-as-you-go system to a privately managed mandatory savings programme coupled with a mechanism that, upon a worker's retirement, converts the funds accumulated in the savings account into indexed annuities. It is too early to evaluate the benefits of the new system, since only about 10 per cent of retired workers belong to it and the value of their pensions has been strongly influenced by the way the Government has acknowledged their contributions to the old system. Nevertheless, the high rates of return obtained so far, if maintained, should guarantee a replacement rate of over 70 per cent. The system was also supposed to facilitate the workings of the labour market by making workers more conscious of the connection between their contributions and the pensions that they will receive in the future, thus reducing evasion and increasing coverage. The induced employment-creating effects will be weak, however, if most workers enjoy only the minimum pension and heavily discount its present value, because their current consumption is constrained by their current money holdings.

Against these benefits, the operating costs of such privately managed systems have been seen to be much higher than in a government-run system. This is inevitable due to the absence of economies of scale present in a system without individual free choice. Advertising costs, costs of managing millions of personal accounts and the absence of sensitivity to price variations—which is typical of insurance markets—explains positive mark-ups by providers. Indeed, insufficient awareness about returns and fees makes providers use gifts and forms of current consumption to attract customers. Management costs may be reduced by group choice and long-term contracts; these are alternatives being explored at the moment.

The effects of the pension funds, which are worth nearly one half of gross domestic product, on deepening capital markets is beyond dispute. Fears that this may unduly increase the concentration of wealth, however, have led to more careful regulation of conflicts of interest and a gradual expansion of the assets eligible for investment.

The political economy implications of the Chilean reform are new rules for redistribution, with four characteristics. First, regressive redistribution becomes more unlikely. Funds are no longer taxed to redistribute benefits to specific groups based on their political clout. The requirement that redistribution be transparent makes demonstration effects strong enough to prevent attempts except when there are strong reasons acceptable to public opinion at large. Second, stocks—not flows—must be distributed in a capitalization system. In pay-as-you-go systems, a promise involves a flow and does not require issuing explicit government debt. Third, the benefits of redistribution take time because as they must accumulate in an individual account. Fourth, it is difficult to tax pension rights because funds are privatized and deposited in individual accounts. The new system also minimizes the costs of adapting to change due to changes in real wages, rates of return or demographic factors. Indeed, it also offers a new role for the labour movement, since teachers' unions, copper-mine workers and bank employees, among others, have created their own pension funds and manage them with less marketing expenses than in traditional pension funds.

The reform of the pension system may also help reform other areas, such as unemployment insurance, which are subject to moral hazard. Individual accounts help to overcome the problems of severance payments and unemployment insurance to the extent that they can be in part substituted for a special deposit in the pension account. In 1993 the Government of Chile proposed a reform of the unemployment insurance system that would have lowered the replacement rate to 50 per cent of income over four months, financed by mandatory savings contributed by the employer and employee. If the savings are not sufficient to ensure the unemployment benefits, the worker receives a credit to cover the difference. This savings credit scheme lessens the problem of moral hazard and fraud for government expenditure and the administrative costs of countering them.

The financing of the transition involves an average deficit in the social security funds of 3 per cent of GDP over more than 40 years. The existence of an initial surplus in the overall public budget has made this transition easier in Chile, but it is by no means necessary, since all such reform does is transform an implicit into an explicit debt. In other words, privatization does not require true funding but only apparent funding.[19] Overall, it is the capacity of the fully funded system to adapt to change and its higher degree of insulation to unfavourable shocks that may make it more sustainable than the pay-as-you-go system in countries facing a competitive worldwide environment in both economic and political terms.

In Chapter VII, Augusztinovics describes the situation of the Hungarian welfare state and warns against the danger of transition fatigue. She places revenues and expenditures of the general Government in the overall setting of income redistribution among factors of production, and then discusses gestation and retirement financing with reference to the ongoing debate about reform options.

Under the "old deal" between the State and the citizens when State ownership of capital was dominant, the net wage share was deliberately kept low, and instead of taxing individuals the State drew on the high surplus share of the economy to satisfy social needs. The State also provided full employment at the price of tolerating low endog-

---

[19]See World Bank (1994), p. 138; Kotlikoff (1996); and note 12 above.

14

enous labour productivity in the economy, but possibly avoiding the social cost of exogenous unemployment. All this created the image of the paternalistic State that provides for its citizens.

The transition to a regime in which the State has limited access to both labour and capital income because private property is now dominant has had only limited results. In fact, the State has managed to preserve its primary share in final consumption, as well as in primary income: that share was 15 per cent in 1993, an increase in real terms over 1985 levels. Whatever it takes and gives is just shuffled between labour and capital. But capital accumulation stands at only 15 per cent of 1985 levels, so that the State has lost its control of and access to capital income to a much larger extent than justified by the amount of actually privatized capital.

On the other hand, the after-tax wage share has spectacularly decreased, while job safety and a chance—however meagre—to obtain modest but decent housing, which were two important factors of adult life security, are gone. Hence, the prerequisite of a new deal has not been created: citizens are now more dependent on the State for their consumption than before. The State, for its part, cannot find the resources to meet its obligations.

Augusztinovics goes on to propose a system that she claims is (a) longitudinal, actuarially fair for efficiency as well as demographic reasons; (b) purely life-cycle oriented, clearly separated from poverty relief and other redistribution objectives; and (c) self-sustained without government intervention. This combined system is made up of two insurance agencies, with flows and stocks accounted for in terms of the same *numéraire*, say a unit wage. Stocks would accrue interest at a rate capable of making them fully funded and robust to domestic economic fluctuations. To make the system free from generational conflicts, one agency (the gestation fund) collects contributions and provides loans (not necessarily limited to student loans), while the other (the retirement fund) collects pension insurance and provides benefits as returns on the accumulated funds.

Macroeconomic viability does not imply that the new system will be capable of operating in the specific national and international environment. The current difficulties with changing social security entitlements in Hungary and elsewhere remind us of the importance of institutional reform in this area. Aside from this macroeconomic viability, though, institutions must be devised that allow the system to operate in the specific national and international environment, a point made repeatedly in the present introduction.

In chapter VIII, Evlo reports on the two similar regimes existing in Togo, social security and social protection for civil servants. While he concludes that this system is better than no system, it does depend on national population policy. The Government gains from unconditional and interest-free loans, but 90 per cent of the population is not part of the system. Banks gain liquidity, but whether this contributes to increased activity in various sectors of the economy, such as construction, real estate and utilities, remains to be seen. The system does not provide any protection against natural disasters.

Of course, the cost-benefit analysis hinges on the macroeconomic policy regime of the franc zone, which set Togo and other member States apart from most other developing countries, even after the CFA franc devaluation against the French franc in early 1994, the first since the late 1940s. The ease of administration of the flat rate of contributions was paramount even though the system became less equitable as a consequence, whereas on benefits a positive judgement can be made independently of their level, especially professional risk (4 per cent of total). Also, given differences in riskiness across sectors, the transfer from low risk to high risk raises equity issues.

The economic (as opposed to the legal) incidence of the corporate income tax in an open economy is on the fixed factor, labour not capital. The wage tax used to finance social security in Togo may thus recognize the structural reasons why labour may pay the part of such taxes that is supposed to be paid by employers, especially the mobility of capital or the importance of foreign direct investment from France. How these aspects interacted with the common monetary regime of the franc zone and the nature of the structural adjustment programmes agreed upon in the early 1980s will have a decisive impact on the ability of the Government to design and implement social security reform in Togo.

The paper by Wenruo deals with urban and rural pension insurance, the topic of chapter IX, but also covers health insurance, work-related accident insurance and unemployment insurance in China. Most economic indicators suggest a rapidly developing country with a greater supply of public goods in the social spheres, such as health and education, than per capita income would have suggested. What emerges from the comparison among the available social security arrangements is that their variety—whatever its historical origin and current institutional set-up—ends up mitigating the negative financial consequences of a universal system, albeit at the cost of greatly reduced social protection. Even though the determinants of the viability of the Chinese system—which remains essentially a pay-as-you-go system—do include the rate of economic growth, the fact that it has been very brisk does not eliminate concerns brought about by other features, such as demography, system dependency ratio, wage replacement rate etc. Nevertheless, variety is a feature that any reform of social security arrangements should preserve if it is to be sustained.

4. TOWARDS GLOBAL CONVERGENCE?

Both the focus on system design and governance in part one and the four case studies in part two assume that States are confronted with global challenges in our interdependent world economy. As a result, sustainable social security policies can no longer ignore the constraints deriving from property rights and international exchange, but they also face constraints coming from expectations. Policies that cannot be sustained without future tax increases elicit negative reactions from voters and financial markets. The sustainability of policies without future tax increases is in turn required for their credibility.

The protection of the property rights of both residents and non-residents and the promotion of international trade in goods, services and assets is a credible signal that no surprise taxation is intended. Such a signal may be required, even though the movement of people remains the exception rather than the rule, both nationally and internationally. The reason is that more and more people are exposed to realities beyond their immediate horizon in space as well as in time. The importance of market perceptions of national policies, alongside voter sentiment, is reinforced by personal mobility.

Increased sensitivity to global trends means that interdependence has become a structural feature of the international system. It can no longer be ignored in the design of mechanisms that used to be purely domestic concerns, such as taxes, social security and other budgetary procedures, let alone their monetary counterparts. Moreover, it can make reform more costly or less enduring, to the extent that mechanisms of peer pressure and multilateral surveillance are weaker than free ride and regulatory capture. This is why forms of regional association have emerged among both developed and developing nations. It is fair to mention Europe as the geographical domain of the most ambitious such association, but there are other cases in point in Africa, Asia and the Americas, such as the Southern African Development Community, the Asia Pacific Economic Cooperation Council, the North American Free Trade Agreement, the Southern Cone Common Market etc.

Interdependence brings a tendency for convergence in economic, political and even social behaviour, as a means to preserve a society's values in a competitive global environment. In contrast to the global reach of the market and the technological forces that make protection inefficient and inequitable, preferences between private and public goods used to be seen as local. This was supposed to rationalize severe spatial differences in taxation among developed nations in the so-called first and second worlds. The developing nations of the third world were supposed to choose the market or plan model based on

17

preferences. Not any more. In spite of the wide variety of institutional arrangements, there is widespread consensus that economic and social development is associated with policies of open economy and polity, whereas underdevelopment or stagnation stems from policies of economic autarchy and political repression.

The demise of the former USSR put an end to the ideological debate between market and plan. The balancing act between market and government failures under imperfect information must be performed on a case-by-case basis. It cannot neglect history, but it is also more and more determined by expectations. Expectations, in turn, include the tendency towards convergence so that they impose tighter and tighter constraints on inadequate policies.

Even though future generations are not represented in majority voting, greater awareness of the need to implement sustainable policies brings pressure on elected Governments to clarify the intergenerational effects of current policies. This applies to the physical and cultural environment as well as to the provision of public goods and transfers through taxation. The awareness that excessive taxation, overt or hidden in the form of inflation, discourages saving and stifles growth is also rising. As growth prospects fall due to the absence of incentives to save and invest, so does employment, making future consumption lower and social deprivation higher. In due course such policies are bound to be corrected. Yet, without adequate institutions, there may be reversions to inadequate policies.

Policy reversions may in turn prevent the poorer countries from growing more rapidly than the richer countries to bring about convergence in living standards and an increasing cohesion in the world economy. If the rich get richer and the poor get poorer, cohesion—be it global, regional or even national—will be threatened. Reforms will stall.

If only countries with an adequate initial level of human capital endowments can take advantage of modern technology to enjoy the possibility of convergent growth, then they form a club.[20] A recent contribution by Sachs and Warner (1995) suggests that looking at the initial level of human capital as the basis for long-term growth potential is unduly pessimistic.[21] Rather, one should look at reasonably efficient economic institutions as the major requirement for economic growth and convergence.

Poor economic management stems from the absence of secure property rights, or from autarchic trade policies and inconvertible

---

[20]Evidence that membership in this club is determined by a combination of geography and history is presented in Macedo et al. (1996).

[21]The idea is reviewed favorably by Bertola (1996), even though doubts have been expressed about the econometric methods used.

currencies. The failure to grow may be explained by reversible policy failures rather than by technology or human capital. Thus, the convergence club is better defined according to policy choices rather than initial levels of human capital. Moreover, poor policy choices are not irrevocably linked to low levels of income. A well known aphorism of Adam Smith's can be invoked in favour of this philosophy of an open club of policy convergence: little else is required to carry a State to the highest degree of opulence from the lowest barbarism but peace, easy taxes and the tolerable administration of justice.

A sample covering approximately 90 per cent of the world population is used to establish that countries with appropriate policies display a strong tendency towards economic convergence, with countries with an initially low per capita income growing more rapidly than the richer countries. Countries whose policies concerning property rights and the integration of the economy in international trade are deemed not appropriate do not display any tendency towards convergence.

With the exception of one regime in which property rights were obviously not protected, every developing country (<$4,000 per capita income in 1970) with an open trading system grew by at least 2 per cent annually from 1970 to 1989! No case was found, therefore, to support the frequent worry that a country might do the right things in terms of overall policy (both politics and openness) and yet fail to grow. This establishes sufficiency. Yet, there are countries that "broke the rules" and achieved high economic growth. The seven exceptions can be interpreted in terms of conditional probabilities, using a Rawlsian "veil of ignorance". If a poor country found itself back in 1970, the probability of its growing at 3 per cent would be less than 10 per cent, whereas conditional on good policies it would be greater than 80 per cent. A gamble on closed policies would not pay off.

The rejection of the reverse causation (slow growth leads to bad policies) is trickier even for countries in which the policy regime was chosen early in the post-war era before a track record on growth had occurred, because outward-oriented policies in OECD also involved security relations led by the United States. Similarly, reacting against such policies was an imposition of the policy of the former USSR in Europe and elsewhere. If this is true of property rights and foreign trade taxes, is it true of taxes in general and therefore of social security regimes?

Not quite, because a Rawlsian experiment like the one above could serve as a rationalization for the welfare state. According to Barr (1992), it is an insurance contract entered voluntarily by risk-averse individuals under the same Rawlsian "veil of ignorance". *Ex ante facto*, the welfare state is actuarial, since no difference in individual risk has yet emerged. But pooling is impossible *ex post facto*, when the risk has become a certainty. Therefore, the rejection of excessive taxation must be based on a perceived threat to property rights or mobility, and it requires a long time horizon.

This interpretation of the veil of ignorance is more justified when international interdependence fostered by cooperation among all levels of government is favoured relative to defensive measures involving some form of protection against foreign competition. Such multilateral surveillance is based on peer pressure as well as on the threat of sanctions. It certainly needs further improvement in the economic and monetary areas. Nevertheless, global economic policy dialogue may bring about the kind of social consensus that is required to overcome diverging interests and establish national cohesion.[22]

The notion of a time bomb has become commonplace in discussing physical and social environment issues. This suggests rightly that the insecurity associated with the nuclear threat during the cold war period has been replaced by the threat of economic and social deprivation. Since widely accepted values demand some form of insurance against drops in individual or family standards of living over one's life cycle, the central problem shifts from insecurity due to war to insecurity due to poverty and social exclusion.

If social security is to be sustainable in market economies, it will require a front-loaded strategy of fiscal adjustment, making room immediately for future reductions in social transfers. Whether this implies budgetary surpluses, as in the case of Chile, or a change in the mix of public expenditure will depend on the particular circumstances. Indeed, the need to expand coverage, as in Togo or China, may dictate that overall social transfers do not decrease and that other expenditures are reduced instead. The decisive point, however, is that tax and social security reform cannot be delinked without endangering the ability of either change to promote savings and enhance growth in interdependent national economies.

Growing structural interdependence notwithstanding, international collaboration on these matters is unusual, and even when it is decided by policy makers is difficult to implement, because—as the case studies in the present publication show—the competence for social security reform is scattered among various ministries and the culture of the social affairs ministries is sensitive to the need to

---

[22]In Macedo and others (1996), the authors show how variable geometry can have a positive effect on the need to combine deepening and widening in the EU. Indeed, broad principles along these lines were unanimously approved in 1995, when Professor Macedo chaired the European Affairs Committee of the Assembly of the Republic of Portugal.

alleviate immediate poverty but oblivious to the interests of current—
let alone future—taxpayers.[23]

If the United Nations continues to be interested in this approach,
topics beyond those selected in the present publication will no doubt
be covered. A greater impetus for sustaining social security worldwide
may then emerge for the sake of current as well as future generations.

REFERENCES

Barr, Nicholas (1992). Economic theory and the welfare state: a survey and inter-
    pretation. *Journal of Economic Literature*, June.
Bertola, Giuseppe (1996). Convergence: an overview. Paper presented at a CEPR
    conference on regionalism, La Coruña, Spain, April.
Branson, William and Jorge Braga de Macedo (1995). Macroeconomic policy in
    Central Europe. *CEPR Discussion Paper*, May.
Braz, José (1995). Social security: perspectives in the European Union. Unpublished
    manuscript. Lisbon: Instituto de Seguros de Portugal.
Commission of the European Communities (1993). Growth, competitiveness and
    employment. *Bulletin of the European Communities*, supplement No. 6/93.
Diamond, Peter, David Lindeman and Howard Young, editors (1996). *Social Secu-
    rity: What Role for the Future?* Washington, D.C.: National Academy of Social
    Insurance.
Gokhale, Jagadeesh, Lawrence Kotlikoff and John Sabelhaus (1996). Under-
    standing the postwar decline in US saving: a cohort analysis. Unpublished
    manuscript.
Kotlikoff, Lawrence (1995), Privatization of social security: how it works and why
    it matters. *National Bureau of Economic Research Working Paper*, No. 5330
    (October).
_____ (1996). Privatizing social security at home and abroad. Unpublished
    manuscript.
Macedo, Jorge Braga, Barry Eichengreen and Jaime Reis, editors (1996). *Currency
    Convertibility: The Gold Standard and Beyond*. London: Routledge.
Sachs, Jeffrey, and Andrew Warner (1995). Economic convergence and economic
    policies. *Brookings Papers on Economic Activity*.
Sinn, Hans Werner (1995). Social insurance, incentives and risk taking. Paper
    presented at the Fifty-first Congress of the International Institute of Public
    Finance, Lisbon, August.
von Hagen, Jurgen, and Ian Harden (1994). National budget processes and fiscal
    performance. *European Economy Reports and Studies*, No. 3.
World Bank (1994). *Averting the Old Age Crisis*. Washington, D.C.

---

[23]A personal note: because the technical exchange between Sweden and Portugal on social security reform agreed in 1992 between the two ministers of finance
never materialized, the partial reforms carried out in 1993 did not benefit from the
courageous Swedish experiment in reforming its much admired welfare state.

Chapter II

ISSUES IN THE REFORM OF SOCIAL SECURITY: A PERSPECTIVE FROM THE INTERNATIONAL LABOUR OFFICE

Colin Gillion*

Throughout the world, social security systems are in a state of turbulence. The developed countries that are members of the Organisation for Economic Cooperation and Development (OECD), which have rapidly expanded public expenditures on social protection over the last several decades, are now questioning whether they have gone too far, whether future taxpayers will be willing to pay increased amounts for public transfers and social services, and whether their existing systems do not retard economic growth and performance. In contrast, the rapidly developing countries of South-East Asia are anxious to expand and enhance their existing, sometimes quite minimal, schemes. African countries are preoccupied with questions of governance and of expanding the coverage of social protection to include their large informal sectors. In Latin America, the dominant questions concern the structure of pension schemes, with many countries casting eyes on the Chilean reforms of 1981. Eastern and Central European countries are concerned with the problems of economic transition and of recasting pension, health and unemployment compensation schemes to meet the needs of reorientation to market economies. In sum, there is scarcely a country in the world in which the reform of social security—in many cases a radical and major reform—does not figure high on the political agenda.

1. CONTEXT

The list of countries or areas affected is a long one. In China, the Government is planning to introduce major reforms to pension schemes, employment injury insurance, unemployment compensation and eventually health care. In India, schemes for early retirement, unemployment compensation, redundancy and retraining are being developed as a prerequisite for the restructuring of industry. In Thailand and Palestine, for very different reasons and in very different

*Director, Social Security Department, International Labour Office.

circumstances, social protection programmes are being developed from a very limited base. In a number of countries, especially in South-East Asia and East Africa, national provident funds are being converted to pension schemes. Conversely, many countries in Latin America are contemplating a change to privately managed pension schemes based on individual accounts. In Central and Eastern Europe, most countries face an almost complete overhaul of their pension and health-care systems, together with the installation of new programmes of unemployment compensation and social safety nets. Many schemes in Africa, such as that in Madagascar, are undertaking a basic reconstruction of both their design and coverage and their organization and management. Timing differs form country to country. Some countries, such as Chile, introduced major reforms several years ago. Other countries, such as Nigeria, have reform processes that are well under way. And still other countries, such as Viet Nam and Mexico, are just beginning the process of change. Finally, such countries as Cuba, South Africa and Nepal are contemplating future reform. History also differs from country to country: Uruguay has a long history of social security but is now planning a radical change to its existing scheme. Nor are changes confined to developing and transitional countries. The United Kingdom of Great Britain and Northern Ireland and the Netherlands have recently made important changes to their system of health insurance, and the United States of America may do the same. And there is a great deal of discussion among OECD countries about the effectiveness of current systems of social security, their cost and their implications for economic performance.

As the examples above suggest, the pressures for reform and development also vary widely from one country to another. In many countries, the impetus stems directly from a process of economic structural adjustment: expanded systems of social protection are required to deal with the adverse social consequences of structural adjustment and economic stabilization. In a similar context, the huge transformations associated with the transition from a planned to a market-oriented economy, principally but not only among the countries of Central and Eastern Europe, have meant that many of the functions previously located in state-owned enterprises must now be redeveloped as authentic social security schemes. New systems of unemployment compensation and social safety nets must be developed to cope with the large number of workers becoming unemployed in the changed context of a competitive labour market. In some countries, the impetus for change derives from sustained economic growth and urbanization: populations that were previously too poor or not sufficiently industrialized to contemplate social security systems now see them as an essential concomitant of the move towards an affluent society. The process of democratization has also influenced events: in

23

Brazil and a number of other countries in Latin America, new constitutions have included access to social security as one of the basic rights of all citizens, often on the basis of international conventions and recommendations adopted by the International Labour Organization (ILO). And in quite a large number of countries, a restructuring is being undertaken simply because existing systems are perceived to have failed both in terms of their effectiveness and efficiency and in terms of their basic design.

2. THE INTERNATIONAL LABOUR ORGANIZATION

The ILO has been involved in this process throughout its 75 years of history. From its beginnings, the ILO has viewed the provision of social insurance and social security both as a human right and as an essential element to be embodied in concepts of international labour standards. Much of its effort in the early years—say up to the beginning of the 1950s—was directed towards the establishment of the International Labour Standards related to social security, a process that led to the formulation of the benchmark 1952 Convention No. 102 [Social Security (Minimum Standards)] and subsequent conventions and recommendations that enhanced and updated those provisions. The standards reflect the normative view of the world community on the question of the minimum measure of social protection, and remain a basic criterion for establishing the acceptability of proposed reforms: the ILO played a significant advisory role in the preparation of the original Beveridge report. But the ILO has also been involved directly in the development of social security and social protection programmes throughout the world. During World War II, the ILO was particularly active in Latin American countries, and it subsequently played an important role in the establishment of social security systems in the newly independent countries of Africa and Asia. The current tide of reform, development and reconstruction has intensified that involvement, and the disappearance of the communist bloc has extended the area of concern to the transitional economies of Eastern and Central Europe.

3. OBJECTIVES OF SOCIAL SECURITY SYSTEMS

In spite of the diversity of history, circumstances and existing arrangements, almost all systems of social security and/or social protection possess a common set of fundamental objectives, chiefly related to their coverage, the contingencies to be included and the levels of benefits to be provided. Such objectives have evolved over time but were firmly established in Convention No. 102 (1952) of the International Labour Standards. In general terms, the Convention stipulates that social security should be extended to the large majority of workers

24

and their families; that benefit levels should, at a minimum, be sufficient to prevent severe hardship in the case of accident, sickness, old age or other contingencies; and that nine main types of benefit should be provided, namely:

(a) Medical care;
(b) Sickness benefit;
(c) Unemployment benefit;
(d) Employment injury benefit;
(e) Old-age benefit;
(f) Maternity benefit;
(g) Invalidity benefit;
(h) Family benefit;
(i) Survivors' benefit.

The Convention also gives broad indications on the financing of such benefits, chiefly in the direction of a sharing of contributions between employers and employees. And it places clearly with the State the responsibility of ensuring that the stipulated benefits and services are in fact provided. The Convention has subsequently been extended by further conventions and recommendations, which have enhanced its benefit and coverage provisions.

Given that basic commitment, however, subsequent conventions display considerable flexibility in their provisions, in their requirements for ratification by member States, and most especially in their terms of administrative and financial organization, which allow for a variety of concepts of protection. In the view of one of its drafters, the Convention regards social security as an end and accepts any means that effectively attain that end, namely, the guarantee of adequate benefit under conditions that respect personal dignity. In effect, the Convention endorses a variety of different types of social security mechanisms, including pluralistic structures that embody mixed forms of financing and delivery.

As far as developing and transitional countries are concerned, the International Labour Standards, together with more general international declarations, should be read as statements of ambitions and objectives rather than as a reflection of the world as it is. Although social protection policies in developed countries have mostly gone well beyond what is required by the conventions, in developing countries there is not only a great diversity in what is actually available but also a great divergence between aspirations and reality. For although more than 146 countries throughout the world possess some form of social security, compared to just under 50 countries in 1950, there are many deficiencies. Few developing countries treat all the main contingencies; in many, the population covered by the schemes is restricted

25

to a small minority of workers in the formal sector of the economy (sometimes only public employees); the level of benefits is often minimal and far from adequate, even where incomes are generally low; and such deficiencies of structure, coverage and benefit levels are frequently exacerbated by operational failures of management, administration or financial organization or by excessive costs, and sometimes by corruption, so that even the intended benefits are not delivered.

It is that gap—between international ideals and actual outcomes, between legislation and practice, between needs and reality, and between the advanced and the developing countries—that adds tension to other pressures such as structural adjustment, economic transition and democratization, and explains the current momentum of reform and development.

Appreciating the need for change is relatively straightforward, but implementing it is more difficult. There are a number of constraints to the process of reform.

4. CONSTRAINTS

An obvious limitation is the proportion of the population that lives and works in the formal sector of the economy. Social security systems that are to be more than simple mechanisms of personal savings or insurance, that is, those that embody a degree of social solidarity and/or income redistribution, need to be anchored in a framework that can ensure compulsory contributions in return for entitlement to benefits. The conventional structure that permits such stability is based on formal employment: employment contracts can be monitored and assessed for the purposes of contributions. Thus, the size of the modern sector broadly sets the bounds for these two revenue bases. Outside that limit, it is difficult for social security schemes of the conventional type to reach out to the population as a whole. In Africa, less than 10 per cent of the active population is employed in the formal sector; in Latin America that proportion is much higher; in Asia, it varies widely. By contrast, Central and East European countries are emerging from planned economies in which almost the entire active population had been incorporated in the formal sector, but are finding that the size of the informal self-employed sector is now growing rapidly. Thus, for many developing countries and increasingly for both transitional and developed countries, a substantial proportion of the population lies outside the scope of contribution-based social security schemes.

An alternative is to use the tax base—both personal and enterprise income taxes and indirect taxes—as the financial base for programmes of social security and social protection. But countries with a limited modern sector usually find that their tax base is also limited. Direct

26

taxes are difficult to collect from informal-sector workers, especially in the agriculture sector, and there is often widespread avoidance and evasion on the part of upper-income groups. Indirect taxes can partially fill the gap but are generally insufficient to fund a generalized social security programme. A compromise that is sometimes reached is to use general revenues to fund basic universal benefits and services—usually basic health services but sometimes family benefits as well—and to restrict the principal cash benefits, such as retirement pensions, to workers and enterprises in the formal sector who can be identified and are able to contribute.

An additional constraint is essentially social and political. Income in many developing countries is frequently distributed very unevenly, a situation that is reinforced by a disproportionate access to political power and influence. It is difficult to persuade the more affluent groups of society—not just the rich but also affluent workers with good jobs, such as the military, public servants and workers in the larger State and private enterprises—to contribute to schemes that imply a significant degree of solidarity and income redistribution, especially where contributions are themselves proportional to earnings. Where benefits are more or less proportional to contributions, resistance to the development of a comprehensive social security scheme may be low, as is the case for certain types of pension schemes or schemes of an insurance nature, in which risks are more or less the same for all contributors and benefits and proportional to contributions. But where benefits are related to needs rather than to means, there is likely to be greater resistance by groups of better-paid workers. This is the case for most types of anti-poverty programme, for pension systems that embody minimum benefit levels for all participants, or for health insurance schemes in which treatment is determined by the illness rather than the contribution history. In such situations, there is a tendency to develop multi-tiered systems that provide higher benefits to higher earners and contributors. Better-paid groups may try to opt out of generalized schemes, depriving them of much of their financial viability, which frequently results in the neglect of schemes directed at lower-income groups and the exclusion of lower-income groups from all forms of social security. In such circumstances, the extension of social protection, even to the limits indicated by the formal sector as a whole, becomes difficult and uncertain.

4.1. *Economic limits*

Total social expenditures not only absorb a substantial proportion of total national income but also account for a major proportion of total public outlays. It is natural that they should form a central area of concern in countries that are struggling to reduce fiscal deficits or to maintain a hard-won fiscal balance. For OECD countries, however,

27

social expenditures appear to be less of a problem now than they did a decade ago. Although there is an almost automatic tendency for fiscal deficits to expand during a recession, such as the recent one, there is little sign that aggregate social expenditures are structurally out of control. The ratio of social expenditure to gross domestic product (GDP) has been roughly constant for several years now, and Governments of OECD countries are consciously avoiding further enhancements to pension entitlements and making strenuous efforts to contain costs in their health-care policies.

But the situation is very different in the transitional economies. Many of the former planned economies are on the horns of a dilemma. On the one hand, the transition to a market-oriented economy not only requires a change of ownership of the means of production but also implies a large-scale reconstruction of physical capital, both of the productive system itself and in terms of public and social infrastructure. At the same time, high rates of inflation require a tight control of fiscal deficits. For both those objectives to be achieved, investment and savings must be increased, resources must be directed away from current consumption, and incomes and the money supply must be constrained. On the other hand, for most such countries GDP has dropped very sharply in the early years of transition, the development of new labour markets has coincided with the emergence of large-scale open unemployment, and where the old labour arrangements have persisted they have led to higher levels of concealed unemployment and declining real wages. Pension benefits have been eroded by rapid inflation, and there is widespread poverty both among the old and among families with children. The social need is for an expansion of social benefits and programmes. But the move towards private ownership and competitive labour markets has also weakened mechanisms for revenue collection: many countries are simultaneously in the process of reforming their tax systems, including both direct and indirect taxes, and implementing new systems of social security contributions. Until they can do so, there is little hope of achieving revenue support for greater social expenditures by means of a progressive system of taxation. Meanwhile, a hard choice must be made between investment in the economy and social protection.

There is no easy remedy for this imbalance, but there is a fear that if expenditures swing too far in the direction of social support, investment and economic recovery will be jeopardized. On the other hand, if insufficient social protection is afforded to those most in need, the political consensus for transition may not be sustained. Clearly, aid and loans from other developed countries and from the Bretton Woods institutions will help, but such aid is unlikely to be sufficient by itself.

If the control of social expenditures is much less of a problem now than it was in previous decades, the control and reduction of non-wage labour costs, especially the social security contributions levied on employers, is a much-talked-about issue. For almost all OECD countries, social charges represent a high proportion of the total cost of employing labour: from 25 to 30 per cent in France, Belgium, Italy, Germany and Sweden, rather less in the United Kingdom and Ireland. The fear is that such costs may reduce the international competitiveness of countries, resulting in a loss of both export earnings and productivity and indirectly leading to higher unemployment.

Neither the validity of this proposition nor the chain of argument that supports it is entirely clear, although it is a view that is widely held. That social charges form part of production costs in a nominal accounting sense seems beyond dispute. What is not clear is who ultimately absorbs such costs and whether they ultimately affect the cost of domestic goods and services as measured at world prices. Social charges may be absorbed by the employer, passed on in the form of higher prices, or borne by workers in the form of lower real wages. They represent a means of financing social transfers or services in the same way as other forms of taxation, and do not automatically add to the real costs of production. As far as foreign trade and investment are concerned, international competitiveness has to be seen through the veil of the exchange rate: to the extent that the exchange rate does not reflect or respond to changes in social charges or real productivity, then domestic costs will be misrepresented on world markets. But normal expectation would be that the exchange rate would take into account and offset nominal social charges. Anything else would appear to be a problem of foreign-exchange mechanisms rather than social costs. The international experience is in any case mixed: there are countries with high social charges that are competitive, such as Germany; there are countries with low social charges that have become less competitive, such as the United Kingdom; there are countries with low social charges that are competitive, such as Japan; and there are countries with high social charges that are uncompetitive, such as Norway.

Perhaps the most important adverse effect of high social charges is that they drive a wedge between the formal and informal components of the labour market, particularly as regards low-paid jobs because of contribution ceilings, inducing labour to flow to jobs and occupations in which social charges can most easily be avoided, rather than to jobs that are most productive or profitable. If all employers in a country, including the self-employed, faced the same social charges and complied with them, the misallocation of resources would be minimal or non-existent. But the development of an informal or black labour market has been an issue of concern for some time now, not only because of the productivity and revenue losses that it implies but also because in some areas and for some contingencies, lack of compliance leads to a loss of social entitlement.

In a similar vein, there are a number of general concerns that over-generous systems of social protection may inhibit the economic performance of a country, chiefly through distortions in the labour market that reduce the supply of labour and hence lead to larger than necessary levels of unemployment, partly through effects that reduce the supply of savings, driving up interest rates and reducing real investment and growth. On the labour market side, the argument is reinforced by comparisons between Europe and the United States. Over a long period, employment in the United States has grown more rapidly than it has in Europe, although in both areas the growth of output has been much the same. Unemployment in Europe is much higher than in the United States, and the difference in labour market performance has been attributed in large part to the difference in social protection benefits: social security is less generous in the United States, unemployment insurance benefits are less and their duration shorter, and there is a less resilient safety net. The argument has been extended to include protective labour market regulation generally, as well as income replacement measures.

5. AGEING

The world's populations are ageing, partly because of earlier declines in fertility rates, partly because of current and expected improvements in life expectancy and mortality. The trend affects all regions: for the world as a whole, the proportion of the population over the age of 60 will increase from approximately 9 per cent in 1990 to just over 16 per cent by 2030. But it especially affects the transitional socialist countries, China, and the OECD countries, where the proportion will increase from about 18 per cent to nearly 31 per cent by 2030.

Although a number of aspects of this transition are to be welcomed—greater longevity and a reduced pressure on resources from lower overall population growth—the shift raises a fundamental question about how the older population will be supported if it does not work (does not wish to work, is not allowed to or cannot find jobs). At any given point in time, the inactive retired population must be supported by a transfer of resources from the active, working-age population, so that the simple arithmetic of greatly increased numbers of inactive elderly implies that, relative to current retirement arrangements, either contribution rates must be increased, replacement rates must be reduced or the actual age of retirement must be increased. There is no other solution except an immediate and very rapid increase in fertility rates, which demographers view as extremely unlikely and which in any case would not offset the ageing that has already taken place. It is necessary to emphasize, however, that these difficulties are to be measured in relative rather than absolute terms, and although we can be confident that demographic assumptions are reliable, we know very little about the economic and social context in which the ageing process will take place. Who, in 1900, would have accurately predicted the situation in 1950? Who, in 1950, would have accurately predicted the economic and social circumstances at the end of the century? In 50 years' time, even at an average growth rate of 1.5 per cent a year, real GDP per capita will have doubled, so that all sections of the population will be greatly better off than they are now, even if transfers from the active to the inactive must be doubled to take account of the support required by the retired elderly. So economic capacity to support the old does not appear to lie at the heart of the problem. What is at stake is whether or not current arrangements, chiefly stemming from existing social security schemes, will be sufficiently robust to cope with the ageing process, whether they will continue to command a widespread social consensus in the face of greatly increased contribution rates, and if not, what alternative means of accommodating the ageing process can be found. What is clear is that, whatever basic design is adopted to confront the ageing process, the existing combination of basic parameters—contribution rates, relative benefits and retirement age—cannot simultaneously be sustained.

Among academics and policy analysts, and increasingly among politicians as well, the debate about the implications of the ageing process has been particularly fierce. It has not resulted in any conventional wisdom but has instead polarized participants into two opposing camps: those who see the adjustment to the ageing process taking place within an adapted and revised social security structure of the type that currently prevails throughout Europe, that is, pay-as-you-go financed public schemes with defined benefits; and those who favour a radical shift towards mandatory retirement savings schemes, that is, schemes that are fully funded, based on individual accounts, managed by non-government pension funds and designed to deliver benefits based on defined contributions. There are other reasons besides the ageing problem for weighing the relative merits of the two alternatives, and of course there are an infinite number of different options that lie somewhere between the two extremes. Other questions concern issues already raised above, such as the harmful economic effects of high contribution rates, the economic consequences of current schemes and the pressure that they maintain on public finances; these are discussed below.

As far as ageing is concerned, while it is clear that the existing structure, if it is retained, will necessarily undergo a painful adaptation to altered circumstances, proponents of the shift to a mandatory retirement savings scheme argue along the following lines: if pension schemes were formulated in terms of a compulsory, defined contribution scheme in which workers accumulated savings in an individual account which, when they retired, would enable them to purchase an indexed annuity, then the ageing problem would in a sense be pre-financed. Reserves and funds would be built up when the age-bulge was of working age. When the age-bulge reached retirement, those funds could be withdrawn to provide the necessary income in old age. Such a scheme would provide a closer connection between individual contributions and entitlements than current social security arrangements, would lead to fewer labour market distortions, and would promote savings and investment in productive (i.e., private-sector) undertakings.

There are two relatively unsettled questions concerning the potential of such a system to offset the ageing process.

In the first place, it is not clear how a mandatory retirement savings system would alter behaviour in capital markets. During the build-up of pension funds, the flow of new savings from pension funds into financial markets would necessarily be large: on the order of 15 per cent of aggregate wages and salaries. Although some of those funds might flow into new investments that would otherwise not have taken place, it is likely that they would also displace existing forms of savings and influence the volume and cost of financing Government bonds, and could lead to a downward pressure on interest rates. Such developments would in turn influence the rate of return that contributors could expect in the long run, and hence the ultimate value of their annuities or pensions. The risks of fluctuating or declining returns would be borne by contributors and beneficiaries via the uncertainties of the capital market, rather than being absorbed by the contribution rates of current workers via the operations of a social security institution. Ultimately, of course, just as in a pay-as-you-go scheme, the transfer of resources to the old must necessarily be subtracted from the resources (standard of living) of the active population. During a run-down or stagnation of net savings flows, which would occur when the age structure stabilized or began to decline, reverse effects might occur, leading to interest rates higher than otherwise and a reduction in real investment.

The second question concerns the effects of either scheme on the distribution of income between the active and the retired, bearing in mind that some adjustment of that distribution is a necessary consequence of population ageing. Under a pay-as-you-go structure, the nature of such a rebalancing would reflect a social and political decision: the burden would be consciously shared between workers, employers and retirees. Under a mandatory retirement savings system, changes in the distribution would be largely determined by market forces whose outcome would not be at all clear.

Nevertheless, it is entirely possible to conceive of a mixed system that combines some of the merits of both social security and mandatory savings schemes.

6. THE PRIVATE/PUBLIC DEBATE

Switching from social security pension schemes as traditionally conceived to a system of mandatory retirement savings schemes is a strategic option that is currently the subject of much debate. As indicated in the previous section, that debate has partly been fostered by the prospect of ageing populations and the need to provide for a larger proportion of older people in society. But there are a number of other reasons for considering the merits of these two radically different approaches. Ultimately, of course, the options need to be judged in terms of their ability to achieve the fundamental objectives of retirement pension schemes. In recent ILO documents, these have been broadly defined as:

(a) The provision of a minimum basic pension to all citizens, regardless of their current circumstances or history of contributions, which would prevent poverty in old age;

(b) The establishment of a compulsory pension insurance scheme, financed by contributions from both workers and employers, which would ensure an adequate replacement of earnings during retirement;

(c) The provision of scope for voluntary participation in a complementary pension scheme that would supplement the provisions of the compulsory scheme;

(d) Protection of all components of the retirement package against their erosion by inflation.

There is a general consensus about the first objectives which is frequently covered as much by programmes of social assistance as by basic pension arrangements, and also about the third and fourth objectives, providing scope for individual initiative and indexing against inflation. But there is considerable debate about how the second objective might best be achieved, and it is this component of pension arrangements that covers most workers in the middle range of incomes and is most important in terms of ensuring an adequate replacement rate. Of course, the objectives as stated above still leave much to be defined, in particular what should be defined as an adequate replacement rate to be provided by the compulsory scheme, and the choice of different arrangements depends as much on the quantitative levels of benefits to be provided as on the design of the schemes.

Under a pay-as-you-go social security scheme, contributions are levied on both workers and employers during working life, which

33

entitle the worker to a pension on reaching a specified retirement age. The contributions are proportional to earnings, although frequently subject to a ceiling. The retirement benefits are defined in terms of previous earnings and the number of years of contribution (defined benefits). Contribution rates are the dependent variable in such schemes: the schemes are financed on a pay-as-you-go basis under which the contributions collected in any year are pooled to meet total benefit payments to be made in the same year. There is little build-up of reserves to meet future liabilities. If the number of current pensioners is low or benefit rates are low, contribution rates will be correspondingly low; conversely, if the number of pensioners is high or benefit levels are high, contribution rates will be correspondingly high. After retirement, pensions are indexed to earnings and/or prices, and in calculating entitlements, previous earnings are normally revalued in line with the index of average earnings.

Under a mandatory retirement savings scheme, compulsory contributions from workers and employers are placed in an individual account for each worker, possibly with a private pension fund rather than a public agency. Savings in these individual accounts are accumulated and invested. At the point of retirement, the worker may use the accumulated fund to purchase an annuity that will provide income during retirement. In that case, it is the benefit level that is the dependent variable. Contribution rates are fixed in advance (defined contribution) and what is often highly uncertain is the value of the annuity that can eventually be purchased: that will depend not only on the investment income received during the build-up of the worker's individual fund but also upon his or her life expectancy at the point of retirement, as well as the current interest rate, a crucial variable for calculating an annuity. Mandatory retirement schemes, especially in a number of developing countries, most commonly take the form of national provident funds, but more recently a number of countries, especially in Latin America, have been replacing existing social security schemes wholly or partly by a mandatory retirement savings system.

As they are currently practised, there are a number of deficiencies in both pay-as-you-go social insurance schemes and mandatory retirement savings schemes that are essentially unrelated to their basic design. The essential pros and cons of the two systems are the following:

Social insurance

Benefits are defined, so individuals know with a fair degree of certainty what replacement income they will receive in retirement, but system costs may rise over time, and policy decisions

34

may be taken without adequate consideration of future cost increases.

Solidarity can help to enhance benefits for the less well off, e.g., by crediting periods off work due to unemployment, maternity or sickness, by disregarding periods of exceptionally low earnings, by establishing a minimum pension or using a weighted benefit formula etc. But the better off may succeed in turning such provisions to their own advantage, either by influencing policy or by manipulating the amount of earnings and the periods of employment that they declare.

Since benefits are paid out of current contributions, indexing benefits to earnings and thereby linking the living standards of pensioners to that of the active population raises no technical problems.

When a scheme is introduced or improved, the elderly may benefit within a very short time by having previous periods of work recognized as periods of pensionable service. But unfavourable policy changes, such as increases in pension age, tightening of other eligibility conditions, tax changes etc., may, in the absence of proper transitional arrangements, adversely affect pensioners' and workers' existing entitlements.

Economies of scale in administration and the absence of marketing costs allow efficient social insurance systems to devote close to 100 per cent of revenue from contributions to paying benefits, but some schemes, particularly in undemocratic societies, may have much higher costs due to inefficiency and/or corruption.

Mandatory retirement savings

The costs to the contributors are fixed and thus entirely predictable, but benefits are highly unpredictable because of the investment risk and because of the variables affecting annuity rates (individual life expectancy and the current interest rate), and the community may be saddled with a heavy bill to pay if many poverty-stricken pensioners have to claim social assistance.

From the point of view of the individual contributor, there is a high degree of transparency, but the absence of any risk-pooling or solidarity means that some workers, particularly those in low-paid and precarious jobs, are more likely to end up with an inadequate income in old age.

Benefits can be indexed to inflation provided that the State will undertake to issue index-linked bonds, but otherwise such schemes are unable to guarantee inflation-proof pensions and it is not possible for them to increase pensions in line with current real earnings.

Workers' savings are not exposed to the risk of adverse changes in social security policy, although changes in tax policy may still affect them, but workers will benefit fully from a mandatory retirement savings scheme only if they have had the opportunity to contribute to it throughout their working lives.

Competition between different funds creates an incentive to provide good service and to secure a high return on investments, but it also results in high expenditure on marketing and in high administrative costs for contribution collection, with the result that about 30 per cent of contributions do not go to paying benefits.

A compromise between these two approaches, which could avoid the worst features of both, might involve the development of a three-tier structure, as follows:

A mixed system

A flat rate, possibly means-tested, basic pension, chiefly as an anti-poverty measure.

A middle tier comprising a compulsory defined-benefit pay-as-you-go social security scheme, perhaps providing benefits of more modest scope than would be the case if this were the only mechanism for providing for old age.

The development of a third voluntary tier comprising personal or occupational defined-benefit or defined-contribution schemes, operated through non-public pension funds, which would enable workers, individually or through collective bargaining, to supplement the provisions of the compulsory public social security scheme.

Such a proposal might provide flexibility missing in current schemes or in reliance on a single type of pension scheme. But it would also be more costly and require a more elaborate and intricate involvement by the State, which would have to be responsible for the regulation and monitoring of the activities of private (fully funded) complementary schemes.

6.1. *Transition*

Finally, there is the problem of transition. To move directly from an existing pay-as-you-go scheme to a fully-funded mandatory savings scheme would involve a heavy cost to the current generation of workers and employers. They would face a double burden: not only would they have to finance their own future pensions but they would still have to pay for the current generation of retirees and for new retirees who had acquired entitlements under the existing pay-as-you-go scheme. And their obligations to do so would continue until all existing entitlements were exhausted, which might take some time. Those costs might be attenuated if the transition was introduced gradually over a relatively lengthy period of time (50 years or more); but they would have to be faced, and for some countries, the cost of meeting the entitlements accumulated under existing social security arrangements constitutes a major obstacle to a shift towards fully funded defined contribution schemes.

7. GOVERNANCE

Alongside these questions of structure, economics and demographics is the problem of governance. Social security systems are necessarily complex. They rely on accurate record-keeping—in the case of pensions, over a long period. They rely on full compliance with the regulations on the part of both employers and employees, and prompt and reliable disbursement of benefits on the part of the social security institutions. They rely on good management and a reasonable level of administrative costs. And they rely on the Government not to divert social security resources to other purposes; to ensure proper investment opportunities for social security funds; and to monitor, regulate and control the operation of non-public schemes. In many developing countries, those arrangements either do not function or function so badly that the scope and effectiveness of the schemes falls far short of the coverage and benefits that are intended in the legislation. Management skills are in short supply, staff are insufficiently trained, computer technology and record-keeping are limited, indexation procedures do not exist, health care costs are uncontrolled, and administrative costs can be very high, sometimes on the order of 20 to 30 per cent of premiums paid. In some cases, corruption can be significant. Government management of the supply, delivery and cost of health-care services is frequently weak. Pension schemes may be obliged to invest in Government bonds, very often at negative rates of interest; in other cases, social security funds are simply expropriated.

There would appear to be no single means of improving management and administrative functions. A range of measures is needed, including:

(a) The improvement of financial management, especially concerning the investment of social security funds;

(b) Regular actuarial monitoring of social insurance schemes, including health care and other programmes, as well as pensions;

(c) The development and implementation of electronic data-processing techniques, and their application to record-keeping;

37

(*d*)   Greater efforts to ensure compliance on the part of workers and employers, and sometimes Government, and greater willingness to pursue legal enforcement;

(*e*)   Implementation of training and personnel development programmes, particularly at middle-management level;

(*f*)   Greater attention to relations between central, regional and local offices, and better relations with clients, both contributors and beneficiaries, in terms of both managing overall operations and costs and providing greater information and transparency;

(*g*)   The creation of policy analysis, forecasting, monitoring and survey units close to management and as the basis for diagnosis and planning, and greater control and supervision of health-care providers and the cost and quality of their services.

Where several agencies undertake the task of providing a pluralistic structure of social security and health-care programmes, it may also be necessary to establish an overall supervisory body, at arms length from both government and the various agencies involved, to ensure coordination between the different tiers and to regulate and monitor both the public and non-public forms of provision.

8.   CONCLUSION

There are clearly many other issues of significance to the reform of social security, including issues related to health care, unemployment compensation, social assistance and the provision of social services. Their relative importance throughout the world varies from region to region and from country to country, depending on individual circumstances, background and social structure. The discussion above reflects only some of the major and most controversial issues. It is also clear that there is no single agenda for reform nor a unique process by which to achieve the political consensus for it. If there is a common thread, it concerns the role of the State in the provision of social protection. In the area of retirement pensions, one of the main options concerns the possible development of non-public mandatory retirement savings schemes as an alternative to existing public social security pensions. Similarly, in the area of health-care programmes, there is frequent discussion—and in some countries a movement towards—systems based on managed competition rather than direct universal provision by the State. In programmes of unemployment benefits and social assistance, there are questions about the relative degree to which individuals should rely on themselves or on the State to maintain incomes and to find employment.

Consideration is being given to a possible modification in the role of the State, because in any case the overall weight of social expenditures—on social services, education and labour-market programmes as well as on pensions, health care and social assistance—now appears in some countries to have reached its limit. To some, it may even appear to have exceeded what is desirable. Obviously, no precise boundaries can be set. What is clear, however, is that social expenditures are perceived to be placing pressure on the management of public budgets and fiscal policy, and there is little consensus for, say, a growth of social expenditures that might exceed growth of GDP. Allied to that general concern are a set of issues concerning the effect of high social expenditures on economic performance, some of which, such as the consequences of high contribution rates or the implications for distortion in labour and capital market, may be adverse. But there are also positive effects that need to be taken into account, especially the effect of better social safety nets on the flexibility and redeployment of labour in the context of structural economic adjustment. And where there may appear to be significant economic costs of public social expenditures, these need to be weighed against the substantial social benefits and successes that have been achieved in the provision of health care and in the prevention of poverty and hardship among the elderly, families with children and those excluded from employment and earnings.

Particularly important has been the contribution of welfare-state expenditure to the maintenance of social cohesion. It is significant that, at least for the countries of Western Europe, high and growing levels of unemployment have not resulted in the social and political upheavals that accompanied the depression and mass unemployment of the 1930s. Clearly, development of the welfare state has helped Governments to fulfil their responsibilities with respect to both social justice and the maintenance of social cohesion.

What might a modified role of the State look like? The main role would be what it has always been in relation to social protection, namely, to ensure social justice, social cohesion and social consensus by guaranteeing people a reasonable standard of living. What may change are the means to be used by Governments in a pluralistic society. There will need to be a greater emphasis on sound governance of both public and private institutions based on transparency, strict financial controls, regulation and supervision, and greater responsibility for protecting the most vulnerable groups by ensuring a decent standard of living for all in a way that is respectful of human dignity.

Part One
SYSTEM DESIGN AND GOVERNANCE

Chapter III

THE IDEA OF SOCIAL PROTECTION

Lars Söderström*

1. INTRODUCTION

A society's members naturally experience periods of reduced or non-existing working capability (childhood, old age, illness). They also experience periods when capabilities cannot be used to their fullest (lack of demand, unemployment) or return from work is unexpectedly low (for example, due to crop failure). In addition, they are sometimes faced with exceptionally large consumption needs, such as in connection with natural disasters, fire or illness.

To solve this kind of problem is one of society's basic functions, perhaps the most basic. During normal conditions, under which life actually requires a great deal of labour, such problems must be solved through cooperation. The solution is to create pools that make it possible for several persons to share in the fruits of each other's labour. How these pools are organized is very important for the character of a society and its possibilities for development. An extreme case is the pure socialist model, in which earnings are put into one common pool and shared according to need. Another no less extreme case is the pure market model, in which all resources are allocated through different financial arrangements (banks, insurance companies etc.) to the extent that individuals decide through mutual agreements. Between these two extremes are models with varying degrees of cooperation. One of the most important mechanisms for the pooling of resources is the family.

Pools can be studied from a long-term or short-term point of view. From a short-term perspective (which dominates in the general debate) it is natural to emphasize differences between people and view the pooling of resources as a means to change the distribution of income in society. It seems, then, that the aged, sick and unemployed receive a benefit at the expense of people who are young, healthy and employed. However, when pooling arrangements are viewed from a long-term perspective things look different. As pointed out above, no one can rely on being healthy, employed, and lucky for an entire lifetime. From the long-term perspective, the pooling of resources is

---

*Professor, Department of Economics, University of Göteborg, Sweden.

43

clearly seen as a mutual concern in which the objective is not to redistribute income but to render more effective the use of every individual's income in society. The idea is that one should have access to consumption possibilities when they are most needed.

The present paper stresses the efficiency aspect of resource-pooling.[1] Hence, the basic issue is how a system of pools can be arranged that is favourable for everyone involved. What do private pooling arrangements look like? What can the State do to support them? What is the role of public insurance? In discussing these questions, we distinguish between the problem of spreading consumption possibilities over an individual's life cycle and the problem caused by loss of income and unexpected expenses due to illness, unemployment etc. This distinction is motivated by the fact that spreading consumption possibilities over the life cycle is achieved mainly through the pooling of resources among generations, whereas safeguards against risk of illness, unemployment and similar situations are achieved mainly the through pooling of resources within each generation. However, because certain risks are related to age, there are pools, such as health insurance, that function both across and within generation boundaries.

In order to enlighten transfers between generations we shall use a life-cycle model with overlapping generations. For the sake of simplicity, we make the following assumptions: (a) an individual's life cycle is made up of four equally long periods: childhood, lower middle age, upper middle age and old age; (b) the population grows exponentially; (c) income from labour appears only during middle age. The basic question is how consumption during childhood and old age, respectively, is to be financed out of one's surplus income during middle age. The snag is that this surplus appears at another point in time. One has to rely on a corresponding surplus for those individuals who are middle-aged at the same time as one is oneself experiencing childhood or old age.

We shall in turn look at the family, the market and the State as pooling institutions. The discussion proceeds in two stages. First, the situation without uncertainty is discussed. Then we discuss problems caused by uncertainty about length of life, size of income from labour and need of consumption goods, respectively. By the term "social protection" we refer to the entire system of arrangements, private as well as public, informal as well as formal, for spreading consumption opportunities over the life cycle and handling the risks under discussion. By contrast, the terms "social security" and "social insurance" refer to public provisions only.

---

[1]The redistributive effects of various pools are discussed in Söderström (1988).

44

2. THE FAMILY

The classic method of arranging a resource pool is that individuals belonging to several generations live in a common household. The individuals do not have to be related to each other, but blood relationships certainly contribute to strengthening their ties. This is the family model, in which transfers take the form of gifts.[2] Children and the aged are supported by the middle-aged, who voluntarily refrain from consuming all incomes themselves. This does not mean that these persons are motivated by altruistic reasons. As mentioned above, everyone can expect to become dependent on the support of others. By being generous themselves today, the middle-aged can hope to meet generosity from others tomorrow. This probability increases if children are brought up to regard giving as a duty.

For purposes of this study, we assume that each family is self-supporting. A family's consumption cannot thus exceed the family's total income, in any case not for any significant length of time. An economically interesting question is how a family acts to obtain the greatest possible benefit from its consumption possibilities. A general answer to this question cannot be given here, but we shall look closely at an example in which all members of the family have the same preferences and are also, to the same extent, the object of each other's solicitude. This is a situation in which it would be rational to maximize the utility of an average piece of the family budget. For the sake of argument, let us assume that people are selfish in the sense that an individual's utility does not depend on anything else but his own consumption.

To start with, we disregard problems related to uncertainty and assume that everyone lives through all phases of life. Since the rate of population growth has been assumed constant, in the long run there will be a clearly defined age structure in the population. At each point in time there will be a certain fraction of children, lower-middle-aged, upper-middle-aged and old-aged persons.[3] The average income (standard of living) is proportional to the average income (wage) of gainfully employed family members during a particular period of time, denoted W_t. We assume that this income increases $100z$ per cent per period, that is to say $W_{t+1} = (1+z)W_t$.

2.1 Optimization over the life cycle

Thus, the question is how a typical family member, assumed to live during the periods t, $t+1$, $t+2$ and $t+3$, prefers to use his share of

---

[2]The family is now used as a prototype for all voluntary resource pools that have some permanence.

[3]If at a certain point in time there are N elderly, there are also $N(1+q)$ upper-middle-aged, $N(1+q)^2$ lower-middle-aged and $N(1+q)^3$ children.

the family income, given that the consumption path that he prefers must be available to all family members. The optimal consumption vector thus defined can generally be written:

$$C_{ij} = (C_{0,t}, C_{1,t+1}, C_{2,t+2}, C_{3,t+3})$$

Here C_{ij} denotes consumption for family members belonging to the ith age group ($i = 0,1,2,3$) during the jth period ($j = t, t+1, t+2, t+3$). It should be pointed out that the optimal consumption vector does not have to mirror the family's income path. That a family's average income grows at a certain rate per period does not mean that the consumption of individual family members must grow at the same rate per period. Individuals can be allocated any rate of increase in their consumption, simply by deciding what share of the family income should be consumed by each age group.

What the optimal consumption vector looks like depends on what the typical individual receives in terms of utility from consuming in a certain period rather than another, as well as what it costs him to transfer consumption opportunities over time. Suppose first that the latter is of no significance. The question then is how the individual may obtain the greatest possible utility from a given amount of consumption. There are two factors that decide this: the marginal utility of consumption (denoted MU) and the individual's rate of time preference (denoted ρ).

When individuals are indifferent to the time aspect, the optimum condition is, not surprisingly, that consumption is to be allocated so that its marginal utility is the same in all periods. Normally, however, people are not indifferent to the time aspect. They have a time preference in the sense that consumption is valued more the earlier it comes. The time preference can be expressed as a discount factor $(1+\rho)\tau$, where τ is the distance to the period in question. If the time preference is taken into account, then the optimal consumption path should be decreasing just enough for the marginal utility of consumption to increase at the rate $(1+\rho)\tau$.[4]

The cost of transferring consumption opportunities will depend on circumstances. In the present example, this cost is determined by the population growth (at the rate q) and the growth in productivity (at the rate z). Due to the former, there are more younger than older individuals in a family and therefore relatively more people with whom to share consumption early in life. For one unit of consumption as a child the individual can receive $(1+q)$ units in lower middle age, $(1+q)^2$ units in upper middle age and $(1+q)^3$ units in old age. This is a reason

---

[4]The consumption path should have the following property: $MU_{t+i} / MU_t = (1+\rho)\tau$.

to postpone consumption. Increasing productivity in the economy is another argument to defer consumption. For each unit the individual consumes as a child, he receives $(1+z)(1+q)$ units in lower middle age, $(1+z)^2(1+q)^2$ units in upper middle age and $(1+z)^3(1+q)^3$ units in old age. Taking the time preference, the population growth and the growth in productivity into account, the optimal consumption path is characterized by the following condition:

$$MU_{t+\tau}/MU_t = (1+\rho)^\tau / [(1+z)^\tau(1+q)^\tau] \qquad (1)$$

According to this condition, the marginal utility of consumption should increase over the life cycle if $(1+\rho)$ is larger than the product of $(1+z)$ and $(1+q)$. In this case, consumption will successively diminish. At each point in time, a relatively large share of the family income is consumed by children. This would be typical of a stationary society. If there is a moderately rapid development of income, because of either an increasing population or increases in productivity, it will be favourable to allocate a larger part of consumption opportunities to older family members. Each individual will then experience that his own consumption grows more rapidly than the total family income (see figure III.1).

Some observations

We have seen how selfish (but loyal) family members act to maximize their own utility. As long as conditions regarding ρ, q and z are the same, the optimal consumption profile will be the same from generation to generation. To realize this consumption profile requires transfers (T_j), as shown in table III.1. Evidently, these transfers are rather large. Under present assumptions, about one half of the family income has to be taken into account. In our model, children and elderly persons account for about half of the population. The level of consumption for these groups will not differ much from the average for the total population. If the level for children is, say, lower than the average, then according to the condition (1), the level of consumption for the aged is above the average (and vice versa).

Table III.1. Income distribution and transfers within the family

	Childhood	Lower middle age	Upper middle age	Old age
Labour income	—	W_2	W_3	—
Optimal consumption	C_1	C_2	—	C_4
Deficit	$T_1=C_1$	—	—	$T_4=C_4$
Surplus	—	$T_2=W_2-C_2$	$T_3=W_3-C_3$	—

Note: A dash (—) indicates that the amount is nil or negligible.

47

Figure III.1. The optimal consumption profile
(*p*= Subjective rate of discharge)

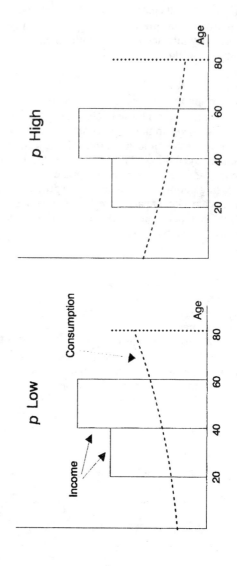

48

For a family, it seems natural to use transfers in kind. For example, children and the aged may be given shelter, food, clothes and other necessities to the extent deemed suitable. For a family living in a monetary economy, an alternative would be that transfers are given in cash, either as a lump sum or as a voucher for certain consumption. Of course, different types of transfers can be mixed. For a child, one can supplement food, housing and other benefits in kind with special accounts for the purchase of clothing, etc., as well as a lump sum to be used freely. In this way, the receiver is given discretion over at least some of his consumption (and even its timing). Whether this is a positive or negative feature of supporting grants will for now be left an open question.

Formally, transfers are decided by a family's middle-aged members. They are in control of resources and can decide what shape the transfers should take. Why should they guard the family as a pooling instrument in the best interest of *all* family members? Many would say that this is a natural duty. The economists' traditional answer is, of course, that middle-aged people do so as long as their alternatives appear worse. If they have a better alternative, then they choose that one, perhaps not immediately but eventually.

3. THE MARKET

Are family members able to obtain a better standard of living for themselves through the market system? In this section, we shall see what the market has to offer. The market's main alternative to family-based transfers is a system of *loans* that crosses generation boundaries. In order to clarify this alternative, let us imagine an economy without any private real capital. Real assets are limited to stores of foodstuffs etc. for immediate consumption.[5]

A conceivable possibility in this case is that transfers take the form of bilateral loans. One borrows during childhood, saves (paying back child loans, issuing new loans) during middle age and dissaves (has loans paid back) during old age. In our model, the loan can have a duration of one or two periods. A one-period loan is used by lenders in upper middle age (to children). Repayments, which are the lender's "pension", are in this case made when borrowers reach lower middle age.

What does the optimal consumption profile look like in this case? For obvious reasons, condition (1) no longer applies. In the loan model,

---

[5]It is easiest to imagine this example as an economy where all real capital is owned by the State, but one can also think of an economy with no real capital whatsoever, such as a typical so-called gathering economy, in which people survive by gathering fruit and fishing, among other activities.

the (private) cost of deferring consumption is (formally) independent of growth in population and productivity. Instead, this cost is determined by the rate of interest prevailing in the credit market. If r is the relevant rate of interest,[6] then for one consumption unit as a child one can receive $(1+r)$ units in lower middle age, $(1+r)^2$ units in upper middle age and $(1+r)^3$ units in old age. In the loan model, the optimal consumption path satisfies the following condition:

$$MU_{t+\tau}/MU_t = (1+\rho)^\tau/(1+r)\tau \qquad \tau = 1,2,3 \qquad (2)$$

If ρ is larger than r, then this condition means that the marginal utility of consumption should increase as the individual gets older. This is achieved by a gradual reduction of the level of consumption. The opposite applies when the rate of interest is relatively high. One should then avoid loans and allow consumption to grow over the life cycle.

Equilibrium

In order for the loan market to be in equilibrium, a balance between total demand and total supply is sufficient. It is not necessary that all loans must have the same appearance or that everyone borrow equal amounts. There can be both large and small loans, and one person can have or give many small loans as well as one large one. However, if individuals have the same preferences, there will still be a homogeneous outcome. The outcome is determined by the time preference and the age structure (that is, population growth), as well as the growth in productivity. These factors influence the market's total supply and demand. For example, an increase in the rate of population growth (that is, a greater q) would mean that the number of children, and thus the number of borrowers, increases. The result is an excess demand for credits. Competition will then force the rate of interest to increase. According to condition (2), this leads to a deferral of consumption that, in turn, decreases the demand and at the same time increases the supply of credits.

It is worth noting that loan conditions can be rather poor. Take as an example the case in which children are cared for by their parents and therefore do not demand any loans for themselves. For people of upper middle age, the only possibility to obtain a pension is then to lend money to those who are lower-middle-aged. Of course, there is no guarantee that the lower-middle-aged have an immediate interest to consume more. One reason could be that a major part of earnings is realized when individuals are lower-middle-aged. If so, the upper-middle-aged may have to pay them to accept a loan, implying a negative rate of interest. For persons of upper middle age the situation

---

[6]For the sake of simplicity, the rate of interest on loans and deposits are assumed to be equal.

can clearly become very distressed. At the same time as they need to give loans in order to secure support for their own old age, presumptive borrowers are far from willing to get into debt.[7]

So far, we have assumed that lending is an individual's only form of savings. If there are other possibilities, such as to buy gold, the situation might be less problematic. Gold can be bought by both lower- and upper-middle-aged persons, and then sold during old age. Should the distribution of income be unequal in favour of the lower-middle-aged, then again the upper-middle-aged may be sellers of gold. In this case, an individual can buy a large amount of gold as lower-middle-aged, and sell some as upper-middle-aged and the rest during old age. There is no guarantee, however, that savings will be profitable. For that to happen, the price of gold must be increasing over time. With a given stock of gold (and a constant time preference), this will not be the case unless the economy itself is growing (q or/and $z>0$). In the opposite case, with no productivity growth ($z=0$) and a declining population ($q<0$), there will be a persistent excess supply of gold, and therefore a gradual downward pressure on the price of gold. Of course for an individual saver, a falling price of gold is equivalent to a negative rate of interest.

3.1. Defection

We have assumed that individuals act selfishly. Let us look more closely at the temptation to abandon one's family for the market. First, consider a person who has just entered upper middle age. According to the plan shown in table III.1, he will consume C_3 and save $T_3 = W_3-C_3$. These savings are placed in the family pool and used, among other things, to support old-aged parents. If these savings are deposited in a bank (or otherwise invested), the rate of return will be equal to the rate of interest, r. During old age, the person will then have access to $(1+r)T_3$. By staying with the family, he will instead receive $T_4 = C_4$, according to table III.1. The return on savings during upper middle age is in this case $100[(T_4/T_3)-1]$ per cent. This yield can evidently be both larger and smaller than the rate of interest. As an example of a situation in which the upper-middle-aged profit from remaining in the family, we may think of the case in which a major part of labour incomes are received by the lower-middle-aged. In this case, the living standard for people of upper middle age would certainly decrease if they left the family.

The lower-middle-aged have a different situation. Because they have the entire lifetime income in front of them, their benefit from the family and the market, respectively, is independent of how income

---

[7]For a more detailed discussion of this case, see Samuelson (1958).

51

from employment is spread out over the life cycle. Whether they profit more or less from the family or the market will just depend on the long-term yield in each case. As stated earlier, consumption possibilities increase at the rate $(1+q)(1+z)$ in the family, while they increase at the rate $(1+r)$ on the market. Hence, for lower-middle-aged persons to prefer the family before the market, it is sufficient, generally speaking, that the sum of population growth (q) and productivity (z) be large in relation to the market rate of interest (r). The condition for this is:

$$(1+q)(1+z)>(1+r) \qquad (3)$$

Obviously, people living in a growth-oriented environment with many children receive a comparatively large benefit from the family, while the opposite is true for those who live in a more static environment with few children. It is the latter category who might choose the market before the family. Notice that a defection of lower-middle-aged family members does not have to be harmful to the standard of living enjoyed by remaining family members. All parties stand to gain as long as $T_2 \leq 0$ (see table III.1). In this case, the lower middle-aged earn no more than they themselves (and their children) consume.

3.2. Net savings

Before we leave this comparison between the family and the market as institutions for the pooling of resources, a word should be said about the effect on aggregate savings in the economy. That savings are explicit and visible in the market model, while implicit and difficult to see in the family model, may give the impression that people save more in the market model. However, appearances are deceptive. That the market model shows large gross savings is no guarantee that an increase in wealth actually occurs in this model. If all savings, as we previously assumed, take the form of (domestic) consumption loans, then the national net savings rate will be zero. In order to have a growth in wealth for the entire population, savings must take the form of investments in real assets (buildings, machinery etc.), foreign loans or the purchase of foreign property.

With respect to the aggregate rate of savings, there are two major differences between the family and market model. First, the optimal consumption path may be different. It might even be the case that one model has an optimal consumption profile that decreases over time and therefore requires a low level of savings, while the other model has an optimal consumption profile that increases over time and therefore requires a high level of savings, *ceteris paribus* (see figure III.1). For the market model to generate a higher level of aggregate savings than the family model, it is required that q be positive and

$(1+r)>(1+q)(1+z)$.[8] Second, incentives to save are also qualitatively different. What a person saves in the family model does not give him any particular entitlements. The extent to which savings today put him in a better position tomorrow will be decided by his children and grandchildren. The family model is based on charity. In this respect, the market model is quite different. What a person saves today goes unreservedly (and with interest) to his own future consumption. He acquires certain entitlements. The question, then, is whether or not this feature of the market model gives a stronger incentive to save. We leave that as an open question.[9]

4. THE STATE

It is high time to bring the State into the picture. The State can take part in the pooling of resources both directly, by administering grants, loans etc. itself, and indirectly, by making it easier for families and other private institutions to implement their transfer plans. For this purpose, the State can use its power to tax and other powers that are not available to individual families, companies or institutions.

4.1. Four main tasks for the State

General stable conditions

The State's primary task is to contribute to stable conditions in the economy at large, including protection against foreign aggression, maintaining law and order, and various other components of macro-economic stabilization, not least measures to maintain a stable value for the currency. It is self-evident that failures in these tasks would have severe consequences for all citizens. In this context, it would be going too far to discuss defence policy, national security and stabilization policy from a social policy viewpoint. We have to be content with the comment that the State should be concerned with transaction costs, adopting measures that make transfers between individuals of different age as cheap and secure as possible. An example is that the State uses its instruments of power to make sure that borrowers, if possible, fulfil their duties. Negligent borrowers can be threatened with legal action of various sorts.

---

[8]When individuals have uncertain lifetimes and there are unplanned bequests, aggregate savings may be positive even in a stationary economy with no population growth; see Söderström (1982).

[9]In discussions whether a public pension scheme of, for example, the United States social security type, increases or decreases aggregate savings, one should keep in mind that the private alternative looks quite different with the family model than with the market model.

Regulations

Another and equally important task for the State is to support private transfer arrangements. The family, for example, can be strengthened through laws that set a standard for the relationship between spouses. Regulations can be introduced on adults' obligation to support children, aged parents etc., as well as each other, lest the family be dissolved. Because the State takes measures against negligence, the family gets a backbone that is difficult to create voluntarily.[10] Similarly, the State can prescribe laws to strengthen the banking system etc.

Subsidies

Greater support for private institutions can be provided by subsidies, the State paying part or all of certain arrangements. For the family's sake, such subsidies could take the form of a child allowance, a housing allowance etc. to be paid according to certain rules, perhaps with preference for people who live in a formal marriage. Furthermore, the State may partially or wholly provide for day-care centres, schools or nursery homes. Also, the private banking and insurance system can be subsidized; subsidies can apply to specific activities (construction work, regional priorities etc.) or specific categories of recipient (for example, students).[11]

As previously indicated, people have a special interest in obtaining "child loans" in one form or another. In the market model, children are potentially the most important group of borrowers. In the family-only model, no loans exist, but it is not difficult to imagine a mixed model in which parents take loans for the purpose of supporting their children. Such loans, more or less subsidized by the State, would be an alternative to the kind of child allowances (or tax deductions) used in many countries. Notice how the burden of bringing up children changes in these cases. In the pure family model without any external support or when parents are borrowers, the parents carry the entire cost for their children. To the extent that bequests are reduced, however, certain parts of the cost will be passed on to the children themselves. When children are supported out of public funds, the cost is borne by the population at large. In the case of formal child loans, the responsibility for repayments rests with each child. What approach is best is

---

[10]An interesting example is the Swedish system of maintenance advances. This system was introduced in the 1930s as a tool to improve conditions for children at first but later for women as well. As the name suggests, maintenance allowances are paid by the State, which then tries to cover as much as possible of the cost by charging the fathers (in case they are known). If a father is unwilling to pay, he can be threatened with legal action.

[11]For a discussion of the Swedish family policy, see Söderström and Meisaari-Polsa (1995).

54

debatable. Depending on which model is used, a child is faced with three quite different prospects: (a) to pay the cost of his own children, no matter how many, (b) to pay a higher tax in order to finance subsidies to children in general, or (c) to pay back his own child loan. In the two latter cases, the expense is independent of the number of his own children.

Administration

The State's involvement may also be directed to replacing private institutions. One step in this direction is for the State to introduce its own banking activity or insurance company. For example, the State may set up special bodies to provide student loans, subsidized housing loans etc. Another step is for the State to assume part of the role played by the family. This is done when child care, schools, pensions, nursery homes etc. are not only subsidized by the State but also produced by government agencies. This does not necessarily mean that the pooling of resources must be strongly centralized: part of the administration can be handled by municipalities and other local authorities with their own political backing.

4.2. The welfare state

The State's involvement in the transfer system can evidently be very varied, and there are indeed also great differences among countries. At one extreme are countries classified as welfare states. Here, the responsibility for an individual's security and well-being rests primarily with the State, which means a less important role for the family and other private institutions. It is distinctive of the welfare state that (a) entitlements to benefits like child care, schooling, nursing homes and health care are given by virtue of citizenship, refugee status etc. and not on account of merit; (b) benefits are preferably produced by public agencies, provided in kind and distributed to promote equality; and (c) benefits are financed by progressive taxation.[12]

Compared to the traditional family model, the welfare state has a clear advantage and a just as clear disadvantage. The advantage is that everyone is included. There are no inequalities caused by differences between families in the rate of growth of family members (q) and productivity increases (z). Individuals are not required to have children of their own in order to get provisions for old age. Furthermore, there is no risk that defectors could cause a setback in the standard of living for those who remain in a family. Defection can also

---

[12]For a description of the Swedish welfare state and comparisons with Denmark, Germany, the Netherlands and the United Kingdom of Great Britain and Northern Ireland, see Olson et al. (1993).

55

happen in a welfare state—as emigration—but the effect is likely to be negligible.[13]

The disadvantage with the welfare state is that benefits are expensive. In a small family, it is not a burden to take care of children and the aged—one's own flesh and blood. The well-being of children and parents is part of the reward one receives for hard work and thrift. Within the small family, it is quite clear that everyone works for his own benefit. It is different in the strict welfare state. No immediate advantage is obtained from exerting oneself. To the extent that an individual's and his family's benefits are independent of what he does, the value of these benefits tends to be forgotten in decisions on the scope and direction of work, savings etc. Hence, people behave as if their jobs and savings are worth less than they actually are. This will most likely lessen people's interest in education, work, savings and other economic virtues, and be harmful to economic development.[14]

It is not only the financing of benefits that is more expensive in the welfare state. An extra cost lies in the uniformity of benefits. The principle of equality means that everyone should have the same benefits, such as child care. The problem is that different individuals have different needs and interests. Insufficient differentiation is inefficient, whereas a higher level of differentiation makes it possible to reach the same level of utility with fewer resources. In the family model, possibilities for differentiation are better. In this model, there can be inequalities among families reflecting differences in climate, job, religion etc., and also even greater inequalities within each family, depending on differences in taste and interests. Because family members live near each other, it should also be easier to take individual preferences into account.

We have now been referring to an advanced welfare state. In reality, the State's involvement in these matters has a less extreme design, among other things to keep costs down. One deviation is that certain benefits are given as a voucher or as a cash benefit. Receivers have in this manner the possibility to influence the concrete content of the benefit. This applies *a fortiori* if the State does not have a monopoly on producing child care etc. Another deviation from the strict welfare state is that certain benefits are paid according to merit, which makes them appear as a wage and salary component. For example, old-age pensions are differentiated, at least partly, according to earnings earlier in life. Through these types of deviations, the welfare state takes on a different

---

[13]This is not to say that the brain drain that is a result of people moving out of the country would lack economic meaning. What we mean is that moving does not cause acute problems. In other words, the effect is on the economy's rate of growth rather than its immediate income level.

[14]For an overview of these issues, see Sandmo (1991) and Barr (1992).

character. An extreme alternative is that the role of the State is reduced to the administration of commercial transfers in which all transactions are made according to the principle of *quid pro quo*. As in the market model, this means that each person directly pays for his own welfare.[15]

5. PUBLIC CHOICE: AN EXAMPLE

There are many theories about what decides the State's behaviour in different situations. Many of these theories concern the State as an instrument for pursuing the interest of a particular individual or group in society. To give a few examples, this particular individual/group can be the prince (Machiavelli), the capitalist class (Marx), the bureaucrats (Niskanen) or the median voters (Bowen, Black).[16]

It would be going too far in this paper to attempt to discuss such theories more closely. We shall limit ourselves to giving an example illustrating how the median voter theorem can be applied. This theorem states that it is the median voter who in his own interest decides how the State's powers should be used. The theorem gives an intuitively simple interpretation of the idea of democracy, and makes the State appear in glaring contrast to the family and the market. According to earlier assumptions, the family is steered by a well-meaning despot with the ambition of maximizing benefits for a randomly chosen family member, while the market can be described as a "catalytic" (Hayek) procedure, by which partially conflicting interests are concretized into mutually beneficial contracts/transactions.

The pension system will be used as an illustration. As discussed earlier, the private alternative is either an unfunded family-based pay-as-you-go system or a funded market-oriented capital reserve system. The difference is that whereas an individual pays his own pension in the latter, he pays his grandparents' and parents' pension in the former. For the sake of the argument, we assume that $(1+r)>(1+q)(1+z)$, and thus that the capital reserve system dominates. How large the capital reserves are depends on how large a pension is desired, as well as the expected rate of interest.

The State can enter the picture by taking over the existing system or by starting its own competing system. The result is similar, in any case, if the State requires that everyone should join the public system. In both cases the part that is administered by the State becomes a mandatory basic pension (not necessarily flat rate) that individuals may supplement as they like. Supplementary pensions can be organized collectively, that is, through wage negotiations, or can be obtained

---

[15]A system of this type is used as reference alternative in order to assess the welfare state's redistributing effects in Söderström (1988).

[16]There can be several median voters, in principle one for each question.

57

on an individual basis; we leave that question open. The issue before us is what the basic public pension will look like. What does the median voter want? Will it be a maintained capital reserve model or will there be a shift to the pay-as-you-go model?

Windfall gain

That the market rate of interest is relatively high is no guarantee that a political majority wants to preserve the capital reserve system. A shift to the pay-as-you-go model, which does not need any funds, gives rise to a windfall gain for the present generation. For those who have had time to obtain capital reserves in the old system, the profit is visible, in that they can receive two pensions provided that they do not prefer to increase their immediate consumption by reducing savings in the private capital reserve system.

Roughly calculated, the windfall gain is as large as all existing capital reserves in the basic pension system. It can amount to perhaps a fourth of people's lifetime income, that is to say about 10 years of earnings. The temptation to obtain additional income of this size is naturally hard to resist. If we think that the transition will be immediate and without special exceptions, today's pensioners are strongly tempted to vote for a reform. They would receive a double pension. It is just as clear that the lower-middle-aged would vote against such reform. Because they have not had the time to save in the capital reserve system, they have no part in the windfall gain. Because the market interest rate is relatively high, according to our assumption, they will be worse off under a pay-as-you-go system (see condition (3)) and will therefore prefer the capital reserve system. With pensioners in favour of and the lower-middle-aged against such reform, the decision will rest with the upper-middle-aged. As the windfall gain rises with age, the oldest would be the most favourably disposed to a reform. The median voter would (in our model) be a person around 50 years of age.[17]

Tax rate and pension level

It must also be decided what level the pension should have. In the pay-as-you-go model (unlike the capital reserve model), this is a collective concern. If pensions are financed by a proportional income tax (or payroll tax) with the tax rate s, the budget equation for the pay-as-you-go model takes the form:

$$RP = sAW$$

---

[17]There is a snag in this analysis. That people gain more the older they are is in itself an argument to postpone the shift from capital reserve to pay-as-you-go. However, at the same time one should realize that if voters behaved accordingly, there would never be a reform. For a discussion of this problem, see Sjoblom (1985).

or rather

$$s = (R/A)(P/W) \qquad (4)$$

Here, R denotes the number of pensioners, P an average pension, A the number of employed persons and W average earnings. According to condition (4), the tax rate is equal to the product of the *dependency ratio* (R/A) and the *replacement ratio* (P/W).[18] What tax rate and thus pension level does the median voter prefer? A person who is at the beginning of his career has a situation that is similar to the one under discussion in the family model. He wants a trade-off between impatience and costs according to condition (1). This trade-off implies, we assume, that the tax rate should be s_0. For a randomly chosen person who has to pay for each penny of his pension himself, this is the optimal level for the tax rate and thereby for the pension. However, a majority of the population has a different position. For obvious reasons, most people want a higher tax rate and pension. Most of those in favour of raising the tax are pensioners who receive a correspondingly higher pension without having to pay anything at all. Older upper-middle-aged persons are the next most favourably disposed to a higher tax rate. In exchange for paying a higher tax, in a few years they receive a higher pension for the rest of their lives. Each age group has its own preferred level for the tax rate, which we denote s_j. The younger the individual, the lower is s_j, but everyone is above (or at) the level s_0.

Figure III.2 illustrates the situation. The curve drawn in the figure shows how the level of the desired tax rate (and also the pension) rises with age. The median voter is placed in the middle. If his desired level is s^*, then half of those who have the right to vote (or rather half of those who vote) would want a lower tax rate and as many would want a higher. At the tax rate preferred by the median voter, the pension will be higher than in the family model or in the private capital reserve model. Thus, the young generation is forced to have an inefficient consumption profile, consuming too little when young and too much when old.

Promises of future pensions

The transition to the pay-as-you-go model and the resulting tax increase does not have to be made so that pensioners are the most favoured group. It is possible to get the majority to vote for a reform that means that a major part of the windfall gain goes to those who are middle-aged. This is achieved by allowing the transition to be made

---

[18]If, for example, there are 6 pensioners for every 10 employed, $R/A = 0.6$, and the pension makes up 70 per cent of an average salary, $P/W = 0.7$, then the necessary tax rate is equal to 42 per cent, $s = 0.42$.

Figure III.2. Desired tax rate (and pension) in different age groups

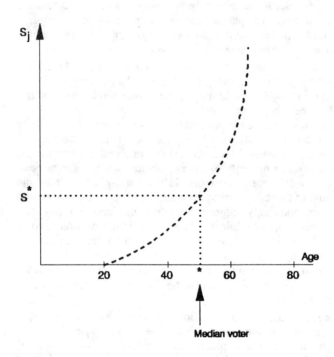

Note: After retirement (at 60) the desired tax rate becomes (in principle) infinite.

through promises of future pension benefits. An example is the Swedish ATP system,[19] in which a qualification time of 30 years of employment is required to receive a full pension (in relation to one's salary). Such requirements prevent pensioners from receiving anything of the windfall gain, and at the same time the gain for upper-middle-aged persons is cut back.[20] An arrangement of this type is significant for the pension level. Because the main focus among decision makers is shifted into younger age groups, preferences for tax increases lessen. The pension system will lie more in line with the desires of the youngest generation, which means lower pensions and a correspondingly reduced burden on the national economy. Notice, however, that we are still discussing an over-dimensioned system, that is, forced savings from the point of view of the youngest generation.

How the transition from a capital reserve model to a pay-as-you-go model influences the national net savings has been mentioned in the previous section. We have no reason to believe that a public pay-as-you-go model would have a less damaging influence on savings than the family pay-as-you-go model. In both cases, the incentive to save is very weak.

6.   UNCERTAINTY OF LENGTH OF LIFE

We shall now discuss two problems that are rather different from one another, related to uncertainty of length of life. One problem is that people contributing to the support of a family, we can call them breadwinners—may die early. If this should happen, there would be a difficult setback for the family's income. Another problem is that ageing members of a family may live much longer than average. This does not mean a loss in income but certainly a requirement for increased expenditures, which can be as difficult. We shall look at the latter problem first.

6.1.   *Risk of a long life*

In order to illustrate the problem of extreme longevity, we return to the utility-maximizing lender of section 3. Suppose that he cannot exclude the possibility that he will live yet another period, that is, that he may die at the age of 100 instead of 80, and that the probabilities for either outcome are 10 and 90 per cent respectively. The probable length of his life will thus be 82 yearse. What should he do?

---

[19]ATP = general supplementary pension, introduced in 1960 and presently under revision.
    [20]However, in order to ensure a broad majority in favour of the ATP reform, the aged were given generous transitory benefits.

Trying to solve this problem by himself will not be particularly successful. To make sure that he will not starve to death he must act as if he is certain to become 100 years of age. Roughly estimated, he would then have to double outstanding loans during working age. The consumption plan would have to be modified accordingly, that is, lowered about 25 per cent during all days of life. Something may then happen that is not entirely unexpected: he may die anyway at the age of 80, leaving about 20 per cent of his entire lifetime income unused. This is of course highly unsatisfactory.

If people in this situation cooperate, they can all improve their standard of living. The market solution is that a fund is set up to cover the additional cost for those who *de facto* live a long time. In our example, it would be sufficient if everyone set aside an amount corresponding to about two years of consumption. In exchange, those individuals who live longer receive a compensation covering 20 years of extra consumption. In this manner, the price for avoiding starvation is reduced considerably, to just about 1/10 of the price one needs to pay without cooperation.[21]

Insurance

The type of cooperation described above is an example of an insurance arrangement. What we discussed in earlier sections are rather simple transfers such as gifts and gifts in return; loans and mortgage payments; and taxes, grants and subsidies. An insurance is more complex, being a so-called contingency contract: one pays a premium for the right to receive a certain compensation if something happens, a "damage". For example, the condition can be that a person must live to a certain age, after which the compensation can be paid as a fixed annuity, that is, a certain annual amount, possibly for the remainder of his life, but the compensation can also be a lump sum. How the compensation is constructed is a matter of convenience. Frequently, old-age pensions take the form of a fixed annuity for as long as the policy holder lives, but there are also pensions that come as a lump sum or a fixed amount for a limited period of time.

For an insurance policy to break even, the sum of the premium that is paid by insured persons must be at least as large as the sum of compensations that may arise. A special case is when premiums are being differentiated on an actuarial basis, meaning that each insured person pays a premium that is at least as large as the value of compensation claims that he himself is expected to have. For the ith type

---

[21]Note that the cooperating group is assumed to be large. In a small group, such as a family, one cannot take for granted that the average age will be 82. Consequently, in this case one must make larger appropriations in order to meet the risk for long life.

person, this principle can be written: $p_{i \geq p_i} K_i$. Here, p_i designates the premium, while π_i designates the likelihood that the insurance condition will be fulfilled, that is, that a damage will occur, and K_i designates the compensation that is given in case of a damage. These amounts can vary for different categories.

To illustrate this point, let us imagine that an insurance applies to one type of damage with a simple identifiable risk. As an additional simplification, assume that there are only two categories of insured persons ($i = 1,2$). The difference between them is that they have a different likelihood of experiencing a damage. There is a low-risk group, with likelihood for injury π_1, and a high risk-group, with likelihood for injury π_2 ($>\pi_1$). For example, in a pension insurance, π_i can be a measure of the ith category's expected length of life above retirement age. Expressed differently, π_i is the expected number of years of compensation for the ith category. As to the size of π we know that women normally live longer than men, better educated people live longer than poorly educated people, white-collar workers live longer than blue-collar workers etc. To bring our example one step further, assume that members of the high-risk category die at the age of 90 on average, compared to just 75 for members of the low-risk category. Then, with actuarial insurance premiums, people in the high-risk category pay twice as much as individuals in the low-risk category. The difference reaches an amount corresponding to about four years' consumption.

We have now assumed that each individual insures himself against the risk of having a long life. This is closest to the loan model described in section 3 above. Of course, this is not the only possibility. An alternative is that children may insure themselves against their parents having an extra-long life. This alternative fits well into the family model, in which children have a responsibility for supporting the elderly. In the welfare state, no measures are needed at all. As long as the total number of elderly does not change, uncertainty about the length of life does not call for any changes in the public transfer system. The same tax rate will be sufficient to finance the same annuity for as long as each individual stays alive. If there are fluctuations in the average length of life etc., these are likely to be small.[22]

---

[22]We are not now discussing changes in trends. If people tend to become older, which seems to be the case, then a growing amount of incomes must be set aside for pensions. Whether consumption during other phases of the life cycle needs to be reduced depends on what happens with available jobs and productivity. If people choose to work longer, for example, this can naturally compensate for decreases in mortality. On problems related to an ageing population, see Cutler et al. (1990).

6.2. *Risk of early death*

We turn now to the other problem, that the breadwinner may die early. The solution in this case is to buy life insurance. In the actuarial case one pays a premium that is proportional to the compensation chosen and the estimated risk of death. The former is suitably set so high that survivors are compensated for loss of income etc. A rough estimate of the risk of death can be seen in demographic tables showing the risk of death for men and women in different age groups, sometimes subdivided based on region and socio-economic status. For a more thorough calculation, information on people's occupation, health status, body weight, smoking habits etc. would be necessary. The compensation may be paid as a lump sum or a fixed annuity for surviving spouse and under-aged children.

Life insurance may be a part of the transfer system in a welfare state. However, it is worth noting that providing support to survivors, in particular widows, is one of the more controversial features of the social security system. For men and women to be treated differently is seen to be as out of date. It is sometimes argued that there is no need whatsoever to have a survivors' compensation for adults. In Sweden, for example, steps have been taken to abolish the public compensation for widows. An objection against the compensation of children losing a parent is that the compensation is normally differentiated with respect to the deceased's salary level. Since it is hardly the case that children of wealthy parents have greater needs than other children, critics wonder why taxes are being used for the purpose of preserving this inequality.

6.3. *Problems in insurance markets*

If people are able to obtain insurance of the kind we have described, then uncertainty about the length of life is no great problem. However, it is not certain that a functioning insurance market will develop spontaneously. It is also possible that the insurance that people buy may be costly to the national economy as a result of unfavourable behaviour changes (in particular, moral hazard). We shall now look at some of the typical problems in this area for insurance markets.

Free riding

There may be no great demand for insurance. One reason is that many willingly act charitably. By counting on this behaviour among fellow citizens, one's expenditures for insurance can be saved and used for something more pleasant; one thus becomes a free rider. Since the uninsured are extremely vulnerable, one effect of free riding is that a need for charity emerges. Another effect is that the insurance market becomes thin, which is a problem in itself. We have previously pointed out how important it is that as many as possible partake in insurance pools. It is through the law of large numbers that uncertainty is reduced for the group as a whole. Free riding can therefore lead to more insecure and expensive insurance for those who stay with the pool.

Should free riding be considered a serious problem, a straightforward solution would be to make the insurance in question mandatory. Car insurance is an example at hand. By making such insurance mandatory, one avoids meeting uninsured fellow road users. This is a strong argument. That pension insurance and sickness insurance should be mandatory is not as easy to argue, since in these cases the absence of insurance usually affects only the uninsured person himself. The most important argument for making insurance mandatory is that people are normally distressed by having to witness old and sick people suffering from lack of resources.[23]

Collective risks

It may also be the supply that is lacking. Insurance pools work best with easily identifiable risks and independent damages, but this condition is not always fulfilled. For example, in the case of life insurance there might be many deaths at one time because of a natural catastrophe, epidemic, war etc. In such cases, the risk is causing a damage to many or even all members of the pool at the same time. In relation to such collective risks, there is nothing to win by cooperation. There is nobody or too few left to cover damages. Consequently, insurance companies try to avoid including collective risks in insurance contracts by having certain exceptions to the right to compensation *(force majeure)*. An alternative solution to the problem of collective risks is to build a system of reinsurance, under which insurance companies buy and sell insurance to each other. In this manner, risk-sharing can be spread globally and practically all risks become manageable.[24]

Exclusion

An additional problem in insurance markets is that there are people who want to insure themselves but cannot afford to pay the required premium. This applies primarily to people with high risk exposure when insurance premiums are priced actuarially. It is not difficult to visualize such cases. Take as an example the case that an insurance policy should cover expenses for placement in a nursing home for the aged. For an individual judged to have a great need of care, the premium may be well above his annual income. To avoid

---

[23]Some countries have mandatory insurance limited to low-income workers; those who have higher incomes are assumed to be taking care of themselves.
[24]See Borch (1990).

people in this situation becoming dependent on charity, there is no other possibility than to give a subsidy. This can be done explicitly so that the State (or a private charity, such as a church) pays part of the premium, possibly with a voucher. However, subsidies are often given implicitly through one regulation or another. For example, insurance pools may be told not to differentiate premiums at the same time as they welcome anyone who wants insurance. This is a regulation that is sometimes forced on friendly societies running sickness funds and unemployment funds.[25]

Adverse selection

The problem of exclusion is (at least partially) due to the fact that there is public knowledge of the exposure to risk. A potentially more severe problem in insurance markets is that such knowledge may instead be private. If actual risks are known only to individuals, insurance companies cannot identify what risk category a person belongs to. Insurance companies then have no alternative but to give all policy holders the same premium, corresponding to the expected compensation for the entire population, plus a mark-up for administrative costs and profit. This is attractive for people with a high risk exposure, who then gladly insure themselves, but not for those with low risk exposure. People in the latter group find the premium too high and give up insurance altogether. The insurer then discovers that he has misjudged the amount of claims. Among those who buy insurance, the average-risk exposure is higher than for the population as a whole. As a consequence, the insurance company will take a loss. Raising the premium is no way out of the problem. Each time the premium is raised there will be more defections until the market shrinks to insignificance.

This may sound worse than it is. In practice, insurers have many opportunities of finding out what risk group people belong to. An example is to give a bonus to those who seldom use their insurance, either so that a part of the premium is paid back or so that they get a lower premium in the future. An alternative that can be taken into consideration is that the insurance in question may be made mandatory. This would set a stop to defection and thus increase the sum of premiums, but people with a low risk exposure will probably feel that they are treated unfairly.

---

[25]It is not certain that people with high exposure to risk are actually helped. It is possible that insurance pools, irrespective of whether they are run as a cooperative or a company, will try to avoid unprofitable policy holders. To that end, they can make use of more or less subtle harassment. There is also a risk that the pool may have to be closed down.

Moral hazard

Because people insure themselves against a certain damage, their interest in avoiding this damage lessens. As a consequence, the exposure to risk and the frequency of damages is likely to increase. This reaction is called moral hazard *ex ante*. For example, the frequency of suicide may increase due to people buying life insurance in order to lessen the effect of their death on survivors. A possible response from insurers would be to introduce a clause in the insurance contract that compensation will be reduced if suicide is suspected. Another reaction to insurance coverage is moral hazard *ex post*. For example, the utilization of health care may increase when people buy (or get) health insurance covering expenditures for seeing a doctor etc.

It is hardly possible to avoid moral hazard altogether. However, its extent can be limited by using an excess in the form of coinsurance, a deductible (franchise) or a reduced premium bonus in the future. To the extent that the compensation is less than the value of the damage according to the policyholder's own evaluation, he is burdened with a part of the cost himself. If he can avoid this cost, at least partly, he will certainly try to do so.

Rand Corporation's Health Insurance Experiment (HIE) will now be used to illustrate the behavioural implications of the conditions stated in an insurance contract. HIE, which is one of the largest randomized experiments ever carried out in the social sciences, was designed for the comparison of some 15 models of health-care financing with a focus on the role played by patient charges (out-of-pocket-costs). Participants in the experiment were adults of working age not (substantially) enrolled in social welfare programmes and their families. There was an income-related cap on the amount of charges a person had to pay, for example 2 per cent of annual income.[26]

Some results of HIE are shown in table III.2. The demand for health care (= consumption) varies with different caps (z) and subsidy rates (s). Demand in the case of totally free care, $z = 0$ (equivalent to $s = 100$), has been set equal to 16 per cent of an average annual income. The cap on out-of-pocket-costs varies between 0.5 and 10 per cent of the same income.[27] Three subsidy rates are considered—0, 50 and 75 per cent of health-care costs. The corresponding coinsurance rates are 100, 50 and 25 per cent, respectively.

---

[26]For a description of the Health Insurance Experiment, see for example, Manning et al. (1987), and Keeler et al. (1988).

[27]All results reported in Keeler et al. (1988) are based on observations with the cap on out-of-pocket costs given in absolute terms as US$ 50, 100, 1,000, 1,500, 2,000, and 3,000, all in 1984 prices. For convenience, these amounts are here expressed relative to the taxable income per capita (with some approximation).

Table III.2. Demand for health care with different subsidy rates and caps on out-of-pocket costs
(Percentage of average annual income)

Subsidy rates(s) (Percentage of health-care costs)	Level of demand based on out-of-pocket caps (z) of:					
	0	1/2	1	2	5	10
0	16.0	13.5	13.0	12.2	11.6	9.8
50		13.9	13.3	12.8	12.4	11.2
75		14.0	13.5	13.2	13.1	12.1

Source: Author's calculations, based on E.B. Keeler et al.,
"The demand for medical treatment in the Health Insurance
Experiement", Rand Corporation documents,
No. R-3454-HHS.

It is evident from these results that patient charges have a negative effect on the demand for health care. This is seen most clearly in the case of unsubsidized care, which there is a 15 per cent decrease in the demand already at a very low cap (z =0.005). Raising the cap will decrease demand to less than 60 per cent of its "satiation" level. Notably, there is hardly any effect from raising the cap above 10 per cent; few individuals have expenditures for health care above this level.[28]

It is worth pointing out that even substantial decreases in health-care consumption do not necessarily cause a major deterioration in health, at least in the United States of America. HIE findings indicate that variations in the consumption of health care due to a changed coinsurance rate have only marginal health effects, a conclusion based on observations during five years.

7. PERMANENT LOSS OF INCOME

This section will discuss compensations for a permanent loss of income before retirement age. In the welfare state, this compensation takes the form of a separate disability pension, distinct from the old-age pension. Some disabilities originate at birth, others are caused by accident or illness. Traffic accidents in particular cause a large number of cases.

---

[28]Keeler et al. (1988) estimate that 10 per cent of individuals would have patient charges in excess of the cap in this case. Raising the cap to $z = 0.15$ would decrease this proportion to 7 per cent and lowering the cap to 5 per cent would increase the proportion to 18 per cent, and to 6 per cent if the cap was lowered to $z=0.02$. These estimates apply when there are no subsidies.

What qualifies as a disability is debatable: no one is perfect and different environments have different requirements, while disabilities that were once insurmountable may be overcome by rehabilitation and new technological aids. At the same time, disabilities evidently limit the quality of life. From this perspective, it is not meaningful to classify people permanently as more or less handicapped. The same person can be both more and less handicapped: he can be handicapped in an environment with certain requirements, while he is not in another environment with other requirements. Thus, the assessment of the damage caused to traffic accident victims and others should take various environments into consideration.

Traditionally, a disability pension compensates only for loss of income. As a rule, it is not especially difficult to identify such loss. When possible, one can use information about the individual's previous salary. In certain cases, however, especially when a handicap applies to a young person, one is forced to make a rather stereotyped estimate. What is loss of income for someone who just graduated with an MA in engineering who is badly injured in a motorcycle accident? If authorities do not find a better solution, this person will receive compensation with a minimum amount just above the subsistence level. Possibly, this will remain his only income until retirement age, when the old-age pension takes over.

Let us look more closely at traffic injuries. An alternative to a public disability pension is for loss of income to be compensated from one's car insurance. This would mean raising premiums for traffic insurance, and raising them even higher if pain and suffering are to be compensated, while taxes could be somewhat reduced. If nothing else, this would have an effect on the distribution of income. While the disability pension can be supposed to be financed by a tax that is more or less proportional to income, premiums for car insurance are differentiated with respect to differences in risk exposure. For people without a car, the cost will surely be lower. Who pays more is hard to say, but it can be assumed that, for example, a young man driving a sports car belongs to this category. As has been mentioned earlier, actuarial premiums can be produced by the use of a bonus system. The differentiation of premiums provides an incentive for avoiding risky cars and driving carefully, thereby reducing traffic hazards, which results in fewer accidents, deaths and injuries. Such positive effects are not reached when injuries are compensated within a traditional disability pension.

In case a person's disability is caused by work hazards, a special compensation scheme might be used. Provided that this scheme is being financed by premiums that reflect the work hazards in question, this arrangement can have a positive effect on people's behaviour. There are two possible models for work injury insurance. One model has companies as policy holders, the other model has workers themselves as policy holders. A decisive factor in choosing between these models is who should have the incentive to reduce risk exposure in society. Generally speaking, this incentive should lie with whoever has the most influence on the matter. If negligence on the part of employees is the main problem, then individual insurance is most suitable. If, on the other hand, injuries depend on deficiencies in the work environment and organization problems, then it is more suitable for the firm to be policy holder. A combination is also possible, with each department or work team having its own insurance. Of course, different industries could use different models.

A differentiation of premiums in line with expected damages will have an effect on competition and economic development in general. For firms that have their own insurance, those with low risk exposure (and premium) have an improved situation compared to those with high risk exposure (and premium). In the case of individual insurance, there is a corresponding change in the comparative advantages for different employees, since premiums will vary with how careful and conscientious one is. For those who are typically accident-prone, it would be an advantage to find a job with relatively low risk exposure. Otherwise, a large part of their salary will be consumed paying the insurance premium.

In this area there is evidently a great risk of free riding. When insurance premiums are very high, it is tempting to take a chance on charity. This is more serious, since damages often involve outsiders who demand an adequate compensation. Mandatory insurance could be a solution. Primarily, it is work injury insurance and traffic insurance that should be mandatory. One can also consider requiring insurance, for example, for people skiing, climbing mountains or otherwise taking a deliberate risk. Such insurance can for the most part substitute disability pensions. This would not only have a positive effect on preventing injuries but would also mean that such financing would be moved outside the tax system, thus lowering the excess burden of taxation.

As to the problem that some are born with handicaps or acquire them during childhood, a possible solution would be for parents to have a suitable insurance policy against that event validity. However, since it might be difficult to make sure that all parents buy such insurance,[29] a better alternative might be for all children to be protected by the State. In this case, there are hardly any incentive effects to worry about.

---

[29]Sometimes it is even difficult to know who is the father of a child.

8. TEMPORARY LOSS OF INCOME

We have now reached the last subject in this paper: the temporary loss of income. The most important reasons for a temporary loss of income are childbirth, illness (oneself and others) and unemployment. Is this something that has to be compensated? If so, how?

The family is actually well suited to handle temporary losses of income. As long as amounts are small—seen from the perspective of the entire life cycle—the family needs no large buffer to deal with the problem. Should the family purse occasionally need to be reinforced, there are possibilities for taking out a loan. Providing such loans could be a task for local governments, as a form of social assistance. However, more formal insurance arrangements cannot be avoided entirely. They enter the picture because unemployment, etc. may have more than just a marginal effect on life-cycle incomes. As time goes by, a family can experience many and long-lasting losses of income, with a quite noticeable effect on the standard of living. For a single person, the pain threshold can be rather low.

Traditionally, the family has acquired complementary insurance by organizing friendly societies. Members of such societies have often been people who work in a certain workplace. Other possibilities are for members of a particular union or those living in a certain area to organize a society. Friendly societies function as ordinary insurance providers. Members deposit part of their salary into a common pool when they work and receive a compensation from the pool when they become ill or are unemployed. The compensation for illness may include health care.[30] Because members of a society know each other well, it is relatively easy to prevent abuse of the system.

Note that abuse and moral hazard are not the same thing. An example of abuse is that someone claims to be ill without being so. Moral hazard deals with the incentive to avoid risk exposure and thus limit the size of the damage. Because of insurance, people can be less careful in protecting themselves against infections (or even pregnancy), or can be more brazen in dealings with their employer. They can also be less eager to find a new job or to take medicine as prescribed. This increases the amount of legitimate loss of income. However, it should be pointed out that insurance presupposes that people follow some standard of conduct. Social norms are essential for establishing a system of social protection.

Both abuse and moral hazard become less of a problem when compensations are paid with a sizeable excess in the form of coinsur-

---

[30]Taking care of the mentally ill has by tradition been a responsibility of the State or the church.

71

ance, a deductible (franchise) or reduced premium bonus in the future. A firm limit on the period a person may be compensated, such as 300 days, has a similar effect. As abuse of the system becomes expensive for the individual himself, it becomes profitable (a) to avoid illness and unemployment and (b) to return to work as soon as possible. Such behaviour keeps premiums low and strengthens the society's ability to resist strain. A question is whether the excess should be progressive or regressive. If an excess is progressive, it grows with the size of the compensation, that is, the permanence of loss of income. This means that one receives less compensation over time, which might intensify people's efforts to return to work. In the regressive case, it is instead the compensation that increases over time. This has the advantage of compensating the loss of income proportionately more the larger it becomes, but at the same time the incentive to return to work becomes weaker. The risk in this case is that people become accustomed to being out of work ("learned helplessness") and that the population will be segmented into employed and unemployed.

During the 1920s and 1930s, resources of both health insurance funds and unemployment funds were greatly strained. Increasing premiums threatened to create problems with free riding, exclusion and adverse selection. Even collective risks made themselves felt. For unemployment funds, the 1930s mass unemployment was a clear reminder. For health insurance funds, it was more a question of technical developments increasing medical costs. Problems of this sort can be eased by various public measures. One option is to grant a subsidy to a number of friendly societies in proportion to the total amount of compensation, possibly on the condition that they have a moderate premium and be available to everyone, even people who are not members of a union or live in a different neighbourhood. [31]

Notice that unemployment funds owned by such societies are designed for those who are normally employed. Young people who become unemployed after leaving school and older workers whose compensation possibilities from such funds have been emptied must be compensated in another manner. The option of social assistance is always necessary as a last resort.

---

[31] This is the model still used for unemployment insurance in Sweden. Unemployment funds are administered by unions. Friendly societies in the area of health insurance, on the other hand, were abandoned in the middle of the 1950s when a general health insurance plan was introduced. This plan is financed by taxes and gives compensation in the form of sickness benefits as well as medical care.

REFERENCES

Barr, N. (1992). Economic theory and the welfare state: a survey and interpretation. *Journal of Economic Literature*, No. XXX, pp. 741-803.

Black, D. (1958). *The Theory of Committees and Elections*. Cambridge University Press.

Borch, K.H. (1990). *Advanced Textbooks in Economics*, vol. 29; *Economics of insurance*. North-Holland.

Bowen, H. (1943). The interpretation of voting in the allocation of economic resources. *Quarterly Journal of Economics*, No. 58, pp. 27-48.

Cutler, D. M., et al. (1990). An aging society: opportunity or challenge? *Brookings Papers on Economic Activity*, No. 1.

Keeler, E. B., et al. (1988). *The demand for medical treatment in the Health Insurance Experiment*. Rand Corporation document, No. R-3454-HHS.

Manning, W. G., et al. (1987). Health insurance and the demand for medical care: evidence from a randomized experiment. *American Economic Review*, No. 77, pp. 251-277.

Niskanen, W. A. (1971). *Bureaucracy and Representative Government*. Aldine and Atherton.

Olson, S. E., et al. (1993). Social security in Sweden and other European countries: three essays. *Swedish Ministry of Finance Documents*, No. 1993:51.

Samuelson, P. (1958). An exact consumption loan model of interest with or without the social contrivance of money. *Journal of Political Economy*, December.

Sandmo, A. (1991). Economists and the welfare state. *European Economic Review*, No. 35, pp. 213-239.

Sjoblom, K. (1985). Voting for social security. *Public Choice*, No. 45, pp. 225-240.

Söderström, L. (1982). The life cycle hypothesis and aggregate household savings. *American Economic Review* No. 72, pp. 590-596.

Söderström, L. (1988), The redistributive effects of social protection: Sweden. In *The Crisis of Redistribution in European Welfare States*. J. P. Jallade, ed., European Institute of Education and Social Policy.

_____ and Meisaari-Polsa, T. (1995). Swedish family policy: economic aspects. In *Scandinavian Population Studies*, vol 10, *Demography, Economy and Welfare*, Ch. Lundh, ed., Lund University Press.

73

Chapter IV

REFORMING SOCIAL SECURITY: EFFICIENCY AND GOVERNANCE

Diogo de Lucena and Jorge Braga de Macedo*

1. INTRODUCTION

The reform of the welfare state as we have known it in recent decades has been more and more on the agenda of policy makers and academics. In addition to the aggregate financial constraints felt by a great number of States worldwide, microeconomic efficiency also bears on this problem. In section 2 below, we address efficiency issues, with specific reference to old-age pensions and unemployment benefits. Both provide social security via insurance, the latter against states of nature.

Sustaining social security is thus a worldwide challenge for policy, in an environment in which reform at the national level is a response to pressure on domestic firms and ultimately on individuals to escape excessive taxation or regulation. Even if policies broadly converge to some efficiency norm, the response may not be immediate for a variety of reasons, including political cycles. Lack of national cohesion on development strategy may benefit incumbent policy makers or existing generations at the expense of voters or future generations. The pattern may be countered by appropriate policies that are supported by institutions, accounting methods and monitoring devices. This problem of governance is covered in section 3. Finally, combining efficiency and governance, we try in section 4 to infer some lessons on how to reform current systems.

Governance is decisive because most social security systems are very dependent on the State. It is thus pure rhetoric to separate the discussion of their financial equilibrium from the discussion of public finances in general. The question is whether or not current policies are feasible in the long run without threatening macroeconomic stability. Governance also impinges on the desirability of redistribution policies and their financing. While one aspect of providing benefits has to do with managing underlying political options, the costs of current—or alternative—social security systems do affect the functioning of

---

*Professors, Faculty of Economics, Nova University, Lisbon.

74

economies. To assess how these interactions operate, it must be recognized that the State cannot raise revenue, for whatever end, by lump-sum taxation. The unavoidable excess burden of taxation creates a trade-off between redistribution and efficiency, which must be reckoned with in political terms.

Yet this type of effect is far from being the whole story: some of the roles fulfilled by modern social security systems do contribute to economic efficiency. And when they do not, there is still the problem of minimizing the losses for given redistribution objectives. Different designs of the way a system operates and is financed can mean widely different costs for the economy. By affecting the incentives to save and work or by solving problems of asymmetric information in insurance markets, a social security system affects the functioning of the economy both negatively and positively .

Solutions must be equitable but also efficient; they must be incentive-compatible and promote growth. Otherwise, they will magnify the social problem that they were supposed to cure and increase social deprivation. If not replaced by more efficient policies, nationally agreed equity objectives will become more difficult to attain as time goes by.

Macroeconomic stability is a prerequisite for sustained growth, and social consensus on a stability-oriented policy is necessary to avoid financial instability in the form of "stop and go" policies. As the current situation in most countries is one of serious problems of efficiency and equity within and among generations, the threat to sustained growth may also extend to national cohesion.

Only firms, not States, can go bankrupt. The notion of the competitiveness of nations must therefore be handled with care. Nevertheless, attempting to foster international interdependence by encouraging cooperation among all levels of government, instead of defensive measures involving some form of protection against foreign competition, is a vital challenge for the State because it helps to sustain reform.

In discussing reform issues, we will take as a reference the most frequent arrangement in the OECD countries: a universal, compulsory public system, financed through a payroll tax and general tax revenue on a pay-as-you-go basis. Reforming universal social security systems can be seen as solving a problem of macroeconomic and microeconomic efficiency, given the values about equity that prevail in a given society, which are in one way or another responsible for the particular institutional mix available.

In the European Union (EU), the mechanisms of multilateral surveillance are based on peer pressure to comply with the annual broad economic policy guidelines and the medium-term strategy contained in the *White Paper on Growth, Competitiveness and Employ-*

75

ment approved in late 1993. Although the White Paper fails to distinguish between the arguments for and against tax reform, including social security reform, and ways to lower the excess cost of labour in Europe, the greatest difficulties for the competitiveness of European firms in world markets come from slow implementation of the agreed-upon strategy.

2. EFFICIENCY

2.1. *Old-age pensions*

2.1.1. *Income smoothing and redistribution*

A major component of all social security systems is the old-age pension scheme. We can distinguish two roles for this arrangement. The first is related to savings and income-smoothing. The second is related to redistribution. We will not discuss the second aspect in detail. It is not clear at all, on a priori grounds, that the old as such are in special need of redistribution measures. They are not always the poorest and may well be richer than families with young children. Poor old people should be the target of redistribution measures because they are poor but not because they are old, as argued in detail by the World Bank (1994).

Moreover, most of the equity debate has been centred on measures of income distribution that may not be adequate. Policy implications can be quite different and sometimes in conflict when we look at intra-generational versus intergenerational redistribution or at instant versus life-cycle inequality, as discussed in section 3 below (see also von Weizsäker (1994)).

In any case, this redistribution role of a social security system can be conceptually distinguished from its role of income smoothing, which includes an insurance argument. And our point is that it should be advantageous to do so. In particular, the redistribution element should be financed by different means. Those are political objectives of society as a whole, as represented by its government, and they should be financed by general revenue. Here the trade-off between equity and efficiency should be made clear by having the general redistribution programmes compete for tax funds with other objectives.

In a world of perfect knowledge and perfect foresight, with well functioning capital and insurance markets, there would be no reason for the State to intervene in relation to the income-smoothing objective. Voluntary decisions, insurance contracts and the saving instruments created by the markets would be enough. So the problem must lie in the fact that market failures exist, which raises the question of whether Governments can intervene to improve the situation. But

76

Governments are also prone to failure, and the problem becomes a very complex one of deciding which types of failures are preferable. We live not in a world of potential first-best solutions but in one in which hard choices among imperfect solutions are the norm.

2.1.2. Income smoothing and efficiency

Income-smoothing has quite a substantial economic value. More precisely, people value the consumption-smoothing that results from income-smoothing. Governments all over the world put a lot of effort into stabilizing aggregate consumption. Lucas (1987, p. 26) estimates the potential gains for the American consumer associated with the elimination of variability in aggregate consumption at about 0.5 per cent. The cost of aggregate consumption instability is therefore a small proportion of aggregate consumption. The cost of individual variability of consumption is estimated by the author at close to 5 per cent, a much more sizeable effect. But this cannot be interpreted as the possible gain from improvements in stabilization policy, rather as the potential or actual gain from social insurance. Any system of income-risk pooling that improves the imperfections of capital markets would contribute to reduce this individual variability and therefore have a significant economic value to individual households. The benefit will be greater the greater the initially uninsurable risk, so that the estimate is probably higher for many countries besides the United States.

There is an efficiency case for social security type arrangements. But different arrangements will have different consequences, and the difficult and interesting questions are the ones that concern the design and operation of alternative solutions; in particular, when and how should the State take over rather than allow the markets to solve the situation?

The smoothing of income has to be made for two reasons. The first relates to life-cycle arguments. The ability to earn changes substantially with age, and old people do not command high salaries. Ideally, people would save enough while young to finance their consumption later. But this need will arise even without any uncertainty about people's real income and life duration. The second reason concerns smoothing across different states of nature. Unexpected events, totally or partially outside individual control, will affect income. Most people would like to insure against such risks. We will take each one in turn.

2.1.3. Life-cycle smoothing

Voluntary schemes are the best way to solve this problem because they will cause the least distortion. As long as there are adequate savings instruments, including adequate tax treatment of long-term savings, there should be no reason for the State to impose its choice on the amount of individual saving and its applications. But problems do appear that can substantially qualify this conclusion.

The first problem has to do with life-cycle poverty: total income over the entire life cycle may be insufficient. If that is so, no amount of individual saving will solve the problem. We need to have redistribution, and it can be argued on efficiency terms that it should be concentrated in the old-age period, when the disincentive to work is not affected.

The second problem has to do with undeveloped capital markets and the inability of evaluating the long-term prospects of the particular investment instruments available. This may lead to a lower than optimal savings rate, which may well warrant some forced savings. But it is not a logical consequence that such forced savings should be made through a publicly run system. If funded, it faces similar informational problems. If it is a pay-as-you-go system, other problems will arise, and we address some of them below. Macroeconomic instability and inflation in particular, so pervasive in many countries, also make for inadequate saving instruments. Again, although this may logically lead to some mandatory forced savings, it does not imply the need of a publicly run system.

Finally, there is a moral hazard type of argument. By short-sightedness or deliberate strategic behaviours, people may not save enough and thus become a burden on society, even when they are, in life-cycle terms, above a minimum poverty level. Modern societies, at least in many countries, will find it unacceptable not to help, which means that every citizen benefits from some insurance. If that is the case, then everybody—and not just workers—should be made to contribute. If we accept this universal guarantee as desirable, then one has a case for a universal compulsory minimum pension scheme. The State is the entity offering the insurance policy and so this should be a publicly run system, but only for a minimum pension.

2.1.4. *Retirement and insurance*

It is well known that, owing to asymmetry of information, insurance markets are prone to some specific forms of market failure: adverse selection and moral hazard. Private markets may thus fail adequately to pool risks in the population. When dealing with retirement pensions, two risks that give raise to great uncertainty deserve attention: inflation and uncertainty about time of death. In both cases, the question can be asked whether the State can do a better job of pooling risks than is done by the market.

When there is no inflation or when the rate of inflation can be anticipated, privately run funded pensions are perfectly possible and efficient arrangements. The problem arises with unanticipated inflation, for two reasons. First, being unanticipated, it makes it very difficult to make actuarial calculations unless real rates of return are independent of the level of inflation. Second, because inflation is a common shock and hits everyone in the same way at the same time, no risk-pooling among pensions will solve this problem. The best way to insure against this risk is to maintain macroeconomic stability, in particular price stability; this topic is covered in section 3 below.

Even in countries with the most sophisticated capital markets, there is only a very partial hedging for inflation risk (Bodie (1990), Gordon (1988)). If pensioners are to be protected from it, the Government may need to intervene. But this can be done without resorting to a totally public scheme. Private pensions can be protected by indexed government bonds or simply budgetary transfers, as argued by Barr (1992). Even when the system is government-run, such indexation may not exist, as was the case in Portugal, where for several years in the late 1970s and early 1980s pensions fell in real terms.

Uncertainty about the time of death is a further source of risk. If a system provides for a lump-sum amount at the time of retirement, a late death may mean hardship. Those are private uncorrelated risks that it should be possible to eliminate by pooling. An alternative way to insure against this risk is for the system to promise an annuity at the time of retirement. Again, the main difficulty with private markets is how to hedge for inflation.

2.1.5. *Social security and savings*

In discussing the efficiency consequences of a social security system, the issue that has received most attention is probably the impact of the system on savings. Theoretical arguments have led many authors to argue that the impact should be negative. The implied assumption is that a negative effect on national savings rate will decrease investment and hence the growth rate as well. In the long run, this means that output is smaller than otherwise, and so there is an inefficiency cost. A second aspect of this issue is whether or not the method of financing makes a difference. Does a fully funded system have a smaller impact on the savings rate, as compared to a pay-as-you-go system?

Take the pay-as-you-go case first. People tend to save when they are relatively young and working, to dissave when old and retired. Transferring income from working people to the older should then have a negative impact on total savings. A more careful analysis shows that this argument may not be so compelling as it seems at first sight. One should look carefully at the determinants of the savings behavior along the whole life of each generation after the system is introduced and try to see the consequences. But the first generation of pensioners receives an unexpected gain, financed by a reduction of the income of a cohort that has a higher propensity to save, and the second generation of pensioners also have pension rights attributed to them that are higher than future contributions. In life-cycle terms, one should expect them to reduce savings. We return to this point is section 3.2 below. One argument leads to the opposite conclusion. If people, when young, either because they are short-sighted or because they do not have access to adequate savings instruments, have a savings rate that is less than optimal, the imposition of a mandatory payroll tax may lead to a reduction in consumption. By affecting the retirement behaviour and the intergenerational transfers among numbers of the family (young supporting the old, or bequest behaviour), the introduction of a pension scheme will further impact on the savings behaviour. Given this complexity, the only way to resolve the question is to obtain empirical evidence to decide the issue.

Unfortunately, the evidence is not strong enough to be totally unambiguous. Nevertheless, for the case of the United States, in the view of Kotlikoff (1994a), in using social insurance programmes to transfer ever larger sums from the young, who are in their saving years, to the old, who are in their dissaving years, the Government of the United States of America has reduced the United States national saving to historically unprecedented levels, and United States consumer expenditure surveys and related data show that it is the elderly, the recipients of enormous social insurance transfers, whose increased consumption accounts for most of the decline in national savings.

Take now a fully funded scheme, in which the Government makes mandatory a certain level of savings. If people were saving that amount or more voluntarily, the decision would have no impact. Otherwise it should increase the total amount saved. When compared with a pay-as-you-go system, a funded one should have a positive effect on the savings rate.

But the implication of the argument that higher savings lead to higher investment and thus higher growth rates depends crucially on how funds are invested. In particular, there is ample evidence that Governments are quite bad at managing those funds, getting much lower yields than privately managed funds, as shown by the World Bank (1994). In addition, it is important to understand how the existence of such funds affects the capital markets and the savings behaviour of the Government. If the Government adjusts its behaviour by using the funds to finance cheaply a bigger deficit, the total national savings rate may not increase, despite the positive effect it has on private savings. Even in comparatively disciplined countries, such as Sweden and Japan, the State could not resist the temptation to misuse grossly the funds it managed (Barr (1992)).

80

One further issue, which cuts across this discussion on the funding method, is the possible impact of the annuitization of the retirement benefits on the consumption of the elderly and on their bequest behaviour, and hence on the total savings rate. The issue is taken up at the end of section 3.2 below.

2.1.6. *Effects on the labour market*

If benefits were actuarially linked with contributions, they would be seen as a price for insurance and should have a small distortionary effect on the labour market. When the system is financed on a pay-as-you-go basis through a payroll tax, this link is vague and the payroll tax is like any other tax, bringing important distortions to the functioning of the labour market.

The first important question is the usual one of tax incidence. If we take for granted that the system is funded on a pay-as-you-go basis, then there is no special reason to finance it through a payroll tax. In many countries the payroll tax is earmarked for social security. But in economic terms, this is exactly equivalent to having these counted as part of the general revenue and having the budget finance all transfers. It makes no sense to separate this part of overall fiscal policy and analyze it independently.

The problem of financing the pensions is then simply one of optimal design of the tax system. The overall tax system, including an eventual payroll tax, should be conceived in a way that minimizes the excess tax burden for a given amount of revenue. This is a general equilibrium analysis, and it is sometimes dangerous to try to reach conclusions from a partial equilibrium one. In particular, the above-mentioned White Paper includes a proposal about partially substituting the payroll tax with a bigger value added tax, which should be framed in this light. In a world with two factors, capital and labour, and with perfect capital mobility, we know that the incidence of a tax is always on the immobile factor, i.e., labour. There would be no point in substituting a payroll tax by a value added tax.

The rise in European unemployment may nevertheless be due, at least in part, to the widespread use of payroll taxes throughout the EU. The more rigid the labour supply and the fewer opportunities there are to escape to the informal sector, the more interesting a payroll tax becomes as part of a fiscal system designed for efficiency. But the real issue is that the size of transfers has been increasing owing to demographic evolution and rising entitlements, so that tax revenue was bound to increase.

One important decision affecting the labour market has more to do with the benefits of old-age pensions than with the financing of the system: the retirement decision. In fact, the effective retirement age and the labour-force participation of older people have been decreasing almost everywhere (World Bank (1994)). Theoretical arguments suggest the negative impact of a pension scheme on the labour supply, but empirical studies are inconclusive (Diamond and Hausman (1984) do find some empirical support for this).

A quite different issue that also concerns the efficiency of the labour market has to do with the mobility of the labour force. The issue is specially important for occupational schemes, in which there are sometimes quite long vesting periods and no portability of rights. This has a positive effect by allowing a firm to recover its investment in firm-specific human capital by being able to induce a longer relationship with its workforce. But it also has negative effects, by creating barriers that may stop efficient redeployments of the labour force. A second point is that the insurance benefits are thereby reduced, which may also be an efficiency loss. This last point can be of reduced importance, if the insurance effect is already guaranteed by a basic scheme and the occupational plan is simply a complementary one, as it is often the case. We do not conclude that this type of condition, limiting to some extent labour mobility, should be totally barred. If a basic scheme exists that is portable, it may be efficient to allow firms to attract an adequate and stable labour force by using such an instrument.

This discussion brings us to a last general point of which this one may be seen as a special instance. The detailed rules regulating the eligibility and timing for old-age pensions have important embedded incentives that need to be understood. In Portugal, for example, the pension at retirement age is calculated as a given percentage of a reference salary. The percentage used to be 2.2 per cent for each year of contribution up to a maximum of 80 per cent. The reference salary used to be the average of the best five years of the last 10, in nominal terms. When inflation is high, the replacement rate (first pension/last salary) could be quite low. On the other hand, using only information about the last few years opened the system to strategic behaviour: one could contribute on the basis of a very low salary and make arrangements to have a (fictional) high salary during the last few years. Small family firms could use such a strategy quite easily. With a low total life-cycle contribution, one could qualify for a very high old-age pension. The problem is that such rules ignore a very large amount of information about the past history of each person. Recent reforms have shifted the system in the right direction, so that what counts are the best 10 of the last fifteen years, with correction for inflation.

A second problem with incentives is that no allowance is made for a gradual decreasing of working effort. With such rules, the best strategy is to work as hard as possible in later years, because that has a strong effect on the pension. Working part-time for a while is a self-defeating option. This can have the effect of reducing the actual retirement age and thus the total labour supply. Rules that would not penalize a gradual phasing out from the labour force are not difficult to conceive and might have better embedded incentives.

2.2. Unemployment benefits

One useful way to look at unemployment compensation is to think of it as smoothing income across states of nature. With risk-averse individuals, this has a economic value that can be substantial. There is an efficiency argument here for the existence of an insurance scheme. Notice that this argument is quite independent from a redistribution type of argument. The system might be actuarially fair for everyone, as far as the efficiency argument is concerned; if provided by private markets that would be the case. Again, here the interesting problem lies in the analysis of the reasons that markets fail and also whether the State has a reasonable means of bettering the situation.

One reason that insurance markets may be unable to cope is that risks are correlated. At certain periods, the probability of being unemployed is higher for everybody. This is an aggregate risk that cannot be solved by pooling the individual risks. But no state scheme will solve this problem either, for the same reason. The advantage may be only in a greater capacity of the State to use its budget and the public debt to shift resources in time.

A second reason has to do with adverse selection: some people are simply worse risks than others, and it may be difficult or impossible for private firms to monitor the relevant information. The availability of a past record on employment can partially solve this problem. But then firms will try to seek the best risks and the market will be characterized by separating equilibrium, with full insurance for the good risks but only partial insurance for the worse risks. Eventually, some groups may not be able to make insurance at any price. A pooling equilibrium might be made possible by making insurance compulsory, as happens in other markets (e.g., car accident insurance). But the Government would need to make it impossible for a company to reject any individual, or alternatively, to set up a last-resort public scheme to insure those that no company would accept.

A much more difficult problem to solve is the question of moral hazard. If insured against unemployment, especially with a high replacement rate, a worker may well decide to be unemployed. This is the reason that makes it almost impossible for a general unemployment insurance scheme to be run by private markets. Simple empirical observation shows the almost total absence of such privately owned arrangements. And we do not believe that this is simply a "crowding-out" by the now generally available public systems.

83

While this suggests that it is almost impossible for private markets to supply unemployment insurance, it does not make it a logical conclusion that the State should set a system instead. But, even if only for efficiency reasons—besides eventual redistribution ones—there is a strong case for the existence of such a scheme, as long as we believe that there is involuntary unemployment. But no system of unemployment insurance can avoid the negative aspects related to the strategic behaviour of the insured. A publicly run system is probably very desirable, but it should be designed to minimize the disincentive effects it has on the labour supply. The problem becomes especially serious when replacement rates are high. This is often the case for low-paid workers, who are almost as well off unemployed as employed, and even sometimes better off as unemployed (the so-called poverty trap).

The disincentive effects can be substantial and should be carefully weighted in designing the rules that determine benefits. Very often, this means offering only partial insurance against unemployment, and, in fact, most systems already do so. First, the replacement rate, although sometimes too high, is in general less than one. Second, there are eligibility conditions, in general in the form of a certain minimum period of employment. How the benefits should be defined as a function of the individual past history is an important theoretical and empirical issue requiring more work. Some features, such as maximum duration of benefit, whether benefits should decreased over time, how demanding the rules are on seeking employment and the employment/unemployment record may all be important elements that should probably be taken into account in the designing of this insurance contract.

Hugo Hopenhayn and Juan Pablo Nicolini (1994) develop an interesting model in which they characterize the optimal unemployment insurance contract and evaluate the welfare differential between this optimal contract and the typical current programmes. They find in particular that compensation should decrease with the length of the unemployment period, and that the level of those benefits should depend on past history—i.e., the shorter the last unemployment spell, the smaller the benefit.

In looking at pension systems based on individual accounts, one may be able to avoid some incentive problems by substituting unemployment insurance schemes with access to liquidity schemes. The idea is to allow the worker to have partial access to the funds accumulated in the individual account out of which he will finance his retirement pension. This implies that, to a certain extent, he will have to sacrifice the level of that pension or else choose to retire somewhat later so as to again accumulate rights to a higher pension. In this way, the costs of giving only partial insurance may be mitigated. The optimal scheme probably becomes a combination of partial insurance and access to liquidity. This is an area in which further theoretical and empirical work could have a high pay-off in terms of designing better-performing schemes.

3. GOVERNANCE

3.1. *Institutions*

We have been taking as a reference what is the most frequent institutional mix in the OECD countries: a universal compulsory public system, financed through a payroll tax and general tax revenue on a pay-as-you-go basis. In particular, the peer pressure mechanisms practiced in the EU have been emphasized as an effective way to deal with growing international interdependence. It has also been stressed that the medium-term strategy contained in the above-mentioned White Paper does not contain clear arguments for and against tax reform, including social security reform. One reason may be that taxing and spending powers, as well as the design of budgetary procedures, remain with member States. This is why the principle of no bail-out by the Community or by each other (article 104b) is the basis for the protocol on excessive deficits that is part of the Maasticht Treaty on European Union. The protocol stresses budgetary procedure because the public-sector annual budget helps markets, social partners and taxpayers see the size of the public sector relative to private initiative, and therefore deals with high and rising public debt from below.

European integration will be sustained if policy rules exist to protect the interests of present and future taxpayers. But institutions oriented to the avoidance of excessive future taxation will not take hold unless voters appreciate the unsustainability of current policies. The convergence criteria for stage III of the European Monetary Union can be seen in this light. Without them, the economic regime remains fragile and subject to policy reversals.

Social partners and taxpayers must understand that spending and borrowing by the Government tend to be higher than what would be socially desirable. There are two reasons for this bias. Spending may be excessive because the marginal cost of financing is not fully accounted for. Debt finance may be excessive because the interests of future taxpayers are underrepresented. A high share of open-ended expenditures (transfers to households, interest payments on public debt and government wage bill) increases the bias. Because they create entitlements, open-ended expenditures make it difficult to sort out the effect of economic cycles and the effect of discretionary policy decisions.

Appropriate procedures must include contingent reductions in expenditure and increases in revenue due to uncertainty in forecasting both sides of the budget. On the whole, appropriate budget procedures ensure that the authority representing the collective interest in the efficiency of public finance dominates over spending agencies, including those responsible for open-ended expenditures. The institutional requirements involve the parliament and the court of auditors, both at the national and at the union level, in addition to the independence of the central bank in matters of monetary policy. Basically, an effective multi-annual fiscal adjustment strategy on the part of each member State is necessary.

Strengthening market institutions also requires devising ways of monitoring the implementation of internal market measures, including financial services, as well as the coordination of the implementation of structural measures contained in the White Paper. Structural measures, including tax measures, for removing the obstacles to growth, competitiveness and employment will certainly be part of the transition. They are required in most if not all of the current and prospective member States so as to reinforce the competitiveness of firms located in Europe relative to firms in the United States or Japan, as well as firms in the rapidly growing developing countries.

As von Hagen and Harden (1994) have stressed, the annual public-sector budget must be the locus of conflict resolution. Institutions determine fiscal policies to the extent that they determine strategic roles and advantages. Therefore, they create or destroy opportunities for collusion among groups. Budgetary procedures will be appropriate if they facilitate effective and accountable conflict resolution. On the contrary, if the process leads to non-decision or if conflict resolution is removed from the budget, budgetary procedures are not appropriate and fiscal convergence will be impaired. The budget becomes a mere record of prior commitments and off-budget items spread, compounding the inefficiency of the budget process.

A multi-annual fiscal adjustment strategy can thus be seen as a commitment technology that helps to remedy budget illusion. The commitment will not be credible, however, if appropriate budget procedures are not followed. Appropriate procedures must include contingent reductions in expenditure and increases in revenue due to uncertainty in forecasting both sides of the budget. In countries that need to introduce a stable and broadly based tax system that does not encourage widespread evasion, as an important component of structural adjustment, there will be additional uncertainty on the revenue side.

On the whole, appropriate budget procedures have been successful in bringing some EU economies closer to a sustainable fiscal stance because they ensure that the authority representing the collective interest in the efficiency of public finance dominates.

This implies the strategic dominance by the Prime Minister or the Minister of Finance over spending ministries. It is to be understood that spending ministries include those responsible for transfer payments. The revenues from social security contributions do not suffice in general to make the minister responsible as true a representative of future taxpayers as the Minister of Finance. The tradition of the payroll tax, already mentioned in section 2.1.6 above, may be related to the belief that its revenues should be earmarked for social insurance transfers. In addition to complicating the design of the optimal tax, this tradition also makes it more difficult for budgetary procedures to sustain social security policy.

3.2. Accounting

The introduction of a system of generational accounting should be foreseen as part of the reform of budgetary institutions, including systems of social insurance. Indeed, Kotlikoff (1994b), who has been responsible for the preparation of these accounts for the United States federal budget over the last few years and has applied them to a number of other countries, states that if one were to include only social security benefits and taxes in the construction of generational accounts, one would essentially end up with the *Trustee's Report of the Social Security Administration*. He adds that generational accounting is not some complicated, black-box economic model, but a straightforward means of drawing out the collective implications of the Government's separate fiscal, demographic and growth projections.

In the actual implementation of generational accounting, the fiscal burden of future generations and that of the youngest current generation, namely newborns, are compared in terms of lifetime net tax rates. These are taxes paid (*TAX*) net of transfer payments received (*TRAN*), expressed in terms of share of lifetime labour income:

$$NETX = TAX - TRAN$$

Lifetime labour income grows over time, together with the growth of the economy as a whole. This comparison is justified because newborns, like future generations, have all net taxes ahead of them. Once in place, generational accounting is apt to answer questions on the sustainability of fiscal policy, such as the ones asked by Kotlikoff (1994a), namely:

(a) Is the trajectory of government spending affordable? Or does it imply that current or future generations will be forced to make unacceptably large net tax payments?

(b) Given the trajectory of government spending, are current generations projected to pay enough in net taxes to ensure that the net tax payments of future generations do not become unacceptably large? The intertemporal constraint can then be written as:

$$PVNETX^c + PVNETX^f = PVSPEND + DEBT$$

where PV is the present value operator; c, f are the superscripts for current and future generations, respectively; $SPEND$ is government spending; and $DEBT$ is government net financial wealth.

The zero-sum nature of fiscal policy is clear from the equation. Given the right-hand side, reducing net taxes on current generations implies increasing them on future generations.

The wealth variable measured as liabilities minus assets excludes government capital because it is valued at the present value of its imputed rent and would therefore appear in $PVSPEND$ and in $DEBT$ with opposite signs. There is no presumption about debt retirement in the future, only that public debt will continue to be serviced.

Note that generational accounts place explicit liabilities such as $DEBT$ on an equal footing with implicit liabilities to make promised transfer payments, defined as $PVTRAN$, to both current and future generations.

The introduction of a pay-as-you-go social security system clearly lowers $PVNETX^c$ relative to $PVNETX^f$, since current generations include current and near-term retirees who will receive larger social security transfers without having to pay additional payroll taxes. If transfers are financed by privatization, $DEBT$ remains unchanged but $PVNETX^c$ falls so that $PVNETX^f$ must rise to keep the intertemporal budget in balance.

As an illustration of the bias against future generations, figure IV.1 shows United States generational accounts from Kotlikoff (1994b): lifetime tax rates rose from 24 per cent of lifetime labour earnings for the generation born at the turn of the century to 36 per cent for 1992 newborns. But that increase—more than 50 per cent— pales by comparison with what Kotlikoff estimates that future generations will have to pay: a colossal 82 per cent.

This is used to explain the decline in the United States rate of savings and investment and the rise in consumption by the elderly. The increase in the relative consumption of the old is largely due to health care. At the end of section 2.1.4 above, the relevance of the choice between lump-sum versus annuity was noted. Again, this choice will affect the savings rate (Kotlikoff, Shoven and Spivak (1986)) by increasing consumption in old age and reducing bequests. Indeed, the effect of the form in which the Government has been transferring social security benefits to the elderly—indexed annuities rather than lump-

Figure IV.1. United States of America; lifetime net tax rates of current and future generations

Percentage of lifetime labour earnings

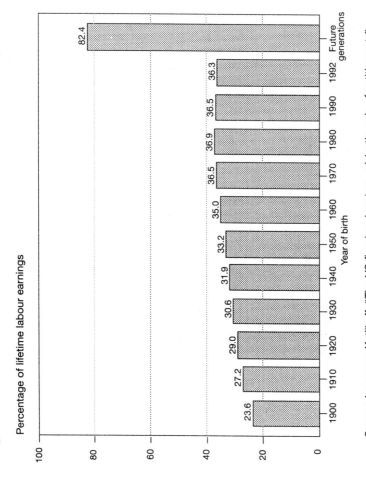

Source: Lawrence Kotlikoff, *"The US fiscal and savings crisis: the role of entitlements"*, Manuscript (Boston University,1994).

sum payments—as well as the effect of Medicaid and Medicare benefits being provided in the form of in-kind annuities have been substantial in the United States, according to evidence presented in Kotlikoff (1994a). The average propensity to consume out of total resources of people in their late eighties rose from less than 0.1 in 1960-1961 to 0.4 in 1987-1990, and the rise is also dramatic for people in their seventies.

3.3. Monitoring

Any evaluation of fiscal policy requires a study of public debt sustainability. However, the lack of a clear distinction between private and public sectors and the lack of data make this difficult if not impossible for most countries. The existence of substantial arrears among public enterprises, the financial system and the Government, with gross debt probably much greater than net debt, makes assignment of debt to sectors conceptually difficult, even if we had the data. The existence of unmeasured future claims on the Government add to the conceptual difficulties with measuring the fiscal deficit, as shown by Towe (1993).

An influential publication by Crédit Suisse First Boston (1993) has helped make the financial community more aware of this problem. Using the estimates made by the Dutch civil service pension fund of unfunded pension liabilities in the 12 EC member States at end-1990, it shows that the hidden debt is of the same order of magnitude as the explicit debt. In the notation above, using a discount rate of 4 per cent:

$$PVTRAN = DEBT$$

Since some of the pensions are taxed, an adjustment also has to be made to $PVTAX$, and an estimate of the "true" debt is arrived at; this is reproduced in table IV.1. The Dutch report goes on to encourage private-sector pensions, along the lines of the World Bank (1994). The magnitudes of pension funds and life insurance company assets relative to gross domestic product in 1992 show a wide range, from zero and 10 per cent, respectively, in Austria, to nearly 80 per cent and 40 per cent, respectively, in the Netherlands. Italy, Portugal, Belgium, France, Norway, Germany, Denmark, Ireland, the United Kingdom and Switzerland rank in ascending order of the first variable, with Norway and the United Kingdom ranking higher on the second. Both reports also claim that asset allocations should be liberalized in spite of possible negative short-term effects on currency fluctuations. Figure IV.2 shows the limited international diversification that exists to date.

Even if generational accounts are not fully implemented, any multi-annual fiscal adjustment strategy will involve major structural

Table IV.1. European Union: "true" debt, 1990
(Percentage of GDP)

Country	Conventional debt	Unfunded liabilities	Tax claim on public pensions	Tax claim on private pension	"True" debt
Belgium	128	112	22	0	218
Denmark	67	97	19	0	145
France	47	106	21	2	130
Germany[a]	44	179	36	5	182
Greece	96	196	39	0	253
Ireland	102	103	21	12	172
Italy	98	184	37	0	245
Luxembourg	7	238	48	0	197
Netherlands	79	210	42	21	226
Portugal	68	167	33	0	202
Spain	45	183	37	0	191
United Kingdom	40	70	14	22	74

Source: Crédit Suisse First Boston, The Remaking of Europe:
Employment and the Hidden Debt (London, 1993).
[a]Former Federal Republic of Germany.

Figure IV.2. Pension funds in selected developed countries
(Percentage of non-domestic assets)

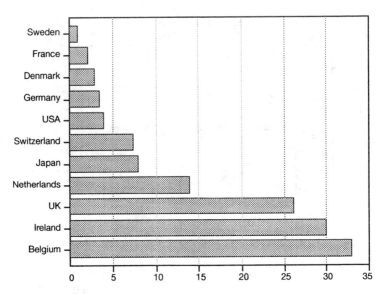

Source: Credit Suisse First Boston, *The Remaking of Europe: Employment and the Hidden Debt* (London, 1993).

changes in the budget. Aside from further improvements in the tax system, measures are needed on the expenditure side whenever the level of publicly provided pensions is very high and provisions for retirement are liberal. Since structural measures are needed for pensions, as well as for many other fiscal issues, adjustment strategies may require some form of social contract to be effective, and they will change the future fiscal position. Indeed, conceptual and practical problems in measuring the public deficit, and even worse, the public debt, make monitoring especially difficult in countries in which the public/private distinction is blurred or is changing by explicit policy, such as the formerly planned economies.

Yet adequate monitoring of the implementation of a given strategy is essential for its credibility: it is the only way that a country can durably join the policy convergence club, which is another reason that the appropriate institutions should be developed. The EU experience in matters of multilateral surveillance is again relevant for a broader set of countries. On the other hand, the difficulties with banking supervision that have become apparent in a number of OECD countries, including EU members, suggest the difficulties associated with any reform process in which the costs may be borne immediately but benefits appear in the medium term.

This is yet another argument for a multi-annual financial adjustment strategy capable of remedying deficit illusion so as to adopt budgetary procedures that avoid the excessive taxation of future generations. A further implication is that such a strategy will probably be front-loaded, that is, deficit reduction may overshoot its long-run target via either tax increases or expenditure reduction. In any event, nominal ceilings on non-interest expenditure, including social transfers, continue to be an important component of any credible strategy.

4. CONCLUSIONS FOR REFORM

We have shown that efficiency considerations alone suffice to make old-age and unemployment insurance mechanisms desirable. A similar reasoning applies to health insurance and other transfer payments within and among generations.

The strategy proposed above is based on the premise that, quite aside from the constraints existing in an international body such as the European Union, entities as the North Atlantic Free Trade Agreement, the Southern Cone Common Market and the Asia-Pacific Economic Cooperation Council will have to confront some of these issues together with their member States. It is also assumed that international institutions, such as the International Monetary Fund, the World Bank, the World Trade Organization and the United Nations system have a role in monitoring progress on these matters.

While the values of proximity to the citizen, national legitimacy and democratic accountability appear to be widely shared, they are not valid worldwide at present. The emphasis on expectations and on future generations allows us, nevertheless, to invoke these values in connection with the set of policies that has brought more and more countries to policy convergence, respecting property rights and an open trading system. In spite of the greater difficulties in monitoring, social security reform must be seen in this light.

The current situation, in which redistribution and efficiency objectives are mixed in a unique State-run system, is quite costly in terms of efficiency. Given that most benefits are also universal, they cannot be targeted to precise redistribution objectives. The insurance component should be made as close to an actuarial component as possible. The redistribution component should be funded from general tax revenue and more targeted. That the current systems are not very good at redistribution is clear from the analysis of the World Bank. The existence of more than one pillar, with different objectives that are managed differently, is probably the best way to fulfil different objectives.

This paper has addressed the reform of universal social security systems by showing in section 2 that equity arguments are not necessary for a social security system to exist. In that connection, the importance of designing incentive-compatible rules was stressed, and two examples were presented of how rules constrain the decision to retire and to be unemployed. In the latter case, the effect of unemployment compensation on long-term unemployment was also addressed. Section 3 stressed the fiscal fundamentals that are present in social security and the effect of alternative institutional arrangements on efficiency, that is to say on incentives and growth. The problem of financing social security is seen as one of optimal design of the tax system, conceived in a way to minimize the excess tax burden for a given amount of revenue. While there is no general case for substituting a payroll tax by a value added tax, the move suggested in the White Paper may help lower European unemployment.

In fact, the general argument about optimal tax reform—that it should be sweeping and infrequent—cannot be applied to social security. Since there are efficiency arguments for social insurance, changes in that direction follow the general argument that by requiring insurance the State can lessen the moral hazard problem. There is no reason for gradualism there. The same can be said about improvements in the functioning of unemployment insurance by adding individual information or allowing a combination of partial insurance and access to liquidity. In connection with redistribution, however, the optimal tax argument for a swift regime change disappears.

A front-loaded multi-annual fiscal adjustment strategy—making room immediately for future reductions in social transfers—suggests itself in this connection. To make such a strategy credible, something like the so-called excessive deficit procedure agreed in the Maastricht Treaty may be required to ensure that national cohesion is not threatened by fiscal overshooting. Forms of multilateral surveillance adapted from the ones found in the EU will also help to make any process of social security reform more acceptable in international financial markets.

The acceptability of the front-loaded multi-annual fiscal adjustment strategy will turn out to be decisive in keeping social security reform on the political agendas, and more importantly, on doing something to sustain social security policy worldwide. We do not attempt to draw country-specific conclusions but rather to present some consequences of global competitiveness among firms for problems that are often still seen as pertaining solely to national decision-making. Nevertheless, both authors were involved in different capacities in the reform of the Portuguese social security system initiated in 1993, and their stand on what has been achieved and on what remains to be done is the same.

As in so many other structural reforms, sustained progress on the social security front will not take place until political forces agree to cooperate in the announcement and implementation of measures that appear unpopular but are far more efficient and equitable that the status quo. In this consensus-building, peer pressure from other States helps tremendously.

REFERENCES

Barr, Nicholas (1992). Economic theory and the welfare state: a survey and interpretation. *Journal of Economic Literature*, June.
Bodie, Zvie (1990). Pension as retirement income insurance. *Journal of Economic Literature*, vol. 28, No. 1, pp. 28-49.
Credit Suisse First Boston (1993). *The Remaking of Europe: Employment and the Hidden Debt*. London.
Diamond, Peter, and Jerry Hausmann (1984). The retirement and unemployment behavior of older men. In *Retirement and Economic Behavior*, H. Aaron and G. Burtless, eds. Brookings Institution.
Gordon, Margaret (1988). *Social Security Policies in Industrial Countries: A Comparative Analysis*. Cambridge University Press.
Hopenhayn, Hugo, and Juan Pablo Nicolini (1994). Optimal unemployment insurance and employment history. Mimeo. Universitat Pompeu Fabra.
Journal of Economic Perspectives (1994). Intergenerational accounting. vol. 8, No. 1 (winter), pp. 73-112.
Kotlikoff, Lawrence (1994a). A critical review of the World Bank's social insurance analysis. Manuscript. Boston University, May 1994.
_____ (1994b). The United States fiscal and savings crisis: the role of entitlements. Manuscript. Boston University, July 1994.
_____ , John Shoven and Avia Spirak (1986). Annuity insurance, savings and inequality. *Journal of Labour Economics*, vol. 4, No. 3.
Lucas, Robert (1987). *Models of Business Cycles*. Basil-Blackwell.
Towe, Christopher (1993). Government contingent liabilities and measurement of fiscal impact. In Mario Blejer and Adrienne Cheasty. *How to Measure the Fiscal Deficit*. International Monetary Fund.
von Hagen, Jurgen, and Ian Harden (1994). National budget processes and fiscal performance. In Commission of the European Communities, Directorate-General for Economic and Financial Affairs, *European Economy Reports and Studies*, No. 3.
von Weizsäker, Robert (1994). Educational choice, lifetime earnings inequality and conflicts of public policy. *CEPR Working Paper*, No. 1014.
World Bank (1994). *Averting the Old Age Crisis*. Washington, D.C.

Chapter V

ISSUES IN MANAGEMENT: COST, ACCESS, FUNDS AND REGULATION

*Po-Hi Pak, Kwang-Ho Yoo, Hye Kyung Lee,
Wonshik Kim and Seong-Sook Kim**

1. INTRODUCTION

Social security systems in many of the Western industrial countries, as well as in the developing countries of Asia, Africa and Latin America, are undergoing a period of reappraisal. Questions of cost, adequacy and equity have been central concerns in this process. How the experiences of the welfare state will eventually come to be viewed is not yet clear at this stage.

The present paper attempts to consider critically some major features of various social security systems from a management perspective, especially with reference to the interrelated issues of cost, access, finance and regulation. For convenience, the conclusions are presented in the order of the issues cited.

2. COSTS

The cost of a social security system is generally subject to three interrelated parameters: the type of system, its substantive content and its management modality. The last parameter is particularly important, but the first two are also matters for managerial discretion. That is to say, the overall costs of social security management cannot narrowly be regarded to mean just the costs of administering the system, otherwise one runs into both conceptual and practical difficulties. The conceptual difficulty is due, among other causes, to the fact that the management of a social security system actually starts at its very inception, when the principles upon which a system is to be formulated and/or designed, its operational objectives, modes of implementation, institutional arrangements and legal framework, among other factors, are decided. It is therefore difficult to separate the management cost

---

*The authors, in association with the Korea Institute for Social Information and Research, were responsible for sections 1 through 5 and the material contained in the conclusion in section 6, but the editor alone is responsible for the actual text presented.

from the overall costs of a social security system. The practical difficulty has to do with data unavailability. Even if one chose to define the boundary of social security management as that coinciding with its administration at the operational level, cost information on such operation is usually not available.

This section therefore deals with cost and equity implications of different social security systems, rather than str* ;tly with those of their management as such. In so doing, it takes the view that social security costs and equity implications vary depending on the basic principle underlying the system (e.g., universal or selective), its operational objectives (e.g., risk and population coverages), funding strategy and fund management (e.g., fully funded or pay as you go), forms of benefit (e.g., cash, in-kind, service or a combination of these), and management structure (e.g., centralized or decentralized, public or private).

2.1. Coverage priorities and cost

Most advanced welfare states insure against the basic risks stipulated in the 1952 ILO Convention No. 102 on Social Security (Minimum Standards) and offer various other forms of social protection.

Social security systems have evolved over time, and benefits have been introduced gradually, in pace with the overall process of socioeconomic development in the countries concerned. Similarly, the extension of coverage has also been gradual, with the groups facing the biggest risk of falling into poverty usually being the first ones to receive some kind of social protection. Eventually, benefits become universal.

From the management point of view, a gradual and population-group-sensitive social security system is complex and costly in the long run. However, it would be difficult for a developing country to adopt a universal approach from the beginning. The scope of initial resource requirements for that alternative is beyond their capacities. A large proportion of the most vulnerable groups in developing countries are unable to meet the insurance premiums, and their employment statuses are diverse, which makes the task of protecting them under some easily manageable and not-so-costly schemes difficult. For that reason, many developing countries take a compromise approach under which the workers in high-risk areas of the organized sector first receive coverage against industrial accidents/hazards and sickness and disability, while the basic needs of the most vulnerable groups, such as the very poor, dependent children, the elderly, the disabled etc. receive protection under public assistance.

Social insurance is an adaptation of the principle of risk-pooling that governs private insurance schemes. The difference is in the nature of the principle guiding the formation of the pool: "equal value for equal contribution" guides private schemes, while a notion of solidarity among various groups facing common risks guides social insurance. Another distinguishing feature of social insurance is the third-party (the employer and/or the State) contribution in the build-up of the insurance fund. In a private scheme, the prospective beneficiary is the sole contributor.

The principle governing the welfare state—or the universal approach to social security—does not directly link benefits received to the payment of a premium. Nor does it involve a means test. All are automatically entitled to benefits in cash, kind or service upon encountering the pre-agreed risks. The welfare state, in other words, is based on the notion of a universal community of people with shared risks, and is usually financed from general government revenues rather than from insurance premiums.

The principle underlying public assistance, with its requirement of means tests and the notion of "deserving poor" as an important qualification for benefit entitlement, is the clearest example of the selective approach to social security. Public assistance is a constitutional right of any citizen in need in most modern States. However, due to varying degrees of ambiguity in related laws, much is left to the discretion of concerned public authorities, so that bona fide entitlement to assistance is not always a guarantee for actually receiving it.

Over the past decades, the universal approach has been more influential than the selective one in countries in which social security systems are well established. This has been apparent particularly in connection with health and medical services and old-age pensions, both of which have spawned diverse benefits.

Risk and population coverages largely (but not entirely) overlap. Poverty has been the first risk covered in most countries, followed by sickness and maternity, industrial accidents and hazards, old age and disability, survivors, unemployment and dependent children, usually in that order. The extent of costs involved can be determined only in relation to the scope of needs and the prevailing costs entailed in responding to these needs in a given country. For instance, if employment insurance is to be taken up in economic contexts in which full employment is not a viable goal, the funding of unemployment benefits becomes undoubtedly a problem as the balance between the insurance contributions and its payments breaks down.

Social security approaches have been shifting from *ex post facto* to preventive, and causal to objective rationale. In keeping with these shifts, social security benefits have been changing from cash to in-kind and/or service types. Such changes have contributed to improving the benefit level but carried high costs. In-kind and service benefits have become important in social security management, since many social risks, including sickness, industrial accidents, old age and disability, cannot be met with cash benefits alone. Special physical facilities, services and provisions—which may be too expensive or unavailable in the market—are also required. Direct generation and distribution of such resources by social security management bodies could, therefore, reduce costs of social security, while upgrading the level of substantive benefits, at the cost, however, of some freedom on the part of individual beneficiaries.

Where social insurance is the prevailing mode of social security, the causal motivation is dominant. Social security benefits in such contexts are organized according to the causes of risks, and the types of benefits payable are directly linked to them. With the expansion in the benefits in kind or service, however, causal motivation has begun to be overtaken by final motivation even where social insurance is the dominant mode. This has been so because modern social security is more concerned with problem-solving than with maintaining strict equity between contributions and benefits. These trends, however, have compounded the problem of social security financing.

Overall, cash benefits rather than benefits in kind, proactive rather than reactive measures and final (objective-oriented) rather than causal motivation have greater advantages for the organization and management of social security. Greater resource requirements, however, make it difficult for developing countries to incorporate these features in their social security systems.

2.2. Social security financing

Countries resorting to the welfare state approach finance the various social provisions from the government budget. In the social insurance context, one or more social security funds are customary. Formerly, such funds were created by the accumulation of social security contributions. However, with the increasing complexity of the social security environment in many countries, especially in terms of inflationary economic trends and political instability, the cumulative method proved inefficient. Consequently, countries switched to pay-as-you-go approaches.

The funded approach proved untenable in developed countries because returns on funds invested were insufficient to cover the benefits due and to protect the purchasing power of the benefits, partly because such funds were usually required to be invested in some public-purpose enterprises that did not necessarily bring the highest possible yields. Even when funds could be invested without restrictions, the returns tended to lag behind the pace of inflation. Developing countries, however, are not in a position to begin their social security financing with the pay-as-you-go method because of their need for development capital. A time-phased progression from the funded to the pay-as-you-go financing of social insurance schemes would appear, therefore, to be the pattern for some time to come. But it is necessary to raise some questions in this connection before accepting the pattern as unavoidable. For instance, which of these two financing modalities has been established as preferable in assuring benefit adequacy and equity among participants? In other words, does the transition from the fully funded to the pay-as-you-go method mean an improvement (or a deterioration) vis-à-vis adequacy and equity issues?

In terms of equity between insurance participants and non-participants, one could argue that the fully funded approach has an edge, since the scope of Government—usually limited to subsidizing the cost of social security administration—would be smaller. Therefore, the burden on taxpayers, including non-participants, would also be smaller. In the pay-as-you-go framework, the balance between the sum of total current contributions by employees and employers and the sum of total benefit payments due to retired workers—whatever the scope may be—must be borne by the Government, which will draw from the general tax revenue. It thus raises the taxpayers' burden, given the need either to lower the deficit or to pay for a higher debt, or both.

Assuming, therefore, that the fully funded approach is preferable, is there a way to keep it viable? It has been noted above that one of the two main reasons why the funds ran into difficulties was their restricted investment options and government borrowing from the funds at interest rates lower than the prevailing market rate. Since the Government takes responsibility for covering benefit payments at a pre-agreed level in both funded and pay-as-you-go contexts, there is really no reason for a social insurance fund to accede to lower interest rates, even when the Government or public corporations are the borrowers. If it is a question of the Government not being able to pay the prevailing interest rates during a certain period, there could be the option of deferring the full payment to some later date.

Assuming that full indexation is not sustainable even if it were viable, inflation is another factor undermining the ability of an insurance fund to protect the purchasing power of its beneficiaries. Lifting investment restrictions, if coupled with the prevention of outright mismanagement, could go a long way towards sustaining the viability of the fully funded approach.

Where social insurance is the dominant mode, how to set the rate of insurance premiums is another important issue. There are two basic methods in force in many countries: flat-rate and graduated rates. The latter is tied to individual earnings, while the former is simpler but operates contrary to the redistribution goals that some social security systems strive to achieve.

As for the relative shares of contribution among beneficiaries, employers and the State, the issue needs to be considered in relation to non-beneficiaries and the overall impact on the economy, since the employers' share eventually gets unloaded onto consumers. Thus, the limits of employers' share would be given by the limits of competitive market prices for particular goods and services. Ensuring fairness between employers and employees is another factor to consider when establishing their respective contribution rates.

2.3. Management modality and cost

Normally, social security systems are managed and supervised by public agencies. In typical welfare states, such as the United Kingdom, the responsibility falls under direct government administration, from a line ministry at the national level down to the bureaus and divisions at the local level. In countries in which social insurance is dominant, a mix of public agencies and corporations manage and/or supervise the operation. As an example of the latter, the German approach has much to commend from the point of view of self-sufficiency in management and organizational transparency. As a management system, however, it is short on holistic integrity and linkage between system components. It also exhibits into higher overhead costs.

Germany, Japan and the Republic of Korea have adopted the costly and cumbersome multi-agency management system rather than a less expensive unitary management system typified in the welfare state context, either for philosophical or sociocultural reasons or to protect diverging group interests.

It is not useful to compare the two management approaches in terms of efficiency. Efficiency is not an independent concept but is value- or criteria-dependent. It is possible, however, to say that in general a unitary system is simpler to run and more likely to promote equity among participants. A multi-agency system, on the other hand, is difficult to run and supervise, and carries built-in benefit inequalities from one subsystem to another. However, it can be more sensitive to the needs of its constituency.

3. ACCESS

3.1. Analytical framework

The access system is comprised of three interacting components: the provider system, the beneficiary system and the intervention infrastructure which eases access to services. In this context, social security schemes represent intervention infrastructures designed to reduce obstacles to people's access to the provider system.

101

The accessibility of a social security scheme depends on three interacting parameters: (*a*) the scope of population coverage; (*b*) the range of social risks covered and the amplitude of available benefits for given risks; and (*c*) the effectiveness of the delivery system. For example, the larger the population coverage, the more available the benefits and the more effective the intervening management system, the better the accessibility.

Within this overall framework, there are some other pragmatic factors that also have an impact on accessibility, such as the characteristics of provisions and their changes over time. In health insurance schemes, for instance, the state of organization of the medical profession is an important factor that determines whether or not to introduce a medical security scheme. As the scheme ages subsequent to its introduction, other issues arise, such as the gap between service entitlements and actual service delivered, the distribution of medical facilities and personnel required to optimize the participants' access, and the production of essential goods and services not yet available.

From another perspective, these may be seen as issues of service demand and supply, and of adequately matching the two. Normatively speaking, service demand would need to be assumed as universal among the entire pertinent population group, so that at the practical level accessibility becomes a question of who is eligible for the service. A social security scheme always reflects a choice between universal or selective approach.

Service supply is of course directly related to resources in terms of available funds, personnel, knowledge, information, expertise, physical facilities and institutional capacity. Matching the demand and supply is one of the functions of management, and the design of an effective service delivery structure is paramount in importance.

Social insurance is an important mechanism to optimize people's access to social security within realistic boundaries. It allows the bulk of the workers, the self-employed and their families to protect themselves against income loss due to various contingencies. It also allows a flexible, phased application in terms of population coverage, selection of risks to be covered, and the qualitative adjustments of benefits according to changing needs and resources.

Even when the population coverage and the size of resources are given, efficient management can improve access. The question then becomes the identification of social security, and management structures are likely to maximize access. The main concerns in this regard will include the development of adequate and efficient linkages between the demand and supply of benefits and services that ensure equity, improve effectiveness and reduce waste. Better planning and coordination therefore become major policy tasks.

Many alternatives exist for the financing and delivery of social benefits. These and more general policy alternatives for health care and old-age pension are discussed below, with emphasis on the issues of equity and access.

3.2. Health care

With the exception of the United States of America, the industrial countries have in effect various national health-care systems to ease and equalize access to medical services. Their systems are roughly of three types: the universal model, such as the British National Health Service (NHS); the social insurance model; and the public assistance model.

The three intervention models, while very different in their ideological and practical characteristics, have fairly common preconditions for improving their access: first, the availability of basic resources for providing health care, such as the necessary manpower, facilities and medicines; and second, an even geographical distribution of facilities and personnel, since too great a disparity in the distance between various groups of people and the health facilities assigned to them—a condition that prevails in many developing countries—will render a universal intervention scheme similarly meaningless. The NHS model rests on the notion that medical services are public goods rather than marketable commodities, and that they should be accessible to anyone who needs them, regardless of age, sex and other characteristics, particularly economic status. Services are usually financed through general taxation, and the model involves nationalizing medical facilities and the medical profession. Under this system, the main challenge is to maintain the adequacy of the services, given the weak incentives provided for the medical profession to develop its practice cost-effectively.

Finally, under the health insurance scheme, benefits are earned entitlements obtained in return for the insurance premiums paid. If health insurance is part of a public social security system, participants are required to contribute compulsorily. The employers and the State are also required to contribute their shares as stipulated by law. The social insurance approach made a major breakthrough in drastically improving people's access to income security and service, and in providing a far more flexible health-care financing than the tax-based NHS or medical assistance.

Since social insurance is contributory, however, it does not cover the total population. For those who do not contribute, either because they are outside the labour market or because they cannot afford to pay the premiums, the scheme is inapplicable. A social insurance–based social security system therefore has to be complemented by social assistance provisions as the safety net of last resort.

103

Public assistance is provided on the basis of individual need and financed by general tax revenues. Management cost can run high because of the means tests. Most countries, other than those with an NHS system, have a dual system of health insurance and medical assistance.

When first introducing a health insurance scheme, existing administrative public and private apparatus should be utilized not only to improve the access and reduce administration costs but also to expedite the process of legitimization of the new scheme. Alternatives, such as "barefoot doctors" and Chinese medicine, for instance, could be integrated in the health-care system, and local governments, banks, labour unions, farmers' cooperatives and other pertinent entities should pay closer attention to such alternatives as resources for securing less expensive access to health services.

3.3. The old-age pension

Poverty in old age is another contingency that societies commonly try to provide some security against. In advanced industrial economies, in which the elderly are supposedly economically independent from their adult children, the former's access to income is largely a matter of entitlements to social security pensions. As with health care, old-age pension can be provided through three different social security approaches: demo-grants, social insurance payments and public assistance. Public assistance is the oldest and pension insurance the most prevalent approach to old-age income security. While the pension insurance approach operates on the insurance principle, demo-grants and public assistance approaches represent fiscally based income-transfer programmes. As indicated, public assistance requires personal means-testing, while the demo-grant does not. The pension is provided mostly in the form of cash benefits, and policy decisions on delivery methods are far simpler than in the case of health-care delivery, in which the health-care profession is involved. Demo-grants, public assistance and pension insurance are considered below, with emphasis on the accessibility issues.

Demo-grants are provided solely on the basis of demographic characteristics, i.e., age. Pension grants are due to all citizens or residents older than a certain age—reflecting society's decision on that specific age—regardless of their income and assets. Access to a pension is therefore open to all the aged and is paid at a flat rate. Its administrative cost is far less than costs for either the insurance or public assistance approaches. Demo-grants have universal population coverage and access costs are usually low. In contrast, public assistance is limited to the poor and its access is relatively costly, as in the case of health care. Public assistance can also polarize a society in the long run.

104

Pension insurance is more flexible administratively and financially than public assistance or demo-grants. Population coverage, however, is limited to those who have paid the required premiums. As in the case of health insurance, old-age pension insurance can expand its population coverage gradually. It can be run with either a single centralized structure or multiple decentralized administrative structures. And, as far as financing methods are concerned, both the fully funded and pay-as-you-go systems can be used, although their basic position *vis-à-vis* collective responsibility and social solidarity differs widely.

The fully funded approach represents the classic insurance principle, which requires that contributions are accumulated before a participant enjoys the entitled benefits. Under the pay-as-you-go system, on the other hand, current beneficiaries (the retired) are supported by contributions from the currently working population. This approach is based on two assumptions: that the scheme will be financed through compulsory contributions and that future Governments will maintain this obligation. Given these conditions, social insurance under the pay-as-you-go scheme can be seen as a form of social contract whereby the young support the old on the assumption that future generations of taxpayers will do the same for them when they are old.

The funded and pay-as-you-go approaches have other contrasting features. The former excludes those who are already old when the pension is introduced. The latter, on the other hand, can provide benefits to the elderly from its inception, and thus has much merit in terms of equitable access to pension benefits. But what if the age structure of the population changes and the proportion of the retired population increases significantly and too much burden is placed on current contributors? For instance, any increase in the size of the retired population would require an increase in the contribution rate for the currently active population so that individual pension benefits can be maintained. If the situation persists and costs continue to rise, the intergenerational contract would become difficult to adhere to and would need to be modified by government action. This problem can arise even if real incomes grow over time, if pension levels are to keep up with current living standards. In other words, the insurance system would collapse into a governmental tax-based income-transfer programme. From the perspective of access, the pay-as-you-go approach clearly has its merits but faces difficulties in keeping the cost of pensions from rising, since benefits are not contribution-determined.

4. FUNDS

The management of social security funds can have several—sometimes conflicting—objectives. It not only needs to seek the highest possible return on investments but also serves a number of public purposes that are preferably directly beneficial to the funds' participants. This poses a dilemma for the fund managers, who need to maximize the funds' ability to guarantee income security for the participants and protect their purchasing power, since investments in the public sector may not necessarily bring the highest financial return. One of the questions that arises in this connection is: are public investments inherently less profitable than commercially driven investments? In country experiences to date, the returns on social security funds invested in the public sector have been disappointing. Funds have been loaned out at interest rates lower than prevailing commercial rates, or were misappropriated in some instances. In other words, it is premature to judge the funded approach to be inherently unworkable. What should come under closer examination is its management.

4.1. *Factors and approaches*

The management of social security funds depends greatly on the level of socio-economic development of a country in general, and on the country's overall development strategy in particular. By and large, privately managed funds would be invested according to the price signals given by the changes in the rate of return in the capital market. Social security funds, on the other hand, must be managed to reduce the burdens of contributors, in addition to accruing higher return on investments, independently of whether the management is public or private.

Subject to the size of the funds, the factors entering into their long-term management include, among others, participants' age structure, changing interest rates, the institutional framework of investment, the characteristics of their investment portfolio and the degree of openness of the capital market. These factors work as constraints on fund management.

Approaches to social security fund management differ considerably between the developed and developing countries. In the former, increases in benefit level and fast population ageing caused pension funds to be rapidly depleted. There was no choice but to change the financing of the pension schemes from a cumulative to a pay-as-you-go method. Funds were therefore placed under government management on condition that the deficit would be met by the Government. The Government, therefore, bailed out the funds. As a result, these funds have been treated as government funds and have been managed as a tool of government policy, at times at the expense of participants.

Developing countries, however, have shorter histories in social security, and their population coverage is limited. In general, they resort to the provident fund system. Participants receive higher returns on their cumulative savings than if they had invested in the regular capital market, without special incentives or pooling advantages. The system acts as a compulsory savings scheme for the participants, and until needs arise—such as wedding, death, illness and retirement—the savings are accumulated in a fund. The system therefore often serves to create investment capital, its social security objective becoming almost secondary. As with social insurance funds, the provident fund is usually managed by government agencies and the Government utilizes or invests these resources as it sees fit. However, there is a general agreement that the funds should be used for public purposes, such as to facilitate long-term economic development.

Privatization of social security is an alternative solution to financing government programmes and reducing the budget deficit, but it also elicits fears, one of which concerns the concentration of economic power and wealth, since vast amounts of financial resources are usually administered by a few large companies managing the pension funds.

In short, some developed countries have been using social security funds as a measure of deficit financing in the context of a pay-as-you-go system. Developing countries, on the other hand, may use these funds as a source of finance to build up their capital stock and increase the output capacity of their economies.

4.2. Investment portfolio

The underlying principles for the investment of social security funds are not different from those for other fiduciary organizations: safety, yield and liquidity. Within these confines, various alternatives of investment exist, such as government bonds, stocks of private firms and public corporations, loans to the fund participants and the general public etc.

Government policies are generally strategic. Their goals are usually efficiency, equity and stability, as well as the maintenance of political power. As for institutions, they are primarily concerned with real safety when determining their investment portfolios. However, each country has its own special requirements. To cite the case of the Philippines, investment of social security funds has been made a requirement under the Social Security System law because of the strategic role these new funds can play in mobilizing capital for the country's economic development.

Given the magnitude of the amounts involved, the management of surplus social security funds may distort the flow of capital funds existing elsewhere in the economy. Higher interest rates and higher business risks are common consequences of distortions in the capital flow.

Managing social security funds can come under the sway of political forces. Various power groups compete to influence their management, such as rich and poor, old and young, employers and employed, covered and non-covered. The funds may subsidize the old at the expense of the young. The poor may be subsidized for political and/or humanitarian reasons. Biases in favour of the vulnerable often run into opposition because doing so supposedly represents consumption rather than productive investment of precious resources. But does this assumption hold in the medium to long term, especially if non-monetary returns can also be taken into account? Some country experiences in the Asian and Pacific region provide contrary evidence.

At times of government change, various forms of propaganda concerning the use of social security surplus funds arise. Politically engineered policies, however, are generally short-sighted and can jeopardize the survival of the funds and the system. A sound management strategy requires transcending the various political forces, because funds must outlast transient forces, Governments and even the interest of any particular cohort of beneficiaries.

Another common wisdom and practice in the management of social security funds is to manage them separately according to the purpose of the funds. The pension fund, for example, should be invested in long-term instruments, while funds for short-term benefits, such as health insurance and worker compensation funds, should be carried in short-term portfolios to ensure their liquidity. In general, however, short-term benefit reserves do not feature strongly in investment portfolios, since their financing is often on a pay-as-you-go basis.

Protecting the purchasing power of social security funds is a major management problem. With the upward trend of prices, the demand on the part of public social insurance beneficiaries to protect the purchasing power of their insurance payments has become pressing. It has hardly been possible to protect the purchasing power in private systems. Generally, inflation is not a risk to be insured against in the private insurance market. But the protection of purchasing power of insurance beneficiaries is a major function of public insurance schemes.

Protecting beneficiaries' purchasing power can lead to serious financial difficulties. It entails substantially raising benefit levels and consequently the contribution rate as well. However, due to strong resistance on the part of contributors, rates cannot easily be raised. The provision of in-kind benefits can be considered as a means of protecting the purchasing power under budget constraint.

Strategies for protecting the purchasing power of social security beneficiaries inevitably vary at different levels of economic development. As indicated, in some countries in which the fully funded approach is in force, funds have lost their viability in part because of mismanagement. It then needs to be asked whether, without the restricting conditions (mismanagement etc.), the funded approach will still be less viable than commercial insurance schemes, assuming that employment and price policies are effective.

This leads to the issue of existing linkages between a social security system and the overall socio-economic context. It is not appropriate to treat a social security system as a self-contained entity. Its formulation, management and efficacy need to be considered in relation to contextual factors. In a highly inflationary and unstable economic environment, for example, indexing the benefit level to the cost of living would be a folly, whereas in less unstable or inflationary environments it would be an astute approach to protecting the participants' purchasing power. Also, in most socio-economic contexts the price levels of various goods and services vary. The selection of the relevant price indexer is not problem-free. Medical service costs are very high, and keep rising in some countries relative to food prices, for instance. For these countries, indexing the benefit level to the rising rate of medical service costs would be a short cut to bankruptcy for any insurance fund.

5. REGULATION

Defining the role of the private sector *vis-à-vis* social protection is difficult. The discussion below focuses only on private-sector schemes related to income and health securities.

Private-sector schemes may be formal or informal. Formal private-sector schemes are provided through the market or by voluntary organizations. Sometimes these may be quasi-public. Typical private-sector schemes are provided by commercial insurance companies. Non-profit organizations with strong public characteristics, such as cooperatives, labour unions, veterans' associations and mutual aid societies, often institute and manage various schemes similar to insurance, usually in protection against financial losses stemming from sickness, death or property loss, and to provide for children's education. All these private-sector schemes are complex, and they have different characteristics in each country. Their regulatory framework is similarly complex and difficult to generalize. Therefore, only a broad grasp of them is attempted here, in terms of their implications for safeguarding the interest of the private-sector insurance holders, with an eye to assessing the private sector's possible role in future social security development.

The role of the private sector in the provision of social goods varies widely from country to country, depending on the overall policy and institutional contexts in which the private sector operates. In most welfare states, for instance, the private sector provides services that are not available within the statutory social security system, although many of its traditional functions have been transferred to the public sector. The private sector has found service spheres in response to emerging needs, and has thus come to complement the welfare state in an important way.

5.1. Public-private partnership

In the social services field, the relationship between the public and private sectors may be complementary or competitive. If a society wishes the private sector to contribute actively in this field, their relationship will be complementary. Even in such a context, however, the Government usually maintains its regulatory function over private-sector activities.

Privatization of social services can involve diverse arrangements, but mostly it includes the transfer of the production of such services to the private sector, enacting private but regulated responsibilities, and stimulating service consumers to greater reliance on private provisions. Generally speaking, large-scale private-sector schemes tend to be more expensive to administer and more complicated to regulate than their public counterparts. Despite extensive regulation, they are also likely to be less fair and less secure than public programmes. Notwithstanding these drawbacks, private-sector schemes have the advantage of management flexibility and accomplish the important public purpose of providing the services while keeping costs off the public budget. This may be important for countries under pressure to keep taxes low while under severe spending constraints due to large government deficits.

5.2. Regulating private-sector schemes

Insurance-related mismanagement and corruption are no monopoly of the public sector. They can just as well occur in the management of private-sector social security systems, and do indeed occur. Abuses of both public and private schemes can be found on the beneficiary side as well as on the management side. Those on the management side, however, are more harmful, since the credibility of the entire social security scheme will come into question and the scope of monetary loss is likely to be great.

The most important and strongest regulatory body standing in the way of possible corruption and mismanagement of private schemes is the Government. This is an important fact *vis-à-vis* the arguments relating to privatization of income-maintenance programmes, because with the regulatory function still remaining with the Government, it is not clear how much public money can actually be saved by such a change. Governments normally intervene in private-sector schemes to sustain equity, adequacy and continuity of the services, but doing so is generally more difficult than regulating public schemes. Public-sector programmes may be more amenable to certain uniform and standardized regulatory measures and processes than the private schemes. Perhaps for that reason, existing regulatory systems tend to be nominal, lacking in substantive supervisory power.

5.2.1. Private insurance

Private insurance, according to whether it is profit-seeking or not, is divided into commercial and reciprocal insurance. In commercial insurance, the insurer tries to make a net profit from the difference between the sum of premiums received plus any return acquired through the investment of these funds, and the sum of insurance payments extended to the insured plus the management expenses. In reciprocal insurance, a group of people constitute a formal organization and contribute toward the build-up of a common fund to share the burden of a risk or risks among them.

Both individuals and groups can institute a private insurance. Many companies offer insurance policies for their employees as fringe benefits, in addition to existing public pension schemes. Government regulates such insurance to prevent abuse and malpractice. Insurance has become a major cog in the working of the free-enterprise system, with the result that it is bound up with public interest. If insurance is not reliable, the free-enterprise system is hampered. Insurance supervision by the Government is directed at preventing such malfunction.

There are three types of governmental supervision or regulation. The first is the public notification system under which the insurer has only to report, on a regular basis, its balance sheet and business results to the concerned public authority. This is the softest approach to regulation, and is not chosen in most countries at present. The second is the normative system. The Government fixes the minimum conditions for the would-be insurer to fulfil. If the would-be insurer satisfies those conditions in form, it is authorized to act as one. The Netherlands has chosen this system. The third is the system of real supervision. The Government keeps supervising the management of all insurance businesses from beginning to end, and thus restricts the insurer's freedom. Recently, more countries have been choosing this system, although with some variations from country to country.

Governments usually regulate and supervise insurance through a public or quasi-public body. Mostly, supervisory bodies intervene in the licensing requirements of insurance organizations, solvency margins and guaranty funds, reserve regulation, investment, product design and approval, rating, reinsurance, liquidation proceedings etc.

The principal objectives of governmental regulation of private insurance schemes are or should be solvency, fair practice and competent service. The greatest of these objectives is solvency. The average buyer does not have knowledge of insurance contract, since it is a complicated legal instrument, but is very much interested in insurance costs being reasonable and the insurer being able to perform when the obligation arises. Accordingly, continued solvency of insurers has become a major consideration in insurance supervision.

The ability of an insurer to meet its obligations depends on its financial condition, which in turn depends on sound investments, accurate estimates of liabilities, and the maintenance of adequate assets to cover liabilities and unforeseen contingencies. In enforcing standards set by the statutes, a supervisory body works through systems of reports, examinations, audits and regulations to make sure that companies do indeed maintain sound investments, accurate estimates of liabilities, adequate assets and adequacy of premium charges.

5.2.2. Private pensions

Private pensions are operated in various ways. They may be handled by insurance companies, but in the case of employees acting as a group, they may have more public characteristics.

Private pensions may be contracted out of the main public pension plans, as in Belgium, Japan, New Zealand and the United Kingdom. As in the United States, the private-plan benefit formula may be designed to complement the social security formula. In contrast, the Netherlands and Switzerland have decided that, rather than continuing to expand social security, every employer should be required by law to maintain an occupational pension plan, privately financed and administered but meeting prescribed minimum standards.

Because policies are different in each country, private pensions can be regulated differently. But all are under government regulation to secure payments to pensioners.

Free of regulation, employers will generally want to minimize the enforceability of the pension promise. Unless tax incentives induce them otherwise, they will generally want maximum flexibility to finance plans as they choose. To the extent that a plan is funded in advance, employers may want to keep such funds unsegregated or at least under their own control. They will want freedom to invest the funds as they wish, perhaps in the company itself, or at least in a manner favourable to the concerns of the enterprise.

These practices can lead to insecure pensions. If a labour union is involved, it may be able to alleviate some of the insecurities by bargaining to impose some restrictions on the employer. A union is likely to seek to ensure that pension promises are binding. In addition, a union may seek advance funding of the pension arrangement, with the funds placed in an account segregated from the employer's other funds. Unions may not bargain strenuously for advance funding, however, if they believe that they must trade away current wage increases in return.

To the extent that plans are funded in advance, unions may seek to share control over the pension assets or at least to ensure that control is in the hands of someone independent of the employer. While shared control or independent trustees may offer some protection, such safeguards are not guarantees against poor investment performance. Furthermore, unions too are capable of misappropriation of funds. Only the Government is able to guarantee completely the payment of benefits in the event of a shortfall resulting from poor investment, misappropriation or bankruptcy.

A private promise may fail because the promisor has insufficient funds to pay the obligation at the time it falls due. A number of countries have sought to address this problem, in different ways. Some have attempted to bolster the pension promise by providing widespread pooling of the risk, as in Sweden and France. Other countries, including Belgium, Canada and the United States, have addressed the problem by imposing minimum funding requirements on virtually all voluntary employer plans. In those countries, an employer must either set aside funds in advance in a segregated account or purchase annuity contracts as benefits accrue.

A number of countries, however, including Ireland and Norway, permit employers to finance plans in any manner they choose, including on a pay-as-you-go basis. Nevertheless, this is not a widely used option. Even if funds are set aside in advance, the obligation may still be unfulfilled in the end as a consequence of poor investment or misappropriation of the funds set aside. If pension assets are held in a segregated fund or are used to purchase insurance contracts, most countries require that the monies be invested prudently. Moreover, the pension promise may still be unsatisfied if the plan sponsor goes out of business, or for other reasons terminates an underfunded plan. To protect against the inability of plans and plan sponsors to satisfy their liabilities, a number of countries have instituted compulsory insurance programmes to guarantee the payment of benefits.

Some countries require the diversification of investment plans. Consistent with this general requirement, some limit the percentage of pension assets that may be invested in the stock of the company providing benefits.

5.2.3. *Voluntary schemes*

Many people have voluntarily formed organizations for mutual aid for various purposes. Examples range from the friendly societies in the United Kingdom in the nineteenth century to the cooperative organizations of workers in various industries of modern-day Korea. Employees working in large firms or public offices also form such organizations to help each other financially during and after their working lives. If the organization is small, its members will manage the fund themselves and the operation of the fund will be self-audited. General legal instruments, such as criminal and civil laws, are the means available to remedy eventual cases of corruption and mismanagement in the administration of such funds.

Cooperative societies may be prone to monopolistic undertakings if organizations, such as those of police or public officials, exert influence over profit-making enterprises. In the Republic of Korea, the Government intervened in such affairs recently to prevent unfairness on the part of the organizations receiving privileges through manipulation. Special laws are therefore introduced to regulate insurance schemes of large organizations, such as agricultural cooperatives and credit unions.

5.2.4. *Informal schemes*

In developing countries in which formal means of financial assistance have not been developed, informal-sector schemes assume this role. Informal mutual loan clubs may be prevalent. Because such organizations are small and informal, they would normally be free from formal regulation, and the absconding of a member with the funds of such an organization is common. Despite the large losses suffered by members of the organizations in question, it is difficult to devise a special regulatory apparatus for preventing mismanagement and corruption of informal schemes. Criminal or civil law is the only practical recourse.

6. CONCLUSIONS

In the foregoing discussion, alternatives were suggested, wherever possible, for making social security systems more responsive to the requirements of the radically changing development environment of today and tomorrow. The main conclusions of that analysis are set out below.

6.1. *Costs*

The cost of a social security system depends on its formula, substantive content and management modality. The above review of the historical experience of countries with advanced social security systems brings to light four facts, described below.

First, the cost of a social security system increases as the number of social risks it seeks to cover increases. Countries with highly developed social security systems providing coverage for a wide range of contingencies expend a high percentage of their gross national product (GNP) on social security. Sweden, the United Kingdom and Germany serve as examples. Under those systems, a diverse range of benefits and services are provided under multiple delivery infrastructures, thus raising the costs of their social security.

The choice of a social security system is closely linked with the socio-economic, political and cultural conditions of a given country, which have a profound impact on the system cost. In such countries as the United States, where the market principle more or less holds sway, and the Republic of Korea, where the prevailing socio-economic conditions are not mature enough to support the egalitarian goals it seeks, the approach to social security can only be conservative.

In the initial and early stages of social security, countries have generally given top priority to the risks of poverty, sickness, maternity and industrial accident/hazard. In the expansion stage, the coverage is extended to old age, disability and death of the breadwinner, and in the completion stage, it is extended to employment and dependent children. Any country wishing to introduce measures to protect against sickness, old age, disability and unemployment must devise them with the greatest care lest the financial predicament of certain Western systems be replicated.

For risks for which private-sector participation is viable, such as sickness and old age, private insurance schemes could be introduced with institutional support on the part of the Government and other public bodies.

Population coverage needs to be expanded in stages, as was found in the case of the Western systems. Starting with universal population coverage has the advantages of structural and administrative simplicity and managerial cost-saving. However, resource-constrained developing countries cannot embrace such an alternative because of the massive initial resources required.

In the consideration of population coverage, it is essential to take a long-term approach. Should a system's eventual objective be to protect the entire pertinent population (universal), for instance, it should avoid creating different administrative and/or management infrastructures and formulating different criteria or regulations for each different population group. As seen in certain Western countries, the group-specific approach has the advantage of being responsive to group-specific needs and interests but suffers from cumbersome and

115

costly management structures and difficult access. Second, as far as cost-saving alone is concerned, developing countries should consider the adoption of a system composed mainly of a number of social insurance schemes, supplemented with public assistance for the poor. That is, those who can contribute the insurance premium should be the first population target, while others should be brought under coverage gradually as they become financially able to participate. Those who cannot be protected under the insurance principle must come under direct public protection.

Third, the trends with regard to the type of benefit and benefit levels, as observed in developed Western countries, have been shifting from cash to in-kind and service benefits, from after-the-event to preventive measures and from causal rationale to objective rationale, which have all contributed positively to the raising of benefit levels. Such shifts are desirable from the point of view of broadening the status of welfare of a society but carry high cost implications.

Fourth, general taxation and insurance premiums are two basic methods of financing a social security system, and there is no clear-cut relationship between financing methods and system types. In France and Germany, whose systems are primarily insurance-based, system maintenance costs outweigh the share of contributions.

Some developing countries have opted for the funded approach in order to raise finance for development projects. The viability of such approach, however, depends on obtaining sufficient returns on invested funds to meet future obligations to the insured. In the event that returns are inadequate, the approach will lead to financial difficulties similar to those now confronting the insurance funds of some developed countries. Protecting the purchasing power of future insurance payments and ensuring their safety are fundamental to the management of a social security system. Some insurance funds have been mismanaged and were mistakenly invested at interest rates lower than in those prevailing capital markets, which compromised their future income and hastened the shift in the financing of insurance schemes from the cumulative to a pay-as-you-go basis.

Simplicity and transparency of the delivery infrastructure are highly desirable in a social security system. In this sense, the establishment of separate organizations and management bodies for different population groups, such as those based on occupational category and class or on geographical location, as well as the spread of administrative functions among different government departments, are not desirable and undermine the integrity of a system, rendering its management costly. A phased evolvement of the delivery system with clearly defined long-term goals and objectives could help to avoid such outcomes.

6.2. *Access*

Social insurance changed the history of social security in that it made the bulk of the workers, the self-employed and their families able to protect themselves against income loss during certain contingencies. Additionally, it allows flexible and time-phased population coverage and financing.

Universal population coverage is an ideal policy choice, but it has often been circumscribed by such factors as financial constraints and political resistance. In an effort to expand population coverage and facilitate the access to benefits, policy makers must consider developing and utilizing alternative resources, including indigenous medicine and health personnel, as much as possible.

6.3. *Funds*

Strategies for managing surplus social security funds should be carefully designed. Many developed countries have depleted their funds, and what remains of their funds have been deposited with Governments on condition that the latter guarantee rates of return that are sufficient to meet the benefit payments due. Governments manage the funds as they see fit, but will have the problem of financing their deficits through general taxation. Handling depleted social security funds in such a manner may be within the resource capacities of some developed countries but is clearly not viable in developing or poorer economies.

Most developing countries have already accumulated and are managing considerable volumes of social security funds. They have run into management difficulties as well, and in some instances are justifying their mismanagement by citing the experiences of the developed countries. In the developing countries that have copied a model of the developed countries, their systems have begun to experience problems earlier than expected. The likelihood is high that their funds will run into deficit and therefore become unable to provide benefits when due. Indeed, in some developing countries this is already taking place. They urgently need to find investments that will generate higher returns.

Adhering to the notion of guaranteeing the purchasing power of social security payments runs the risk of hurting the health of the social security system. Guaranteeing purchasing power could lead to an earlier depletion of funds and the collapse of the social security system itself. A partial consumer-price indexation and in-kind benefits are the preferred modes of attempting to protect purchasing power.

The target in the establishment of benefit levels should be the maintenance of a minimum adequate standard of living. And for the

117

sake of financial stability benefits should be linked to the rate of return of the invested funds.

6.4. *Regulation*

A variety of means have been devised publicly and privately to alleviate financial difficulties common in modern society, which have made the distinction of roles between public and private sectors more and more obscure.

Even though privatization has been progressing in some countries, Government have regulated and supervised private-sector schemes. Privatization may not actually result in less government spending and regulation. Indeed, if regulation is not adequate, privatization may unexpectedly increase costs for the Government.

In the developed countries in which the private sector is active, the Government assumes the regulatory and supervisory roles for that sector. It is thus not clear how much savings the privatization of public social services can generate for the public budget. The emphasis on the choice between the private sector and the public sector may therefore be misplaced, for in most practical situations they will be complementary: private managerial skills can often complement the public sector.

Furthermore, privatization or a strong tradition of private services does not necessarily mean less welfare: privatization can improve social provisions. Indeed, it would even be possible to combine privatization with increases in equality. If privatization is unfair in practice, this reflects the political and social values that generate the pressure for privatization. The choice between the public and private sector as the provider of social services will depend on each country's own economic and political condition, social tradition of mutual aid etc. However, government regulation is required whatever way is chosen.

In most countries, there are government regulations supported by law to prevent the mismanagement of funds. And, despite differences in methods and regulatory regimes, most countries have intervened to make the funds of private-sector schemes secure. However, if regulation is too strong it may damage flexibility and creativity, which are seen as the merits of private-sector schemes, and if regulation is too weak insecurity of scheme funds can result. The choice between a strong and a weak means of regulation is mainly the subjective decision of each society.

REFERENCES

American Enterprise Institute for Public Policy Research (1970). *Private Pensions and the Public Interest*. Washington, D.C.

Bernand, Benjamin, Steven Haberman, George Helowics, Geraldine Kaye and David Wilkie (1987). *Pensions: The Problems of Today and Tomorrow*. Allen and Unwin.

Brooks, Harvey, Lance Liebman and Corinne S. Schelling (1984). *Public-Private Partnership: New Opportunities for Meeting Social Needs*. Cambridge, Massachusetts: Ballinger Publishing Company.

Center, Charles C. (1960). *Insurance and Government*. New York: McGraw-Hill.

Choi, Kiwon (1993). *Insurance Law*. Seoul: Pakyoungsa.

Deaton, R. L. (1989). *The Political Economy of Pensions*. Vancouver: University of British Columbia Press.

El-Farhan, Mohammad Mahdi (1989). Investment of social security funds: comparative report on pension schemes in Asia and the Pacific. International Social Security Association documents No. ISSA/ASIA/RT/89/3(a).

Flora, Peter, and Arnold J. Heidenheimer, eds. (1981). *The Development of Welfare States in Europe and America*. New Brunswick: Transaction Books.

Gilbert, Neil, and Harry Specht (1986). *Dimensions of Social Welfare Policy*. Englewood Cliffs: Prentice Hall.

Health and Welfare Statistics Association (1993). *Trends of Insurance and Pension*. In Japanese.

Heidenheimer, Arnold, Hugh Heclo and Carolyn Teich Adams (1990). *Comparative Public Policy: The Politics of Social Choice in America, Europe, and Japan*. New York: St. Martin's Press.

_____ (1983). *Comparative Public Policy: The Politics of Social Choice in Europe and America*. New York: St. Martins Press.

HMSO, ed. (1994). *Social Welfare*. London: HMSO Publication Centre.

Horlick, Max, and Alfred M. Skolnik (1978). *Mandating Private Pensions: A Study of European Experience*. US Department of Health, Education and Welfare.

International Labour Organization (1984). *Into the Twenty-first Century: The Development of Social Security*. Geneva: ILO.

Kamerman, Sheila B., and Alfred J. Kahn (1989). *Privatization and the Welfare State*. Princeton University Press.

Kertonegoro, Sentaoe (1989). Investment of social security funds: comparative report on provident fund in Asia and the Pacific. ISSA documents No. ISSA/ASIA/RT/89/3(b).

Kim, Seong-Sook (1994). Changing roles of the public and private sectors in managing a welfare state. Doctoral dissertation, mimeo.

Kim, Wonshik (1990). The welfare cost of social security due to changes in private saving: the case of capital income taxation. *The Korean Economic Review*, vol. 6, No. 1 (summer), pp.120-37.

Kim, Young-Ha, Jaesung Min, Moon-Hyung Pyo and Wonshik Kim (1991). *Policy Issues on the Stabilization of National Pension*. KDI. In Korean.

Lampert, Heinz (1991). *Lehrbuch der Sozialpolitik*. Berlin: Springer Verlag.

Lee, Hye Kyung (1994). Social security in South Korea: programs and policy issues. Paper presented at a symposium on the theme "Social security systems in Asian countries: a comparison of problems and perspectives", held by the China Reform and Development Institute and sponsored by Frederich Ebert Stifftung at Haiku, China, 21-23 March.

_____ (1993). Development of the welfare state in an authoritarian capitalist society: the Korean experience. Paper presented at an international conference on the theme "Welfare state: present and future", held by the Korea Academy of Social Welfare at Seoul.

_____ (1990). The Japanese welfare state in transition. In *Modern Welfare Sates: A Comparative View of Trends and Prospects,* Robert Friedmann, ed. United Kingdom: Wheatsheaf Books.

_____ (1993). Safe protection policies for the elderly in Korea. In *Issues in Economic and Social Policy in Britain and Korea,* James Wilkinson, ed. Sheffield, United Kingdom: Centre of Korean Studies and the Management School of the University of Sheffield.

Ling, Frank Kuen-Bau (1985). *Government Regulation and Supervision as Applied to the Insurance Industry in Taiwan.*

Meier, Kenneth J. (1988). *The Political Economy of Regulation: The Case of Insurance.* State University of New York Press.

Ministry of Social Welfare of the Government of Japan, ed. (1994). *Medical Security in Europe and the US.* Tokyo: Society for the Study of Social Security Regulations.

Organisation for Economic Cooperation and Development (1992). Private pensions and public policy. *OECD Social Policy Studies,* No. 9.

Richardson, Jeremy (1990). *Privatization and Deregulation in Canada and Britain.* United Kingdom: Institute for Research on Public Policy.

Rimlinger, Gaston V. (1971). *Welfare Policy and Industrial in Europe, America and Russia.* New York and London: John Wiley and Sons.

Roth, Gabriel (1988). *The Private Provision of Public Services in Developing Countries.* Oxford University Press.

Shin, Sup-Joong (1994). *Social Security in the World.* Seoul: Yoopoong Publications.

US Department of Health and Human Services (1992). *Social Security Programs Throughout the World—1991.* September.

US Government Printing Office (1989). *Economic Report of the President.* Washington, D.C.

Yang, Seung Kyu (1992). *Insurance Law.* Seoul: Samjiwon.

Yoo Kwang-Ho (1983). *Die Entwicklung des Systems sozialer Sicherheit in Deutschland als Orientierungsmodell fur Entwicklungslander.* Linz: Trauner Verlag.

120

Part Two

CASES IN POLICY ANALYSIS

Chapter VI

THE NEW CHILEAN PENSION SYSTEM: LESSONS AFTER FIFTEEN YEARS[1]

René Cortázar *

1. HISTORICAL BACKGROUND

Chile installed its social insurance system, specifically its pension system, in 1924. The system has developed over the years, in terms of both coverage and benefits. By 1980, 60 per cent of the workers employed were contributing to the social security system (see table VI.1).[2] But also by 1980, in a pattern that is not uncommon, the pension system had created different rules for persons who worked in different occupations or industries. These rules differed in the magnitude of required contributions, the age of retirement and the benefits to be received.[3]

Contribution rates including health care, which increased steadily over the years, had reached about 50 per cent of the wage bill by the 1970s. But even that did not prevent large and increasing fiscal deficits.

A major problem was that the political process, frequently on the basis of short-term financing, would increase benefits that could not be sustained in time without leading to either a future fiscal deficit or an increase in contributions. Conversely, real pensions were many times reduced as a consequence of difficult budget positions.

In 1981, the social security system was changed from a government-run pay-as-you-go system to a privately managed contribution system. The new system basically consists of a mandatory savings programme managed by highly regulated private institutions and a mechanism that, upon a worker's retirement, converts the funds accumulated in the savings account into indexed annuities.

---

*Research economist, former Minister of Labour of the Government of Chile.
[1]Basic research for this paper was done as part of a research programme of the Corporación de Investigacións Económicas para América Latina (CIEPLAN) that has the support of the Ford Foundation.
[2]In assessing the significance of the percentage of workers that contribute, one should take into account that about one third of the labour force are self-employed.
[3]There were over 30 institutions with more than 100 different regimes (Arellano, 1985).

Table VI.1. Chile: coverage of pension system, 1981-1994
(December of each year)

Year	Contributors new system/employed (percentage)	Total contributors/employed (percentage)
1981	..	..
1982	0.36	0.58
1983	0.38	0.53
1984	0.41	0.54
1985	0.44	0.57
1986	0.46	0.57
1987	0.50	0.61
1988	0.51	0.61
1989	0.51	0.60
1990	0.59	0.68
1991	0.55	0.63
1992	0.56	0.64
1993	0.56	0.62
1994[a]	0.58	..

Source: Superintendency of AFPs.
Note: Two dots (..) indicate that data are not available or are not reported separately.
[a]September 1994.

Many countries in Latin America are facing similar problems. The countries that first introduced social security in the region (Argentina, Brazil, Chile and Uruguay) produced in time the same pattern of unequal rules, increasing contribution rates and fiscal deficits. The remaining Latin American countries did not follow that pattern until the 1980s because their systems had not matured, their coverage was not so broad and some of them had lower benefit levels. But it was evident that, since their pension systems had the same design as the first group, similar problems were latent and would surface sooner or later (Mesa-Lago, 1994).

The economic crisis of the 1980s aggravated the financial problems of the countries that first introduced social security in the region and created difficulties in the other Latin American countries.

As a consequence of this process, several reforms were made to the social security system in the region. Chile was the pioneer in 1981 and produced the most radical reform: a new mandatory savings programme managed by private institutions that would in time substi-

124

tute the State-run pay-as-you-go system.[4] Other countries followed suit with less radical reforms. Argentina created a mandatory savings programme in 1933 to coexist with the public-sector pay-as-you-go system. In Colombia since 1993, and in Peru since 1992 under certain conditions, workers can choose between joining the new mandatory savings system and participating in the old pay-as-you-go one. In general, in all these countries the new part of the pension system follows basically the same pattern as the 1981 Chilean reform.

2. THE NEW PENSION SYSTEM: A DESCRIPTION

2.1. *Main features*

The three main features of the new pension system are the following:

(*a*) It changed the "benefit formula", that is, the central concept for calculating the value of the pension under the traditional social security system, into a "contribution formula";

(*b*) The State guarantees a minimum pension for workers whose contributions are not enough to finance it directly;[5]

(*c*) The funds are privately managed and there is a free choice of providers (the *Administradoras de fondos de pensiones* (AFPs)).[6]

Workers entering the labour force must enrol in the new pension system, whereas those who are affiliated to the old system can choose to stay in that regime or enter the new one.[7]

2.2. *Benefits*

Workers have access to three types of benefits, as follows:

(*a*) A pension may be received upon reaching age 65 for men and age 60 for women. Workers may choose to receive their pension as a sequence of phased withdrawals or as a real annuity.[8] The annuity must be purchased from an insurance company;

---

[4]There is a basic pension paid by the old system and a supplementary pension paid by the new one. Mexico created a mandatory savings program for private-sector workers in 1992, to be financed by employer contributions of 2 per cent of the wages, as a supplement to the old system.

[5]The sharp distinction between a contribution formula and a benefit formula sometimes hides the equivalence of both systems for a large portion of the labour force. Under the lower pay-as-you-go system in Chile, about two thirds of the people receive minimum pensions equal to the pensions guaranteed for workers under the new system, involving identical prerequisites. For these workers, nothing has changed.

[6]Workers can select any provider and can switch from one to another.

[7]Workers affiliated to the old system who enter the new one receive a "recognition bond" from the Government. The bond measures the value of the contributions made by the workers to the old system. Workers receive the bond upon retirement or when they reach retirement age.

[8]Or they may decide to use a combination of both. In the case of phased withdrawals, it is based on the worker's life expectancy.

125

(*b*) A worker may retire before reaching the established age if the funds saved for this purpose are enough to finance a pension of at least 50 per cent of the worker's average earnings during the past decade and more than 110 per cent of the state-guaranteed minimum pension;

(*c*) A pension may be received that is financed by survivor's and disability insurance.[9]

The State guarantees a minimum pension to all workers who have contributed to the social security system for at least 20 years, even if the funds accumulated in the savings account are not enough to finance this benefit. Unlike real annuities, the minimum pension is not indexed but is adjusted by law, normally on a yearly basis.

A state guarantee also exists in the event of insolvency of the AFP or of the insurance company that provides the indexed annuities, and also for the survivor's and disability insurance.

The Government provides assistance pensions to workers who, even though they have not contributed to the social security system for 20 years, are classified as poor.

2.3. Sources of funds

All covered or "dependent" workers must deposit 10 per cent of their monthly earnings[10] in a savings account managed by a private specialized institution, the *Administradora de Fondos de Pensiones*,[11] which charges the workers a fee in addition to the mandatory 10 per cent in order to finance the disability and survivor's insurance and the costs and profits of the AFPs.[12] The fee, which is determined by the market, has fluctuated at about 3 per cent.[13] Pension funds also grow with the return on investments, which averaged 14 per cent in the period 1981-1994 (see table VI.2).

---

[9]The State guarantees 100 per cent of the minimum pension and 75 per cent of income over that minimum, up to a maximum level (of over US\$ 1,000). The assets that belong to the AFPs are managed separately from the pension fund.

[10]Up to a monthly income of about US\$ 1,500. Workers are allowed to make voluntary contributions in addition to this mandatory 10 per cent. The fact that it is only workers, and not also employers, who contribute to the financing of pensions does not affect the tax incidence of social security. When the new system was put in place, wages were increased so as to fully compensate the greater contribution of workers and the lower contribution of employers.

[11]Social security contributions for independent workers are voluntary.

[12]The fees charged are set by the AFPs.

[13]Workers must also contribute 7 per cent of their wages for health care insurance, and employers pay a fee for occupational accident insurance (slightly more than 1.5 per cent).

Table VI.2. Chile: rate of return of pension fund, 1981-1994
(Percentage)

Year	Average
1981	12.6
1982	28.8
1983	21.3
1984	3.5
1985	13.4
1986	12.3
1987	5.4
1988	6.4
1989	6.9
1990	15.5
1991	29.7
1992	3.1
1993	16.2
1994[a]	18.2
1981-1994	14.0

Source: Superintendency of AFPs.
[a]September 1994.

Table VI.3. Chile: evolution of pension fund, 1981-1994
(December of each year, millions of US$
of December 1994)

Year	Pension fund total value	Fund/GDP (percentage)
1981	270	0.9
1982	852	3.4
1983	1 547	6.0
1984	2 017	7.9
1985	2 817	10.2
1986	3 692	12.5
1987	4 522	14.5
1988	5 514	15.4
1989	6 815	18.5
1990	9 037	24.7
1991	12 790	32.2
1992	14 262	32.2
1993	18 326	39.4
1994[a]	21 482	42.7

Source: Superintendency of AFPs.
[a] September 1994.

2.4. *Use of funds*

By the end of 1994, pension funds amounted to more than 20 billion dollars, i.e., over 40 per cent of gross domestic product (GDP) (see table VI.3). About 40 per cent of these resources were invested in government securities, almost a third in stocks and the rest in mortgage notes, corporate bonds and deposits in private banks. A little less than 1 per cent was invested in foreign securities (see table VI.4). These funds grew with the steady flow of contributions as well as the very high real rates of return. The extent of indexing in Chile is very substantial: Diamond and Valdés (1994) estimate that less than 10 per cent of the portfolios of the AFPs are exposed to inflation surprises.

AFPs can invest only in explicitly authorized instruments. There is a process involving the risk classification of the different instruments that precedes any authorization, and there are also maximum limits to the percentage of the fund that may be invested in each type of instrument, which are determined by the Central Bank[14] and the Superintendency of AFPs,[15] within a range established by law. There are also limits to the portion of the fund that may be invested in instruments issued by any one institution (Superintendencia de AFP, 1994).

2.5. *Role of the State*

As mentioned above, the State guarantees certain benefits, such as the minimum pension and a pension, in the case of insolvency of the AFP or the insurance company. But it also guarantees a minimum rate of return on the funds.[16] If an AFP fails to reach that minimum, it must supplement the difference in the account of each worker out of its own assets. If an AFP becomes insolvent, the State covers the difference. Private social security providers are closely regulated by the State in the investment of their funds and the provision of information and services to their affiliates.

3. THE NEW PENSION SYSTEM: MAIN ISSUES

3.1. *Benefits*

It is too soon to make a precise estimate of the value of the benefits workers will receive under the new system. Only about 10 per cent of retired workers belong to the new pension system[17] (see table VI.5)

---

[14]The Central Bank is an autonomous agency, independent from the Government.

[15]This is the government agency responsible for supervising and controlling AFPs.

[16]The rate of return of every AFP cannot be less than whichever is lower of (*a*) the average annual rate of return of all pension funds, minus 2 per cent, and (*b*) 50 per cent of the average annual rate of return of all pension funds.

[17]About 1.3 million people receive a pension from the old system.

128

Table VI.4. Chile: asset composition of pension fund, 1981-1994
(Percentage, December of each year)

	1981	1982	1983	1984	1985	1986	1987	1988	1989	1990	1991	1992	1993	1994[a]
Government and central bank securities	28.1	26.0	44.5	42.1	42.4	46.6	41.4	35.4	41.6	44.1	38.3	40.9	39.3	39.3
Deposits	61.9	26.6	2.7	12.2	20.4	22.9	27.4	28.5	20.8	16.3	11.7	9.4	6.1	5.5
Mortgage notes	9.4	46.8	50.7	42.9	35.2	25.5	21.3	20.6	17.7	16.1	13.4	14.2	13.1	12.9
Financial institutions securities	0.0	0.0	0.0	0.6	0.4	0.3	0.7	1.0	0.7	1.1	1.5	1.6	1.4	1.3
Stocks	0.0	0.0	0.0	0.0	0.0	3.8	6.2	8.1	10.1	11.3	23.8	24.0	31.8	32.9
Corporate bonds	0.6	0.6	2.2	1.8	1.1	0.8	2.6	6.4	9.1	11.1	11.1	9.6	7.3	6.3
Shares of investment funds	0.0	0.0	0.0	0.0	0.0	0.0	0.0	0.0	0.0	0.0	0.0	0.2	0.3	0.9
Foreign securities	0.0	0.0	0.0	0.0	0.0	0.0	0.0	0.0	0.0	0.0	0.0	0.0	0.6	0.9
Type 1 current accounts	0.0	0.0	0.0	0.5	0.5	0.1	0.4	0.0	0.0	0.1	0.1	0.1	0.1	0.0

Source: Superintendency of AFPs.
[a]September 1994.

and the value of their pensions has been strongly influenced by the way the Government has acknowledged, through a "recognition bond", their contributions to the old system[18] (see table VI.6). But estimates (Marcel and Arenas, 1991; Iglesias and Acuña, 1992) suggest that even though contributions for pensions have been reduced to 10 per cent,[19] the high rates of return should guarantee a replacement rate of over 70 per cent.[20]

Another expected benefit of the new pension system relates to the workings of the labour market. The use of individual accounts was supposed to make workers more conscious of the connection between their contributions and the pensions that they would receive in the future, thus reducing the tax component of contributions to social security, and reducing evasion and increasing coverage, as well as favouring employment creation. But that effect, which has been stressed in the literature, may not be empirically as important as it might seem at first glance, for two reasons: first, a significant number of workers will enjoy only the minimum pension that is guaranteed by the State; second, most workers, partly because of liquidity constraints, are subject to high rates of intertemporal discount, which means that the potential benefits to be received 30 years from now are not perceived as very significant from the point of view of their present value. The fact is that the new system has not caused any significant change in the number of workers who contribute to social security relative to the total number of employed workers (see table VI.1).

---

[18]The average pension of the old system is about US$ 150 per month. The recognition bond was issued to workers who had made at least 12 monthly contributions to social security in the period November 1975–October 1980, or at least one month of contributions in the period July 1979–December 1982. The value of this bond was estimated on the basis of the average income reported in the months for which contributions were paid and the number of months with contributions since affiliation to the old social security system.

[19]The reduction in the contribution rates was in part possible because of the increase in the retirement ages that took place in 1979, two years before the pension system was changed. White-collar workers who could retire after 30 to 35 years of work, in the case of men, and 25 to 30 years of work, in the case of women (workers in the banking sector could retire after 23 1/2 years), would have to be at least 65 years of age in the case of men, and 60 years in the case of women (Arellano, 1985).

[20]Most estimates have used annual rates of return between 5 per cent and 6 per cent, less than half the average rate of the last 15 years. Since the rates of return should be, on average, higher than the rate of growth of GDP, the figures used in these estimations do not seem unduly high for Chile. Chile's GDP had grown more than 6 per cent on average during the last decade, and more than 3.5 per cent in the last 50 years.

130

Table VI.5. Chile: number of pensions paid, by type of pension, 1982-1994
(December of each year)

Year	Age	Anticipated pension	Disabled total	Disabled partial	Widow	Orphan	Others	Total
1982	..	..	791	..	1 108	2 566		4 465
1983	393	..	2 272	..	2 521	5 821	164	11 171
1984	1 730	..	4 058	..	4 340	9 665	292	20 085
1985	2 647	..	5 729	..	5 872	11 768	410	26 426
1986	4 835	..	7 979	..	7 740	14 539	572	35 665
1987	7 980	..	10 620	..	9 797	16 847	671	45 915
1988	11 819	772	12 786	..	11 506	18 669	814	56 366
1989	17 129	2 824	14 388	..	14 245	19 798	1 051	69 435
1990	23 876	5 790	15 777	..	17 214	23 079	1 325	87 061
1991	30 141	15 673	15 479	..	20 472	29 414	1 621	112 800
1992	35 763	26 054	15 404	32	22 810	29 262	1 805	131 130
1993	43 089	37 521	15 189	107	25 848	31 450	2 122	155 326
1994[a]	48 943	48 140	15 534	228	28 565	32 435	2 407	176 252

Source: Superintendency of AFPs.
Note: Two dots (..) indicate that data are not available or are not reported separately.
[a] September 1994.

Table VI.6. Chile: value of average pensions, 1982-1994
(December of each year)

Year	Age	Anticipated pension	Disabled total	Disabled partial	Widow	Orphan	Others
1982		..	402	..	146	42	91
1983	84	..	240	..	132	37	78
1984	93	..	282	..	114	32	64
1985	89	..	260	..	109	31	59
1986	104	..	257	..	110	32	59
1987	109	..	253	..	106	31	66
1988	124	271	265	..	111	32	62
1989	138	238	265	..	116	37	64
1990	139	247	260	..	113	39	68
1991	158	269	271	..	121	39	65
1992	165	278	270	159	129	44	68
1993	162	277	264	231	135	44	74
1994[a]	165	285	267	235	134	49	72

Source: Superintendency of AFPs.
Note: Two dots (..) indicate that data are not available or are not reported separately.
[a] September 1994.

3.2. Costs

The cost of running the new Chilean pension system has been estimated to amount to almost 90 dollars per effective affiliate per year while active (Valdés, 1993). This is not very different from the costs observed in other privately managed pension systems but compares unfavourably with administrative costs in well-run unified government-managed systems (Diamond, 1994).

The contribution system, in which individuals are free to choose the providers, seems to be more costly to run, owing to several factors: (a) It lacks the benefit of the economies of scale that exist in a simple unified system without free choice; (b) the new system involves costs that arise from the need to market the product (such as advertising and hiring of salespersons; (c) there are costs involved in making deposits separately for each worker, managing millions of personal accounts that have to register deposits, the interest on the fund etc.; (d) this market is not very sensitive to price variations and is hence prone to positive mark-ups by providers because this insurance is a product that is difficult for consumers to evaluate, and because the individual worker is not very sensitive to different rates of return on his/her funds. It is precisely the awareness that people are improvident, and that in the view of society they are short-sighted about saving for old age, that justifies mandatory social security contributions. The same trait will cause people, when forced to choose a provider by themselves, to invest too little time in searching for and informing themselves about returns and fees, because the benefits of this search will be received heavily discounted when they retire. Therefore, the AFPs and insurance companies, when they have to transform savings into annuities, will not only try to attract their customers on the basis of elements other than the amount of the future pension (publicity and salespersons), but will use incentives to induce a certain decision through gifts and other forms of immediate consumption.

Costs are lower than they were in the first years of the implementation of the new pension system (see table VI.7). But, as we have argued, management costs still remain very high. There is a need to increase information and competition. Recently, new regulations on the information that AFPs must issue to their affiliates, as well as new norms for publicity, have been put in place. But there is still not enough information issued to workers about potential benefits when the fund is transformed into an annuity by an insurance company. Competition should also increase with the number of AFPs, which has grown from 13 to 21 in the past five years. Another alternative that has been proposed that could reduce marketing costs is to open up the possibility of group choice and long-term contracts. Group choice may be cheaper

133

Table VI.7. Chile: monthly average costs of pension system, 1982-1994

Year	Gross cost (pesos, December 1994)	Average income (pesos, December 1994)	Gross cost (percentage of average income)	Net cost[a] (percentage of average income)	Gross cost/total contribution (percentage)
1982	5 932	116 307	5.1	..	40.3
1983	8 127	98 223	8.3	..	60.8
1984	8 103	93 241	8.7	..	64.0
1985	8 095	121 245	6.7	..	49.2
1986	7 373	121 951	6.0	..	45.1
1987	6 407	116 761	5.5	3.4	41.0
1988	5 295	132 317	4.0	2.1	29.6
1989	4 841	136 542	3.5	1.9	26.8
1990	4 421	140 136	3.2	1.9	24.4
1991	4 673	150 535	3.1	2.1	24.0
1992	4 973	162 042	3.1	2.1	23.7
1993	5 341	173 913	3.1	2.3	23.7
1994[b]	5 505	179 978	3.1	2.3	23.6

Source: Superintendency of AFPs.
Note: Two dots (..) indicate that data are not available or are not reported separately.
[a] Gross cost minus the fee for survivors and disability = insurance.
[b] September of 1994.

134

and better informed than individual choice. The possibility of longer-term contracts between workers and the AFPs could reduce the fear of turnover and diminish marketing expenditures.[21]

3.3. Capital markets and the concentration of wealth

As mentioned above, by the end of 1994 the pension fund amounted to 40 per cent of GDP. There is little doubt that the new pension system has contributed to a deepening of capital markets, although there is some debate about its impact on the overall savings rate. We should recall that even though there are new deposits in personal savings accounts, the Government must continue paying the pensions of workers retired under the old system; the way that those pensions are financed is crucial from the point of view of the aggregate savings of the economy.

The importance that pension funds have been acquiring has raised questions about the necessary regulation of the markets in which they are invested, and about their impact on the degree of concentration of wealth. As to regulations, there has been a gradual expansion in the set of allowable assets (see table VI.4). And a new law was passed in 1994 to regulate conflicts of interest that arise in the management of pension funds, limiting the use of information about the investment strategies of the AFPs, the situation of intermediaries that are simultaneously trading on more than one account, the use of voting shares in firms, the way AFP directors are elected, and mechanisms for the internal control of the AFPs.[22]

3.4. Financing the transition

The transformation from a government-run pay-as-you-go system to a system based on contributions managed by the private sector channels mandatory savings to the new individual accounts and not

---

[21]Not as a specific proposal for Chile but as a more general proposition, it has been suggested that the privatization of fund management need not be combined with the individual choice of fund. Diamond (1994) has suggested that removing the choice of the fund would induce lower costs, and insofar as people do not understand risk-return tradeoffs it may have little or no welfare significance. But even though this could certainly be the case, one should not underestimate the fact that not only is individual choice a mechanism for selecting the best alternatives in the market but it also leaves to the individual the responsibility for some of the elements of the social security system. If there is, for example, a drop in the stock market that reduces the value of the fund, the reaction of the population may be very different if they feel that they have chosen who should manage their investments than if they have someone (normally the Government, either directly or indirectly) to be made responsible for that result.

[22]These issues are present today in many developed countries, where pension funds are rapidly becoming the major source of capital. This situation is raising a whole new set of issues (Drucker, 1993).

directly to the Government, which must go on paying the pensions owed to the affiliates of the old system. This has raised the question of the fiscal cost of the change of system and the need to finance the deficit of the pension system during the transition. The magnitude of the average deficit has been estimated at over 3 per cent of the GDP[23] and the length of the transition at more than 40 years (Marcel and Arenas, 1991).

In the case of Chile, the transition has taken place with very little issue of new (explicit) public debt because the Government created a significant primary fiscal surplus before the reform was put in place.

But in more general terms, it is not in fact necessary to use a primary fiscal surplus or to create a primary fiscal deficit in order to finance the deficit of the transition from the old system to the new one. The pay-as-you-go system makes a promise of pensions to be paid in the future, in what constitutes an implicit debt. That promise may be transformed, with reform, into an explicit government debt managed as part of the pension fund, which may be sold on the capital market.[24] Thus, transition is basically the transformation of an implicit debt into an explicit one; inn other words, privatization does not require "true" funding, only "apparent" funding (Valdés, 1994).[25]

3.5. *Insurance*

Insurance companies use different life-tables for different individuals. This translates into lower pensions for workers with longer life expectancies, in particular for women, who, when they retire (at age 60 instead of 65) have less money saved in their accounts and a longer life expectancy. A benefit-based system provides this insurance automatically.

But on the other hand, most benefit formulas calculate the value of pensions on the basis of wages earned in the latter part of the working cycle. Since higher-income workers have a steeper income profile and a longer life expectancy, this induces a regressive distributive effect.

3.6. *The political economy of the new pension system*

Probably the strongest argument in favour of the new pension system is the political economy of social security to which it gives rise:

---

[23]In some years, the deficit exceeded 4.5 per cent of GDP.

[24]Even though less than 50 per cent of the pension fund may be invested in government bonds, the Government could sell bonds to firms that could issue securities bought by pension funds. Hence, there could be full debt financing.

[25]If a country wants to go beyond the change to a contribution formula and privatization, and immediately create a funded system, then it will have to either use a primary fiscal surplus or create a primary fiscal deficit.

(*a*) the new pension system makes regressive redistributions more unlikely; (*b*) it automatically adapts to change through market forces and not through costly political struggles; and (*c*) it gives a more central role to the private sector and civil society.

New rules for redistributions to take place

One of the problems with the funded or partially funded social security systems in Latin America has been that, in most countries, funds were taxed by the Government to redistribute benefits to specific groups, increase pensions of the current generation or even augment the current public expenditure.

In most cases of intragenerational redistribution, the elderly—who were better off—received a higher portion of what was distributed. Since it was a multiple system, this was done by modifying the benefit formulas so as to favour that specific group of workers. As a consequence of this process, funds were first reduced and then a fiscal deficit emerged. At that point, the value of pensions for workers who did not benefit the most deteriorated in a way that they could not anticipate in time. The smaller the group and the bigger its political clout, the higher the chances of its benefiting from the system.

The new pension system makes this kind of redistribution more difficult because it has four rules regulating it: it has to take place with no disguises; the whole amount of what is to be distributed has to be transferred immediately; in most cases, those favored by redistribution cannot reap the benefits immediately; and it is difficult to tax pension rights.

First rule

Redistributions must take place with no disguises. An improvement in pensions for a specific group of workers, in a system of individual accounts, normally requires an explicit transfer to those accounts, with an identifiable source (a government check has to be deposited in a private account or paid to an insurance company). Conversely, a redistribution in the case of a benefit system takes place by changing the benefit formula for a certain group of workers, displacing into the future the cost of this improvement in an imprecise way.

An explicit transfer to a specific group of workers will not be acceptable to public opinion unless there is a strong reason to justify it, and that will probably not occur in the case of workers who are better off. On the other hand, such transfers would generate strong "demonstration effects", a set of new demands by other groups of workers, unless the target group has specific features that differentiate it from the rest of the labour force in a way that justifies the redistribution. Both these factors favour redistributions intended to alleviate extreme

137

poverty but not those intended to give away benefits to more organized and powerful interest groups.

Second rule

Stocks, and not flows, must be redistributed. In a capitalization system of individual accounts, redistributions must explicitly be for the full amount of the present value of the flows to be received in future (in a pay-as-you-go system, during the first year it is necessary only to consider the flow to be paid on that occasion).

The fact that stocks and not flows have to be redistributed means that each Government has to internalize, to take responsibility for the future consequences of its decisions. It cannot do this by means of a simple promise, as in the pay-as-you-go system; if it wants to make a promise it has to issue an explicit government debt.

Third rule

The benefits of redistributions take time. If someone's pension is to be increased, it is necessary to increase the contributions to his/her account, and it will normally take many years to accumulate a sum that will have a significant impact on future pensions (in a pay-as-you-go system, it is possible immediately to increase the benefits of the relatively few people who are retiring by increasing the contributions of the many that are working). This fact induces less demand for redistributions on the part of workers: if workers have a high rate of intertemporal discount, these benefits 30 years from now are not, as of today, very attractive.

Fourth rule

It is difficult to tax pension rights. The fact that the pension funds are privatized and deposited in individual accounts makes it more difficult for the political system unilaterally to renegotiate pension promises. It is much easier for the Government to modify a benefit formula, with the excuse of fiscal troubles, than to expropriate private property, as would need to occur in the case of the new Chilean pension system.

But is it a good thing to have a system that makes redistributions so difficult? If we consider that a significant part of the redistributions that took place in the past created financial problems for the social security system or were to the benefit of the workers who were better off, it is probably a good idea to make them more difficult or at least more transparent.

On the other hand, redistributions can continue to take place for workers who can be helped undisguisedly. Specifically, assistance pensions and minimum pensions can be increased just as they were under the old pay-as-you-go system. The flow and not the stock must be increased, and benefits may be raised immediately without having to wait a long period of time. So redistribution is made more difficult when beneficiaries are not at the bottom of the income-distribution scale. Consider that, under the old system, only one third of retired workers received more than a minimum pension. It is only redistributions to those workers that are made more cumbersome under the new system.

The political costs of adapting to change

Both the pay-as-you-go system and the contribution system have to adapt benefits when there is a change in real wages, the real rate of return, mortality factors and the ageing of the population and, in the case of the pay-as-you-go system, in the rate of growth of the labour force. The main difference between the systems is how and by whom this is done. In the pay-as-you-go system, the benefit formula must be explicitly reformed, frequently by law, through a usually very traumatic political process; political gridlock in the attempt to adapt to these changed circumstances is not an infrequent situation. In the private contribution system, however, such charge is accomplished automatically by the market for all pensions except for minimum and assistance pensions, basically through changes in the stock of mandatory savings and in the calculation of the indexed annuities by the insurance companies.

New roles for social organizations

One of the attractive sides of the new pension system that is seldom mentioned is the new role that it offers to social organizations, specifically to the labour movement, as participants in the social security system.

The fact that funds are privately managed opens up the possibility for social organizations to create their own AFPs, as has been done in Chile by the teachers' union, copper-mine workers and bank employees, among others. This is especially important for federations and confederations. AFPs run by social organizations have the advantage that they normally require less marketing expenses (advertising and salespersons) than traditional ones.

4. UNEMPLOYMENT INSURANCE: THE MISSING REFORM

The reform of the pension system may make it easier to reform other areas of the social security system, such as unemployment insurance schemes.

Traditional unemployment insurance and severance payment schemes have been signaled as possible causes of the rise in structural unemployment in several OECD countries (OECD, 1994). Some of the same arguments have also been developed in Latin America.

Unemployment insurance systems that guarantee a significant proportion of wages are subject to moral hazard. They make it more likely for workers to become unemployed, remain so for a longer period and even seek dismissal in order to collect those benefits. They also induce informality: people declare that they are unemployed but work without a contract so as to collect unemployment insurance income. Since these benefits are normally financed by the Government, they may also induce significant fiscal deficits.

Severance payments are normally payable only in the case of dismissal due to the economic needs of the firm. Such severance payments contribute to job security, something that workers value. Unfortunately, they also imply several difficulties that are more important today than they were several decades ago when the system was created.[26]

The existence of individual accounts has permitted the development of other social security and labour institutions that help to overcome the problems of traditional severance payments and unemployment insurance (Cortázar, 1993). Labour laws were amended in 1990 to permit workers and employers, if they so agreed, to substitute a month of severance payments payable only in the event of dismissal for less than a month of severance payments payable also in the case that a worker quits or retires. This amount must be deposited in a special account in the AFP where the worker has his/her pension account.

In 1993, the Government proposed a modified version of unemployment insurance to replace the existing system with its very limited coverage and low benefits. The new system would guarantee 50 per cent of income (plus health-care insurance) for up to four months. To provide this benefit, the proposal imposes mandatory savings by the employer and the employee. Each side must contribute 2 per cent of the worker's salary during the first three years of a labour contract. These funds must be deposited in a personal savings account for the worker at the AFP responsible for managing the worker's pension fund, in which the balance is to be used to finance unemployment benefits.[27] If the amount saved is not enough to ensure these benefits, the worker would automatically receive a credit to cover the difference.

---

[26]They increase the cost of hiring, create a tax on employment, make it more difficult for firms to adapt to change, create potential conflicts between workers and their firms, and retain workers in jobs with lower productivity and wages so as not to loose their seniority and potential future severance payments.

[27]There would be separate savings accounts for pensions and for unemployment compensations.

This "savings-credit" scheme guarantees the benefits described above but is not subject to the moral hazard (and the increase of informality) of traditional unemployment insurance. It is that moral hazard (and informality) that induces more and longer unemployment and fiscal deficits.

These reforms and proposals were possible because of the existence of a contribution system with individual accounts. The potential development of these other institutions has some implications for the discussion above of the administrative costs of the new system. If the new pension system is accompanied by reforms in other areas, such as unemployment insurance, then it would be appropriate to compare the total cost of the joint product of both the traditional pension and unemployment insurance (including the impact of moral hazard and fraud on government expenditure and on the administrative costs geared to counter them) with the total costs of the joint production of both aspects of social security in the new system.

Even though no detailed comparisons have been made of the costs of both systems on the basis of these joint products, the importance of moral hazard and fraud in the old unemployment insurance system suggests that such a comparison should prove more favourable to the new system than when only the cost of providing pensions is taken into account.

5. CONCLUSIONS

As in the case of any other social institution, the new pension system, which is characterized by a contribution formula, privately managed funds with free choice of providers, and a state-guaranteed minimum pension, has many weak points but also many strong ones that should be taken into account in evaluating the Chilean experience or using it as a source of inspiration for other reforms. We have mentioned the following:

(a) Weak points: high administrative costs and possible concentration of wealth;

(b) Strong points: deepening of capital markets, complementarity with other reforms (unemployment insurance) and the political economy of the new system.

We wish to end by emphasizing the strong points because they are related to the dynamics of the system. The new pension system makes it more difficult to tax the pension fund, regressive redistributions are more unlikely, it adapts automatically to change through market forces and not through traumatic episodes in the political process, and it assigns a more crucial role to the private sector and civil society.

It is this capacity to adapt to change and its high degree of insulation to unfortunate economic and political shocks that suggest that the system could hold a better promise for countries that expect to face unstable economic and political conditions in the future.

REFERENCES

Arellano, J. P. (1985). *Políticas Sociales y Desarrollo*. Santiago: CIEPLAN.
Cortázar, R. (1993). *Política Laboural en el Chile Democrático*. Santiago: Ediciones Dolmen.
Diamond, P. (1994). Privatization of social security: lessons from Chile. *Revista de Análisis Económico*. vol. 9, No. 1 (June).
_____. and S. Valdés (1994). Social security reforms. In B. Bosworth, R. Dornbush and R. Labán. *The Chilean Economy*. Washington, D.C.: Brookings Institution.
Drucker, P. (1993). *Post-Capitalist Society*. New York: HarperBusiness.
Iglesias, A. and R. Acuña (1992). *Chile: Experiencia con un régimen de capitalización, 1981-1991*. Santiago: CEPAL.
Marcel, M., and A. Arenas (1991). Reformas a la seguridad social en Chile. *Serie de Monografías*, No. 5. Inter-American Development Bank.
Mesa-Lago, C. (1994). *Las Reformas a la Seguridad Social y las Pensiones en América Latina*. Ecuador: INCAE.
OECD (1994). *The OECD Jobs Study*. Paris.
Superintendencia de AFP (1994). *El Sistema Chileno de Pensiones*. Santiago: Superintendencia de AFP.
Valdés, S. (1993). Administrative charges in pensions: Chile, the United States, Malaysia and Zambia. Mimeo. Washington, D.C.: World Bank.
_____ (1994). Earning-related mandatory pensions. *Policy Research Working Paper*, No. 1296. World Bank.

142

Chapter VII

GESTATION AND RETIREMENT FINANCING APPLIED TO HUNGARY

Maria Augusztinovics*

1. INTRODUCTION

Hungary is one of the Central and Eastern European countries in transition towards a capitalist market economy. Geography, history and the transition process have resulted in specific characteristics, among them a controversial demographic situation and the presently dismal state of the economy. Yet the financing of stages of human life through intergenerational transfers has much in common with other regions of the world, particularly with demographically mature, more or less industrialized countries.

The purpose of the present paper is to describe the current situation of the Hungarian welfare system in a macroeconomic framework. Contributions to and expenditures of the general Government will be placed into the overall setting of income redistribution among factors of production. Gestation and retirement financing will then be discussed in more detail, with reference to the ongoing debate on reform options. Other important welfare issues, such as health financing and poverty relief, will have to be neglected. In the final section, a few ideas concerning the possibility of a combined life-cycle financing system will be put forward; they have emerged from an analysis of the Hungarian situation but might perhaps be valid more generally.

The terms "social security" and "the welfare state", both lacking precise definition—will be applied in the broadest possible sense, practically synonymously, as the means and ways of providing economic safety over the entire human life cycle. The term "general Government" in the Hungarian case covers the central and local budgets as well as two formally independent institutions (called funds but run on traditional pay-as-you-go lines), the social security pension and health insurance funds. For the sake of brevity, however, institutional details will not be discussed. The term "current" unfortunately refers to 1993 in most cases; consistent national accounts are

*Professor of Economics, Budapest University of Economics.

not yet available for subsequent periods. Later events will be mentioned briefly whenever they seriously affect the respective issue.

2. DEMOGRAPHIC AND ECONOMIC BACKGROUND

Over the first six decades of the twentieth century, Hungary had been catching up on the demographic revolution. Mortality had been rapidly improving, followed—although with the usual lag—by the decline of fertility.

Figure VII.1 illustrates the stationary survival profile of cohorts in intertemporal and cross-country comparison. It demonstrates that overall mortality conditions in Hungary at the turn of the twentieth century were rather similar to those that prevailed in Sweden a good 100 years earlier. The gap between Hungary 1900 and Hungary 1985 reflects the progress made in catching up. Yet the 1985 Hungarian profile is still visibly steeper than that of the demographically more advanced countries, indicating a higher mortality in the middle-aged and elderly groups.

Figure VII.2 demonstrates that the twentieth-century fertility trends in Hungary seem to be quite close to the general pattern. The sharp drop in the First World War, then the rapid almost continuous adjustment to declining mortality, are indeed quite common. So is the Hungarian version of the baby boom in the early 1950s and its reverberating effect in the late 1970s, as well as the current below-replacement fertility.

In recent decades, something must have gone wrong. Since the mid-1960s, life expectancy at birth has been stagnating at about 70 years and mortality has been increasing in certain age-groups. Unfortunately, there is no reliable published study that would explain these phenomena. Less affluent and recently deteriorating life conditions may have had some effect, but per capita GDP and consumption were always lower in this part of the world than in the West, even in periods when the catching-up process was in full swing. On the other hand, economic indicators were still swiftly improving two or three decades ago, when the halt in mortality seems to have occurred. One has to conclude that if there is a single major reason, it is probably the increasingly neglected position of and unsatisfactory spending on health care.

These past trends have resulted in an ageing population. The reason, however, is not that the elderly *live longer* but that they *were born in much larger numbers* in the first part of the century than the currently active generations, including the baby boomers and their children. Therefore, the cross-sectional share of the older age groups in the population is already *higher* than the weight of old age on the longitudinal life cycle of cohorts. This is an important fact that should motivate the design of the future pension system. The demographic dependency ratio, crucial for social security issues, is expected to peak first after 2010 and then in about 2040.

Figure VII.1 Stationary survival profiles
(survivors out of every 100 births)

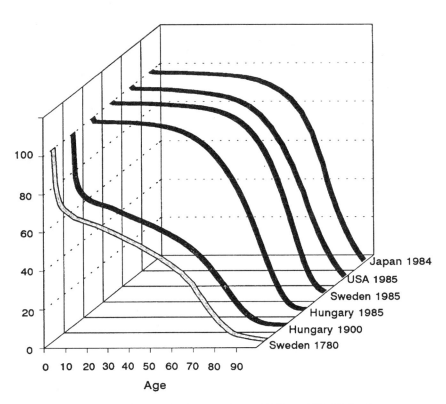

Age

Japan 1984
USA 1985
Sweden 1985
Hungary 1985
Hungary 1900
Sweden 1780

Sources: Pallos, E., *Life-tables for Hungary from 1900/01 to 1967/68*, (Institute of Demography, Central Statistical Office of Hungary): Central Statistical Office of Hungary, *Demographic Yearbook 1985*; US Department of Health and Human Services, Public Health Service, *Monthly Vital Statistics Report*, Vol.34, No. 13. (19 September, 1986); Keyfitz, N. and W. Flieger, *World Population: - An Analysis of Vital Data*, University of Chicago Press, 1968); Central Bureau of Sweden; and the United Nations Statistics Division.

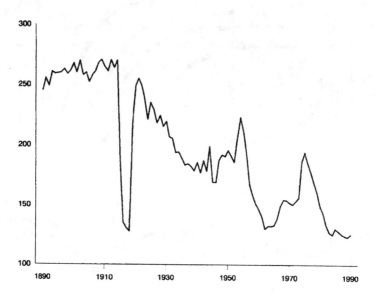

Figure VII.2. Hungary: Number of births, 1890-1990
(thousands)

Source: Central Statistical Office of Hungary, *Demographic Yearbook*,
various years.

Table VII.1. Hungary: major economic indicators, 1989-1993

	Net domestic product (1985=100)	Consumers' prices (1985=100)	Number of employed (1985=100)	Participation rate (percentage)
1989	110	155	98	80
1990	105	199	95	78
1991	86	269	86	70
1992	81	331	79	64
1993	78	407	72	58
1993/1989[a]	71	263	73	73

Source: Central Statistical Office of Hungary, *Statistical Yearbook*, various issues.

[a] Percentage.

The burden of child and old-age dependency, however, does not fall on the middle generation but on those who are actually gainfully *employed*. The dependants/employed ratio has already dramatically increased in recent years because of rapidly growing unemployment (see table VII.1).

The crucial macroeconomic fact of transition is that the net domestic product and employment have dramatically dropped. The collapse is usually explained by the disintegration of the Council for Mutual Economic Assistance (CMEA) markets, recession in the West and losses due to restructuring the economy.

Beyond the decreasing production, deep social structural changes are taking place. When State and cooperative ownership dominated, the State kept the net wage share deliberately low, but then, rather than taxing individuals, extracted a large slice from the high surplus share of the economy to satisfy social needs. With privatization and the bankruptcy wave of State-owned firms, however, the State lost its control over and access to capital income. Hence, it has to rely intensively on transfers from the decreasing labour income, such as social security contributions and personal income tax. Yet people must live, the educational and health-care systems must be sustained at some level, so that welfare expenditures could not be cut proportionally. Consequently, the net gain of the population—or net transfers from the Government to households—through the complex web of redistributive transfers with the general Government, has been increasing since 1989, although it is much less than it was in 1985.

These trends are demonstrated by rows 1 to 13 in table VII.2. The resulting intermediate allocation of income (rows 15 to 17) is very different from its pattern in the 1980s: the Government's share of Net Domestic Product (NDP) has been halved and labour's *share* has

147

Table VII.2. Hungary: macroeconomic income redistribution,
1985, 1989 and 1993
(Percentage of net domestic product)

		1985	1989	1993	1993/1989 Real
1.	Primary income				
2.	Government	11	14	15	78
3.	Labour	62	65	65	72
4.	Capital	27	21	20	68
5.	Labour transfers to government	16	27	32	84
6.	Employees to social security	4	3	4	90
7.	Employers to social security	11	16	17	77
8.	Household to government	1	8	10	95
9.	Government transfers to labour	25	28	37	94
10.	to households in cash	15	16	23	101
11.	to households in kind	10	12	14	85
12.	Labour's net gain[a]	10	1	5	302
13.	Capital to transfers to government	22	12	3	21
14.	Intermediate income				
15.	Government	23	24	13	38
16.	Labour	71	67	71	76
17.	Capital	5	9	16	128
18.	Net unspecified transfers				
19.	Government	-12	-13	2	-11
20.	Labour	-1	-1	11	-1 539
21.	Capital	13	13	-13	-70
22.	Final expenditure				
23.	Government	11	11	15	92
24.	Labour[b]	70	66	82	89
25.	Capital[c]	19	22	3	11

Source: Central Statistical Office of Hungary, Statistical Yearbook,
various issues, and National Accounts, various issues.

Note: Numbers may not add up exactly due to rounding; for details
of Government transfers to labour in 1993, see table VII.3.

[a] Government transfers to labour minus labour transfers to government.

[b] Private consumption.

[c] Net capital accumulation.

148

somewhat increased, although in *real terms* it declined by 24 per cent from 1989 to 1993. Disposable capital income had a share equivalent to 16 per cent of NDP in 1993, an increase of 28 per cent over a period of four years, despite the fact that primary capital income decreased by 32 per cent, faster than NDP itself.

Shares in final expenditure (rows 23 to 25), however, differ significantly from the allocation of intermediate income. On the road from the latter to the former, statistically untraceable income streams must be at work, obviously on the capital markets (rows 19 to 21). While in the 1980s such transfers were directed from the Government—and to a small extent even from personal income—towards capital accumulation via State-financed investments, currently they derive from intermediate capital income: 2 per cent of NDP into public (row 19) and 11 per cent into personal consumption (row 20).

The end result is that: (*a*) the government budget struggles with severe deficit, (*b*) personal consumption has declined in real terms "only" 11 per cent since 1989, while NDP itself decreased by 22 per cent, so that personal consumption has risen to an unprecedented 82 per cent of NDP; and (*c*) net capital accumulation is down to one tenth of its 1989 level. The welfare state is blamed for increases in labour income from its 65 per cent share in primary income (row 3) to the 71 per cent share intermediate income (row 16). Social security institutions are under severe attack, while the further shift from 71 per cent to 82 per cent in personal consumption (row 24), resulting from capital income transfers, goes largely unobserved and remains unexplained.

3. LIFE-CYCLE FINANCING

Conceptually—and most theoretical models are based on this concept—there must be an intertemporal redistribution of income over the life cycle that consists of three major stages: (*a*) *gestation* (childhood, education and professional training), (*b*) *breeding* (when labour income exceeds personal consumption) and finally (*c*) *retirement*. Obviously, in the first and third stages, labour income, if any, does not cover personal consumption; the deficits of these two stages must be covered by surpluses saved in the second stage. Theoretically, the final balance (bequest) should be made zero by utility-maximizing individuals who exercise their preferences when spreading consumption over the life cycle, under the cross-sectional and/or longitudinal budget constraints.[1]

---

[1]The best known archetypes of such models are overlapping generations (Samuelson, 1958), the life-cycle model of saving (Modigliani and Brumberg, 1954), and human capital (Mincer, 1958). For critique, extensions and generalization, see, for example, Tobin (1967), Kendrick (1976), Arthur and McNicoll (1978), Lee (1980), Kotlikoff and Summers (1981), Willis (1988), Augusztinovics (1989) and Jorgenson and Fraumeni (1989).

In practice there are a number of facts to be considered. First, children have no income and do not make independent decisions on their consumption. Longitudinal gestation financing would have to be *ex post facto*, and this could be achieved only by a full gestation loan to be returned over the breeding stage. Apart from the emerging student loans, there are no institutions that would offer such loans. Second, even *ex ante facto* retirement financing can not be fully accomplished at the individual level because of the mortality risk. Third, the population is not stationary demographically, hence either the cross-sectional or the longitudinal budget constraint (or both) must be violated.

In real life, the bulk of life-cycle financing is thus carried out cross-sectionally, in the "pay-as-you-go" models by institutions that redistribute income among generations. It is seldom realized that intergenerational income redistribution—in lieu of life-cycle redistribution—is the major function of the set of institutions, generally called social security or the welfare state.[2]

In Hungary, the generation currently in gestation includes cohorts up to 24 years of age, since labour income exceeds personal consumption only from age 25 at the cohort level. Many members of younger cohorts are enrolled in higher education, and the youth unemployment rate is much higher than the average, while those who work typically earn less than older workers. Retirement age is low: 55 years of age for women and 60 for men. Most women actually retire at age 56, partly by choice but also increasingly because the labour market situation expels them from employment. Hence, at age 56 the majority of a cohort is already retired and labour income again exceeds personal consumption at the cohort level, implying that the generation in retirement includes cohorts from 56 years of age.[3]

In table VII.3, the 1993 primary and final income structure, as well as transfers between labour and government transfers broken down by generations and government transfers, are listed by major items.

In 1993, government transfers to persons represented 37 per cent of NDP (row 20, last column), of which 22 per cent—almost three fifths of the total—can be considered pure *life-cycle redistribution* (row 10), while 9 per cent is related to *health care* and risks and only 6 per cent is devoted to what is usually termed the *"safety net"* (row 19). Naturally, the latter two aspects of the welfare state also include intergenerational redistribution; thus the net gain of the generations in gestation and retirement constitutes 12 per cent and 10 per cent of NDP, respectively (row 21).

---

[2]Kruse and Ohlsson (1994) demonstrate this fact with respect to Sweden.
[3]Allocation of income and consumption among cohorts is based on Baranyai (1989, 1990 and 1994).

Table VII.3. Hungary: generational income redistribution, 1993
(Percentage of net domestic product) [a]

		Gest (0-24)	Breed (25-54)	Ret (55-)	Total
1.	Primary labour income	7.7	50.2	7.5	65.4
2.	Employees to social security	0.5	3.4	0.5	4.4
3.	Employers to social security -	2.0	13.1	2.0	17.1
4.	Persons to government	1.2	7.9	1.2	10.3
5.	Labour to government (2 to 4)	3.7	24.4	3.7	31.8
6.	Education	7.9	—	—	7.9
7.	Children's allowances	3.6	—	—	3.6
8.	Old-age pension on own right	—	—	8.7	8.7
9.	Maternity and orphan's allowances	1.4	—	—	1.4
10.	Life cycle redistribution (6 to 9)	12.9	—	8.7	21.6
11.	Health care	1.9	2.3	2.3	6.4
12.	Sick pay	—	1.2	—	1.2
13.	Disability benefits	—	1.5	—	1.5
14.	Health care and risks (11 to 13)	1.9	5.0	2.3	9.1
15.	Unemployment benefits	—	1.9	—	1.9
16.	Other aid	0.9	1.0	0.6	2.5
17.	Pension-like benefits	—	—	0.8	0.8
18.	Widows' allowances	—	—	1.2	1.2
19.	Aid to the weak (15 to 18)	0.9	2.9	2.6	6.4
20.	Government to labour (10+14+19)	15.6	7.9	13.6	37.1
21.	Labour's net gain (20-5)	11.9	-16.4	9.9	5.4
22.	Intermediate labour income (1+21)	19.6	33.7	17.4	70.7
23.	Unspecified private transfers (24-22)	8.3	1.8	1.0	11.1
24.	Private consumption	27.9	35.6	18.4	81.8
25.	Generations' balance (24-1 = 21+23)	20.2	-14.6	10.9	16.5

Sources: Central Statistical Office of Hungary, Statistical Yearbook; National Accounts 1993 and I. Baranyai, "A generációk Jövedelme és fogyasztása" (Institute of Economics, Hungarian Academy of Sciences), mimeo.
Note: A dash (—) indicates that the amount is nil or negligible.
[a] Totals may not add up exactly due to rounding.

Interestingly, the breeder and retired generations' accounts are by and large balanced by the welfare state transfers in the sense that their final consumption differs very little from their intermediate income (rows 24 and 22). The gap to be filled by unspecified private transfers occurs in practice with respect to gestation financing. This seems to be trivial, since gestation financing is much less institutionalized than retirement financing because the burden of child-raising falls to a large extent on the family. Private intra-family transfers could be expected to play a heavy role in financing gestation.

What is paradoxical, however, is that by the macro-analysis provided in table VII.2, the source of unspecified private transfers is intermediate capital rather than labour income. It would not be reasonable to assume that the bulk of capital income spent on personal consumption is indeed directly allocated to gestation financing. What really happens cannot be traced through the statistical maze of incomplete and fragmentary data. This is thus no explanation of this paradox at present.

4. GESTATION FINANCING

It has often been said that children are the hardest-hit victims of income decrease in the transition process.[4] This might be true in many respects, but it does not mean that they are the biggest relative losers. At least, macro evidence on the subject is mixed.

The current costs of gestation, particularly expenditures on *education*, as shown in table VII.4, have of course been deeply affected by the second baby boom in the late 1970s, as cohorts have proceeded through various segments of the educational system, and are now in the most expensive segments: secondary and higher education. This is the main reason that per capita spending in 1993 is on average almost at its 1989 level in real terms, while per capita spending on most educational levels has been decreasing.

Overhead costs, such as heating and utilities, are sky-rocketing and the Government has not supplemented the budget of educational institutions for the increase in these costs. It would thus be false to conclude that the Hungarian educational system is in splendid shape. On the contrary, the situation is difficult, to say the least. Nevertheless, the fact remains that government expenditures on education have not declined since 1989, and in 1993 they were in real terms well above their 1985 level, a rare phenomenon indeed in the transition process.

In March 1995, the Government announced a fiscal austerity package that introduced changes in the educational system. A significant decrease in the number of teachers and university faculty has been imposed, and tuition fees in higher education are being introduced. A small part of the fee will be mandatory, and universities will be free to charge additional fees at their discretion. This provoked a strong protest by students, who are already plagued by increasing costs of living away from home and decreasing family income. As of mid-1995, a compromise seems to have been reached between the Government and the students, but the situation is fragile and the final outcome unclear.

---

[4]See, for example, Cornia and Sipos (1991).

Table VII.4. Hungary: government expenditure on education, 1989 and 1993

		1989 (1985=100)	1993 (1989=100)	1993 (1985=100)
Total	Number of enrolled	96	96	92
	Real outlays	118	97	114
	Real per capita	123	101	124
Kindergarten	Number of enrolled	92	101	94
	Real outlays	100	97	97
	Real per capita	109	96	103
Primary schools	Number of enrolled	91	85	78
	Real outlays	103	94	97
	Real per capita	113	111	124
Secondary schools	Number of enrolled	111	105	116
	Real outlays	138	96	132
	Real per capita	124	91	114
Higher education	Number of enrolled	102	133	135
	Real outlays	111	117	130
	Real per capita	109	88	96

Source: Central Statistical Office of Hungary, Statistical Yearbook, various years.

Note: Real increase is calculated by deflating with the average consumer price index, and discounting nominal increase in faculty salaries related to the introduction of the personal income tax in 1988.

Speaking in general rather than country-specific terms, there is another institution in gestation financing, a historically new player, the expanding student loan system.[5] Although there are concerns about excessive student indebtedness and in some countries some sharing between grants and loans has recently been regarded as more desirable, the loan system exists and it will remain. It represents a breakthrough, a take-off from the traditional pay-as-you-go (intergenerational, cross-sectional) approach to financing gestation to the funded (intertemporal, longitudinal) approach that has always been present in retirement financing.

Student loans are, however, non-existent in Hungary. This is one of the main reasons for the student unrest: when tuition fees were first mentioned, the Government promised a supplementary, more or less favourable, guaranteed loan system. This promise has been broken: tuition fees have been introduced but not a loan system. If this situation persists, higher education will soon become a luxury, affordable only to the richer segments of the society. Thereby equal—or at least more or less equal—opportunities for education will be gone.

---

[5]See, for example, Woodhall (1990) and Mingat et al. (1985).

Table VII.5. Hungary: family allowances, 1989 and 1993

	1989 (1985=100)	1993 (1989=100)	1993 (1985=100)
Number of beneficiary children	100	104	104
Real outlays	161	77	124
Children's allowance	162	74	119
Maternity allowance	161	88	143
Real per capita	161	74	119

Source: Central Statistical Office of Hungary, Statistical Yearbook, various years.
Note: Real increase calculated by using the average consumers' price index as deflator.

The second largest item in social security gestation financing is family allowances. In Hungary, children's allowances are provided as a citizen's right. They are determined as a percentage of the average net wage, but the rate per child increases with the number of children up to three children in a family. In the case of a family with three children, benefits amount to 61 per cent of the average net wage in 1993; the benefit is somewhat higher for single parents. In addition, there are two optional types of maternity allowances: one is a flat rate that requires some previous employment, the other is wage-related. Both are extended only to mothers who withdraw from active earning for one to three years after the birth of the child.

The 26 per cent drop in the real value of family allowances over the period 1989-1993 has been a substantial blow to the budgets of child-raising families (see table VII.5). Yet, given the considerable real increase in family allowances during the period 1985-1989, the end result is that—as in the case of government spending in education—the 1993 level is still well above the 1985 level.

Once again, the March 1995 austerity package proposed radical changes, i.e., means testing, with a rather low upper threshold of income, and in the case of families with fewer than three children means testing would be required almost immediately, as of July 1995. This was opposed on constitutional grounds and the Government is now trying to find out how to reduce expenditures on family allowances in 1996. As with tuition fees, the immediate outcome of this situation is unclear.

However, although some short-term measures may offer temporary relief, solutions for the longer-term future will require a consistent rethinking of the entire gestation financing system, a reconciliation of family support with educational expenses, and a reconsideration of sources. Generally speaking, at least three types of gestation costs need to be separately considered: private consumption of purchased goods and services by children, the opportunity cost for parents and the financing of education. With respect to sources of financing, earmarking would certainly be desirable. At least, a special separate gestation tax should be legislated and the Government should be made accountable for how it spends that particular money.

Going one step further, however, one is inclined to speculate: is the current pay-as-you-go system of gestation financing economically reasonable and socially fair? After all, building up the human capital of the future breeder generations is a common social investment, so why not treat it as such?

Maybe those who received more as children, such as those who were helped to obtain a higher educational attainment, should pay back their debt. Maybe an *ex post facto* "gestation contribution", at least partly related to previously enjoyed benefits, would be more economically efficient than a tax. Some of the returns on human capital would find their way back to those who advanced the funds, and childless people would not have to be taxed for other people's child-raising.

The problem is, of course, to find the financial resources to be advanced within such a funded, longitudinal system of gestation financing. We shall return to this issue in the final section of the present paper.

5. RETIREMENT FINANCING

Until 1949, three separate large retirement and health insurance systems existed in Hungary for blue-collar and white-collar workers and for civil servants. Farmers and most agricultural workers—over 50 per cent of the labour force in 1949—were not covered at all. All three systems were funded, but their funds were invested mainly in urban real estate, which was demolished or badly damaged in the Second World War. In 1949, a major reform created a *single, unified pay-as-you-go pension system* for these traditionally insured groups.[6] Over the past decade population coverage has been significantly expanded by increasing labour-force participation, particularly of women. In the early 1960s, the system was extended to the entire agricultural labour force and their families, including those already at retirement age. By 1975, coverage became practically universal, 66 per cent of the population in their own right and 34 per cent by family membership.

A comprehensive social security act codified the actual situation in 1975. Rules for the traditionally insured groups and agricultural

---

[6]Health insurance was substituted by free health care and sick pay, financed directly from the government budget.

cooperative members were practically unified, and the entry pension level was established as a more or less continuous function of years served and last earnings. As an *upper limit*, a worker with 42 years completed in service was entitled to a replacement rate of 75 per cent. An annual 2 per cent increase of all pensions was also legislated.

After the second oil price shock in 1978, the pension system was increasingly seen by economists as too generous. Yet, to reduce or eliminate acquired rights seemed politically infeasible, so that inflation had become the major vehicle of reducing (real) benefits. Pensions have never been fully price-indexed, although real wages kept increasing until 1978. Hence, the absolute purchasing power, particularly the relative position of pensions, has always been eroding. The situation, however, was not too serious until 1978, since the annual consumer price index increase never exceeded 5 per cent during that period and was often lower. Inflationary losses became more severe when the inflation rate climbed up into the 5 to 10 per cent range between 1978 and 1988, and even higher, into the 25 to 35 per cent range, after 1988. The 1975 Social Security Act came under repeated parliamentary supervision, with rules changing almost at random and pension increases re-legislated annually (recently twice a year).

Increases were usually biased in favour of the lower pensions (which resulted from earlier retirement with lower wages and a longer period of previous inflationary losses), in order to keep small pensioners alive. Higher rates of increase and/or a lower threshold in absolute terms served that purpose, distorting the proportions of the original entry pensions. The lowest pensions were thereby almost always *overcompensated*, while higher and more recently granted ones, even medium pensions, were increasingly *undercompensated*.

Despite all efforts to reduce expenditures, *aggregate* pension payments as well as the average pension kept growing, even in real terms, until 1990. This was the result of the well known pension paradox or turnover effect: older cohorts of pensioners with smaller pensions leave the system due to death, and new cohorts enter the system at higher nominal levels of last income, as a result of either real wage increase during good times or inflationary nominal increase even when real wages were falling.

The turnover effect was amplified in the Hungarian case by the increase in the average replacement rate, since the passing of time gave more people more and more years served. The ratio of average entry pension to average earnings was almost continuously shifting upwards, peaking at 81 per cent in 1984, compared to 48 per cent in 1965.

Something had to be done to contain the entry pension level. In 1982, it was made step-wise digressive, with successive income brackets adding less and less percentage to a person's entry pension. Since the nominal limits of the brackets have not been changed for many years, while nominal wages have increased rapidly with inflation, ever larger portions of the income gradually fall into higher brackets. More and more medium- and even low-income new retirees suffered heavy losses in their entry pensions; by 1990, the average replacement rate had sunk to 64 per cent, but the pressure on the overgenerous pension system kept increasing.

In 1991, two important steps were made with the seemingly good intention of strengthening the insurance aspect of the pension system. First, universal wage-indexing was introduced in place of the randomly changing previous rules in pension increase, although various upper and lower thresholds were sustained. Second, with respect to entry pensions, a gradual removal of degressivity and lengthening of the time-span of determining last income was legislated. Last income will henceforth be calculated from 1988 to the time of retirement, i.e., the time-span will increase by one year annually. However, a serious trap has been built in: the income earned in the last three years before retirement is excluded from inflationary valorization, meaning that the last income as the base for determining the entry pension is much lower than its real value.

These two steps combined produced an amazing result: they dramatically reversed the direction of the turnover effect (see figure VII.3). Entry pensions that were usually higher on average than previously determined pensions are now lower. Normally, entry pensions push the average pension *upwards*, now they pull it *downwards*—an unprecedented phenomenon.

As a result of the measures mentioned above, the long-desired goal has been accomplished, i.e., aggregate and average pensions have been decreasing in real terms since 1990. The average replacement rate is down to 53 per cent, and the average pension was 62 per cent of average earnings in 1993. Nearly two thirds of all pensions are within or under the minimum subsistence-level bracket. All the same, it would be hardly an overstatement to say that mass poverty is rampant among the Hungarian elderly today. Old-age security is a farther prospect than it has ever been since the early 1950s. Past work history and last income earned have gradually lost significance, and pensions have increasingly been equalized at a low level.

With respect to the *sources* of pension expenditure, a widely publicized and indeed controversial issue is the seemingly outrageous 30.5 per cent statutory pension insurance contribution rate, four fifths of which is paid by employers. This share, however, is based on false arithmetic, by taking wages net of employers' contribution for 100. Actually, the rate is 20.2 per cent of the gross labour cost (income), i.e., compensation of employees, including employers' contributions to pension, health and unemployment insurance.

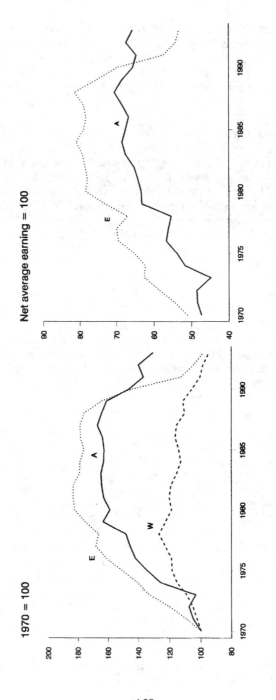

Figure VII.3. Hungary: average and entry pensions, 1970-93

1970 = 100

Net average earning = 100

W: Average real wage   A: Real average pension   E: Real entry pension

Source: Pension Insurance Fund Administration of Hungary, *Yearbook of Social Security*, various years.

Considering that a significant portion of contributions due could not be collected because of bankruptcy and liquidity problems, the actual effective pension contribution rate was 16.3 per cent in 1993. This refers to reported labour income, and evasion by employment in the informal sector is very large by all estimates. Nevertheless, high social security contribution rates are generally blamed by employers for the unsatisfactory competitiveness of the economy.

In sum, we now have a pension system in Hungary that does not satisfy anyone. Low-income pensioners are deprived because they are practically starving. Pensioners in the higher pension brackets (who had previously been middle- and lower-middle income people) are deprived because they justly feel they have been robbed of the fruits of a long life dedicated to work. Business and international financial institutes are outraged because they consider the system too expensive. It is thus generally agreed that a complete overhaul of the pension system, a radical reform to be codified by a comprehensive new pension act, is unavoidable. How, when and in what from this can be achieved is of course much debated.

6. PENSION REFORM OPTIONS

Most of the issues related to pension reform are entirely general, and are widely discussed in the literature with respect to most countries. They include the impending demographic danger; retirement age; incentives to work longer and to contribute while working; and the choice between pay-as-you-go or funded systems, fixed-benefit or fixed-contribution systems, public or private management systems, and multi-pillar or unified systems.

Retirement age is a key issue, since it is indeed low at present. Many experts believe that immediately raising the legal retirement age would do wonders for the efficiency of the pension system and solve the anticipated demographic problems. Others, however, argue that flexibility and incentives to work longer would be socially more acceptable and economically more effective, particularly in times of soaring unemployment.[7]

---

[7]Specific labour market conditions prevailing in a given country should be taken into account when considering the feasibility of pension reforms. Apparently, however, they were ignored by a recent World Bank report when it addressed the need of reforms in the pension system of Eastern European countries and used the case of Hungary as an example of possible shock treatment (see World Bank, "Simulation of an Eastern European transition", *Issue Brief*, No. 12 (1994)). Having asserted that no one retires from 1996 to 2002, it is assumed without further argument that the rise in retirement age increases the GDP, as if the Hungarian economy suffered now from labour shortage and early retirement would be the sole obstacle preventing GDP increase.

The three-pillar system, strongly advocated for example by the World Bank, seems to be gaining popularity. Valid arguments for a unified system[8] are less known and usually ignored in Hungary. The first pillar is often envisaged as a minimum pension as a citizen's right, to be financed from personal income tax. This is a controversial idea in many respects, however, precisely because three quarters of the pensions in Hungary are presently below or within the bracket of the minimum subsistence level. If these become the first pillar, then little would be left for other pillars, and the bulk of social security contributions would thus be converted into personal income tax.[9] On the other hand, if the first pillar provided much lower pensions, it would become meaningless, since one third of the minimum subsistence, for example, would not accomplish anything.

In any case, decisions on the first pillar will basically determine the possibilities of the second pillar, generally seen as occupational, i.e., earnings-related pension insurance. This is where benefits should be tied somehow to previous contributions, and where incentives to contribute must be created, particulary with respect to the large baby-boom cohorts now aged 40 to 45, who will begin to retire around 2010. Opinions are yet seriously diverging on how to implement such a pillar. Should it be a pay-as-you-go or a funded system? Should it be publicly managed by the existing pension fund or handed over to the private sector?

For the second pillar, longitudinal (i.e., funded, actuarially fair) financing seems to be more appropriate for several good reasons. This fact leads many to conclude that it should be mandatory but *privately* managed. The argument is that (*a*) funded public systems usually did not perform well in terms of efficiency, whereas private pension funds boast spectacular returns on the capital invested, for example in Chile (see chapter VI), and (*b*) the fresh capital accumulated in private funds would do wonders for the economy by enlivening capital markets.

Others, however, argue that (*a*) above-average returns are possible only during the maturing period, when capital stock is relatively small, but will be unsustainable later, when the accumulated retirement wealth may well constitute the larger part of the aggregate capital stock; (*b*) redirecting pension premiums to the capital markets would leave already committed pension payments without a proper source of funding, a potential disaster for the Government budget, which would have to finance the old pensions from non-existent additional revenues; and finally (*c*) long-lasting recessions might wipe out the capital

---

[8]See, for example, Falkingham and Johnson (1993).
[9]Attractive for business, which keeps pressing for lower contribution rates, but a big trap for the budget, since income tax is even more difficult to collect than social security contributions.

base of the funded private systems. Hence, there is no better pension guarantee than the unwritten contract among generations, embodied in a public pay-as-you-go system.[10]

The third pillar, voluntary private saving through market-based financial intermediaries, needs little argument, since it is actually not a part of the public system. The only question that will probably be negotiated is how much of a tax incentive—if any—to legislate to induce people to save more.

Secular problems to be faced when designing a feasible pension reform for Hungary are thus not altogether different from the problems of other countries. What is specific in the Hungarian situation, however, is the substandard level of pensions, the distorted pension differentials and the meagre hopes for a foreseeable recovery of the economy.

What seems to be particularly dangerous with respect to various pension reform proposals is that short-term crisis management, such as austerity measures to balance the government budget and lower employers' contribution rate to reduce labour cost, will most likely dominate the debate, while long-term considerations with respect to a reasonable and fair pension system will be pushed into the background.

7. COMBINED LIFE-CYCLE FINANCING?

The large multigenerational family, the institution that has traditionally accomplished the entire task of life-cycle redistribution, is practically extinct. New solutions have been emerging over the past century, responding to needs and expectations that have varied across countries and over time. Most of them have been sheltered in one way or another under one large multipurpose umbrella, the State. This redistributive task undertaken by the State implies that a large fraction of NDP is channelled through the budget of the general Government, thus expanding its revenues and expenditures to an unprecedented magnitude.

There are strong arguments against the paternalistic welfare state. Although it is obviously impossible to push life-cycle redistribution entirely back to the private sphere, there is a vivid impetus to privatize some of the major social security institutions so as to open them up to capital markets. In the thrust to dismantle the welfare state, however, the interdependent nature of its various functions is seldom realized.

---

[10]As a matter of fact, there is a huge literature on inefficiency and risk in private pension plans (Barr, 1992, Frijns and Petersen, 1991) and on incompatibilities in mandatory private saving (Rosenman 1993; Women's Policy Unit, 1993). Even the celebrated 401(k) plans in the United States do not seem to be faring as well as was expected (Papke *et al.*, 1994; Scheiber and Shoven, 1994; Wayne, 1994).

Reform proposals concerning education, children's allowances and pension systems are abundant but never coherent, never considering the mutual links among the stages of life and long-term effects that such proposals might have on life-cycle financing. Looking ahead into the twenty-first century, one cannot help wondering whether a reasonable, combined life-cycle financing system could be designed. Why should funds earmarked for retirement pensions not be invested in gestation loans, thereby providing the necessary capital for gestation financing?

As distinct from current social security arrangements, the combined system should be: (a) *longitudinal*, and actuarially fair for reasons of economic efficiency and also so as to be resistant to impending demographic structural changes; (b) purely *life-cycle oriented*, clearly separated from other redistributional aspects, such as poverty relief; and (c) *self-sustained*, independent from voluntarist government meddling.

The existence of two fully funded insurance agencies could be assumed. Gestation loans—not necessarily limited to student loans—would be financed by a gestation fund and gestation contributions would be collected by it as returns on such loans. A retirement fund would collect pension insurance premiums and provide retirement benefits as returns on the accumulated retirement funds.

All flows and stocks, however, would be accounted for relatively in terms of a selected *numéraire*, say unit wage, that would always be compatible with the actual situation of the economy. All stocks would accrue interest at a fixed internal rate. The system would thus be robust and resistant to economic fluctuations, as well as free from generational conflicts.

The crucial issue is the sustained macroeconomic viability of such a combined system. The viability criterion is that the aggregate stock of gestation loans extended by the gestation fund should never exceed the aggregate stock of retirement wealth accumulated in the retirement fund. Thereby, retirement wealth would always be capable of fully financing the gestation fund. The latter would never need to turn to the Government for help or to financial markets for loans at market interest rates.

The reverse is permissible: assets of the retirement fund might exceed the aggregate loans extended to the gestation fund. The remaining assets—to be called for brevity traditional—would obviously be invested in financial markets.

The magnitude of traditional assets would be crucial for the chances of introducing such a system. It is of course true that the entire accumulated wealth of current retirees and breeder cohorts who have already contributed to the pension system is not tangible or visible.

The same applies to the gestation debt of cohorts currently in gestation and the debt of current breeders. Both stocks, hence the mutual connection between the two funds, could be determined by imputation. However, in order for the combined system to be operational and remain sustainable these traditional assets in the retirement fund would have to exist, invested in financial (or other) instruments.

For number of a years, the author has been carrying out repeated macroeconomic simulations to explore the viability of establishing such a combined system in Hungary during the twenty-first century. The author has calculated that the necessary traditional stock in the initial phase, at the end of the twentieth century, would be about 7 to 12 per cent of NDP, depending on initial conditions and various assumed parameters. This is an insignificant amount compared, for example, to the 11 per cent unspecified unaccounted income transfers in a single year (see table VII.3), or compared to the estimated aggregate stock of retirement wealth, which may be as high as 3 to 4 times GDP. The combined system would thus not be a monopolist, public giant threatening financial markets by its transactions; neither would retirement wealth be dangerously exposed to market fluctuations.

Obviously, macroeconomic simulations are not sufficient to prove the feasibility of a radically new system. Microeconomic, social and legal aspects would have to be worked out in discouraging detail. However, it can be stated, at least theoretically, that there are other and maybe even better ways of cutting through the redistributive maze of the current welfare state than the privatization of its institutions at any price.

Publicly managed life-cycle redistribution does not necessarily imply government meddling. On the contrary, specialized independent agencies should respond to the Parliament rather than to the Government. Income redistribution would thus become transparent, the central budget slimmer and the Government more accountable on how it spends taxpayers' money.

Technical details and ways and means of establishing the rules of any such new system are well beyond the scope of the present paper, along with political feasibility considerations, that is, the existence or absence of political will and social consensus to carry out such a radical reform. The issue is probably not mature. Various fragments of overall life-cycle security, either on the contribution or on the benefit side, exist in almost every country's current social security system. A comprehensive, consistent, economically reasonable, socially fair and sustainable system, however, is still awaited.

REFERENCES

Arthur, W. B., and G. McNicoll (1978). Samuelson, population and intergenerational transfers. *International Economic Review*, vol.19, No.1.
Augusztinovics, M. (1989). The costs of human life. *Economic Systems Research*, vol.1, No.1.
Baranyai, István (1989). Personal income and consumption by age-groups. Budapest: Institute of Economics, Hungarian Academy of Sciences.
_____ (1990). Consumption expenditures by types of households and age-groups: 10 ECE countries and the United States. Budapest: Institute of Economics, Hungarian Academy of Sciences.
_____ (1995). The elderly and pensioners. Discussion paper, No. 4. Budapest: Institute of Economics, Hungarian Academy of Sciences.
Barr, N. (1992). Economic theory and the welfare state: a survey and interpretation. *Journal of Economic Literature*, vol. XXX (June).
Cornia, G. A., and S. Sipos (1991). *Children and the Transition to the Market Economy*. Avebury Academic Publishing Group.
Falkingham, J., and P. Johnson (1993). A unified funded pension scheme for Britain. Discussion paper, No. WSP/90. London: Welfare State Programme, Suntory-Toyota International Center for Economics and Related Disciplines, London School of Economics and Political Sciences.
Frijns, J. and C. Petersen (1991). Financing, administration and portfolio management: how secure is the pension promise? Paper presented at a conference of national experts on private pensions and public policy, Paris (July).
Jorgenson, D. W., and B. M. Fraumeni (1989). Investment in education. *Educational Researcher*, vol. 18, No. 4 (May).
Kendrick, J. W. 1976. The formation and stocks of total capital. *General Series*, No. 100. Columbia University Press.
Kotlikoff, L .J., and L. H. Summers (1981). The role of intergenerational transfers in aggregate capital accumulation. *Journal of Political Economy*, vol. 89, No. 4.
Kruse, A., and R. Ohlsson (1994). Generational accounting: a demographic approach to public-sector expenditure. Paper presented at a European Science Foundation Research Conference on the Economics of Ageing, Sitges (June).
Lee, R. (1980). Age structure, intergenerational transfers and economic growth: an overview. *Revue Economique*, vol. 31, No. 6 (November).
Mincer, J. (1958). Investment in human capital and personal income distribution. *Journal of Political Economy* (August).
Mingat, A., J. P. Tan and M. Hoque (1985). Recovering the cost of public higher education in LDCs: to what extent are loan schemes an efficient instrument?. *Education and Training Series*, No. EDT14. World Bank.
Modigliani, F., and R. Brumberg (1954). Utility analysis and the consumption function: an interpretation of cross-section data. In *Post-Keynesian Economics*, K. K. Kurihara, ed. New Brunswick: Rutgers University Press.
Papke, L., M. Petersen and J. Poterba (1994). Did 401(k) Plans Replace Other Employer-Provided Pensions? *Working Paper Series*, No. 4501. Cambridge, Massachusetts: National Bureau of Economic Research.
Rosenman, L. (1993). Superannuation and the restructuring of women's work, wages and retirement. Paper presented at an RIPAA Conference on "Women and economic policies", Melbourne (October).
Samuelson, P. A. (1958). An exact consumption-loan model of interest with or without the social contrivance of money. *Journal of Political Economy*, vol. LXVI, No. 12.
Scheiber, S., and J. Shoven (1994). The consequences of population aging on private pension fund saving and asset markets. *Working Paper Series*, No. 4665. Cambridge, Massachusetts: National Bureau of Economic Research.

Tobin, J. (1967). Life cycle saving and balanced growth. In *Ten Economic Studies in the Tradition of Irving Fisher*, Fellner et al., eds. New York: Wiley.

Wayne, L. (1994). Shift in pension responsibilities prompts concern about savings. *TheNew York Times*, 29 August.

Willis, R. J. (1988). Life cycles, institutions, and population growth: a theory of the equilibrium interest rate in an overlapping generations model. In *Economics of Changing Age Distributions in Developed Countries*, R. D. Lee, W. B. Arthur and G. Rodgers, eds. Oxford: Clarendon Press.

Women's policy unit (1993). Superannuation for women. Discussion paper. Queensland, Australia: Office of the Cabinet,.

Woodhall, M. (1990). Student loans in higher education, 1. Western Europe and the USA.*Educational Forum Series*, No.1. Paris: International Institute for Educational Planning.

World Bank (1994). *Averting the Old Age Crisis*. Oxford University Press.

165

Chapter VIII

WHO PAYS FOR AND BENEFITS FROM SOCIAL SECURITY SCHEMES IN TOGO?

Kodjo Evlo*

1. INTRODUCTION

1.1. *Historical background and socio-economic context*

The first general social protection provisions were introduced in Togo in the early 1950s. These provisions, which concerned mainly civil servants, were not very harmonized until 1956, when the country got its internal autonomy from France.

There were, however, traditional social protection schemes characterized by a remarkable sense of solidarity within the community (Kagbara, 1977). Social and economic life was organized accordingly, with members of the community sharing what they had, from factors of production to goods, services and income. In such an environment, the social protection of the individual was assured automatically by the whole community. For instance, the health, well-being and education of a child were the concerns of the community and not solely of the parents of the child. Similarly, the elderly, the sick and victims of accidents or any type of mishap (natural or social) were taken care of by the whole community. In this setting, the individual contributed to all aspects of the socio-economic life of the community, from which he received in return the social protection he needed.[1]

The changes in the socio-economic environment caused by the shift from a subsistence to a market economy profoundly altered the traditional social protection system. The old system was no longer fit to provide adequate protection for the population, not even for those who were not employed in the formal sector. Nor was it capable of evolving in order to accommodate itself to the changing socio-economic environment. A new social protection system was called for to complement the old one and accommodate the needs of those employed in the formal sector. The need for a formal system became evident

---

*Professor, Université du Bénin, Lomé, Togo.
[1]Not all aspects of modern social security were relevant in such a system. For example, unemployment benefits could not be provided as such since logically there could be no unemployment.

under the influence of emerging trade union organizations and the International Labour Office (ILO). Gradually, with the assistance of the ILO, compulsory social security schemes were introduced in the formal sector of the economy.

Following the French law of 15 December 1952 creating a labour code in the overseas territories, a family welfare benefit scheme was introduced in Togo on 15 March 1956 for wage earners. This scheme was followed by occupational safety schemes in 1964 and old-age benefit schemes in 1968.

At the same time, a French Law of 1 December 1958 defining the statutes of civil service in overseas territories created two categories of civil servants in Togo, one being the general cadres of French West Africa (expatriates and some specific categories of national civil servants), and the second the local cadres of Togo. The two categories were provided with the same types of social protection schemes in terms of family welfare and occupational safety benefits. In terms of old-age benefits, however, some distinction was drawn between the two categories. General cadres were with the *Caisse de Retraités de la France d'Outre-Mer* and local cadres with the *Caisse Locale de Retraite du Togo*. This two-tier arrangement came to an end after independence, when the new civil service statutes introduced in 1963 instituted a single old-age benefit regime for all civil servants.

The current formal social security system represents the continuation of the two above-mentioned regimes, i.e., a social security regime for employees of the private and parastatal sectors, and a special social protection regime for civil servants and the military.

1.2. *Weaknesses of the formal social protection system in Togo*

1.2.1. *Coverage*

Despite its considerable evolution in terms of both the size of the population covered and the scope of the benefits provided, the formal social security system concerns only a minority, since only 4.5 per cent of the active population are employed in the formal sector (see table VIII.1).

Table VIII.1. Togo: active population and employment, 1991
(Thousands)

Agriculture	Informal	Private sector	Public sector	Total employment	Unemployed population	Total active population
1 044	313	58	33	1 448	603	2 051

Source: Estimates of the Central Bureau of Statistics, Lomé.

So more than 95 per cent of the active population (which includes those employed in the agricultural and informal sectors and those unemployed) does not have any formal social security coverage, which is the situation that prevails in most developing countries.[2] Clearly, it is extremely difficult to extend coverage to a significantly larger proportion of the population in most of these countries because the sectors not covered are not organized in any structure that can link them to a modern social security system. As Guhan (1994) notes, rural populations are spatially scattered, occupationally diffuse and difficult to reach administratively. Similarly, those who are employed in the urban informal sector, where employment is not always well defined but is characterized by a high degree of diversity and instability, are difficult to reach.

Even if the formal system cannot be extended easily to rural populations and the urban informal sector, some forms of social protection still exist for these sections of the population. First, some social protection is provided through broad-based Government transfers relating to publicly funded social programmes such as health care and education. Although the structural adjustment programmes that Togo has adopted since the early 1980s have led to reductions in Government expenditure in the social sectors, the essence of Government-supported social protection remains unaltered.

Second, the informal social protection system mentioned above, although significantly altered by the changing socio-economic environment, still exists, particularly in rural areas. So a comprehensive analysis of social protection should take full account of the traditional aspects of the issue and thus put into the right perspective the role of social solidarity within the African community.

Clearly, given that the traditional system covers a vast majority of the population, an analysis focused only on the formal system cannot give a complete picture of the overall situation. None the less, the organization and the functioning of this system may present some features that could be of interest at least for the purpose of international comparisons.

1.2.2. *Scope of the benefits provided*

The benefits provided remain limited in scope. Only the very basic social security benefits are provided. For instance, the system provides no unemployment benefit and no protection against any natural disaster, and has no poverty alleviation programme. The lim-

---

[2]Coverage rate is particularly low in sub-Saharan Africa, as low as 0.7 per cent in Guinea and one per cent in the Gambia, Chad and the Niger. See, for example, Gruat (1990) and Guhan (1994).

ited scope of the benefits provided is another characteristic that the system in Togo shares with systems in other developing countries. Gruat (1990) found that formal social protection is even more restricted in former British colonies, where it is still often limited to provident fund schemes that do not pay out pensions in the true sense of the term. The protection provided by such schemes is generally judged inadequate by most analysts. Although most of the countries surveyed by Gruat provide some form of old-age and employment injury benefits, only half of these countries provide family benefits, and only one out of 11 countries that have social security programmes statutorily includes unemployment benefits.

The scope of protection cannot be broadened to include most of these benefits because of the socio-economic situation of the country. Guhan has pointed out that widespread poverty and high levels of unemployment and underemployment make it difficult to include such programmes in the social security system in most developing countries. As indicated in table VIII.1, the number of unemployed is nearly seven times larger than the numbers of those employed in the formal sector, which makes it difficult to define any meaningful and feasible unemployment compensation programme.

1.3. *Overview of the formal social protection system in Togo*

As mentioned above, the formal social protection system of Togo has two regimes, a social security regime for wage earners of the private, parastatal and public sectors,[3] and a special social protection regime for civil servants and the military. These are contribution-based social insurance systems covering a total of 90,000 active contributors (60,000 wage earners and 30,000 civil servants or military) and 14,000 pensioners plus their dependants.

Both regimes provide family welfare benefits and insurance against various types of deprivation and/or vulnerability, such as disability due to industrial injuries or occupational diseases, illness, death and the loss of income due to interruption of activity[4] or retirement. With the exception of child benefits, the benefits provided are functions of the contributions paid.

The two regimes are quite similar in the nature and scope of the benefits that they provide. They differ, however, when it comes to the

---

[3]According to its statutes, the civil service has two categories of employees, the *agents de cadre* or *fonctionnaires*, i.e., civil servants, and the *agents permanents*, who are non–civil servant employees of the public sector but are treated as wage earners of the private and parastatal sectors.

[4] Interruption of activity is different from unemployment; it is a situation that arises when, for example, the contributor is on maternity or sick leave, or when he/she stops activity following an industrial injury.

169

contributions, the way some types of benefit are distributed, the quality of the services provided by the agencies that manage the regimes, and the way that these agencies themselves are managed.

2. THE SOCIAL SECURITY REGIME

Togo's social security regime was established during the colonial era in 1956. At the time, the regime had only a family welfare branch. It was extended later to include an occupational safety branch in 1964 and an old-age pension branch in 1968. The regime has not changed much since then. The legal base of the current system is the law of 1973 instituting the national social security code.[5]

The social security system is managed by the *Caisse Nationale de Sécurité Sociale* (CNSS), a parastatal agency with full administrative and financial autonomy.

2.1. Population covered

The regime covers three categories of contributors: mandatory, assimilated and voluntary contributors. Mandatory contributors are all workers who are subject to the national Labour Code, i.e., employees of the modern private and parastatal sectors and non–civil servant employees of the public sector. Assimilated contributors are people enrolled in professional training, rehabilitation or re-education programmes. Voluntary contributors are those who, after a minimum of six months of affiliation to the social security regime, no longer fulfil the requirements for normal mandatory subscription but continue their affiliation to the pension branch of the system on the basis of specific arrangements with CNSS.

The social security insurance system currently covers a total of 124,000 beneficiaries, of whom 59,000 are active contributors, 56,278 are inactive and 8,775 retired. Inactive insured people are those who were formerly employed and were therefore registered at CNSS but have lost or left their jobs. As long as they have not reached retirement age or been hired by new employers, CNSS will keep their registration under this category.

The insured population tripled between 1973 and 1991, as did the inactive group between 1983 and 1991. However, new enrolments in the system have declined significantly, causing the active insured population to fall by 11.4 per cent between 1983 and 1991. The latter trends are due to the macroeconomic difficulties that the country has been going through since the early 1980s and have led the Government to implement International Monetary Fund (IMF) and World Bank–

---

[5]Ministry of Labour and Civil Service, Ordonnance No. 39/73 instituant un code de sécurité sociale, Lomé, 12 November 1973.

Table VIII.2. Togo: evolution of the population covered
by the social insurance system, 1983-1991

Year	Population covered	Active population covered	Inactive population covered	Retired
1983	91 000	66 860	20 582	3 558
1984	94 780	61 766	28 696	4 318
1985	99 100	61 235	32 699	5 166
1986	103 520	62 020	36 262	5 238
1987	108 260	63 944	38 593	5 723
1988	112 300	63 794	42 089	6 417
1989	116 450	58 446	51 344	7 102
1990	119 800	57 341	54 522	7 937
1991	123 800	58 747	56 278	8 775

Source: CNSS, Rapport d'activité, various years.

supported financial stabilization and structural adjustment programmes, respectively in 1981 and 1983. These economic recovery
programmes have put a freeze on recruitment in the public and parastatal sectors and led to a fall in overall employment. Not only was
new recruitment frozen, but also the restructuring or closing down of
many public enterprises caused layoffs and increased unemployment.

The beneficiaries of the social insurance system are the people
directly insured (or contributors), as shown in table VIII.2, and their
families, who are indirectly insured. In 1991, there were 362,000
beneficiaries overall.

2.2. Contributions

The financial resources of CNSS come principally from contributions from or on behalf of its registered workers. Contributions are
proportional to the wage bill paid to employees in the participating
enterprises or institutions, i.e., those under the national Labour Code,
as explained above. Although more than 90 per cent of the participating employers are in the private sector, more than half of the wage
earners covered are employed in the public and parastatal sectors. On
the other hand, about half of these wage earners are employed in the
service sector.

2.2.1. Sectoral distribution of contributions

In 1991, 3,717 employers with a total of 58,747 employees participated in the social security system. Table VIII.3 shows the distribution of participating employers and employees by legal sector, and
table VIII.4 the distribution by economic sector.

Table VIII.3. Togo: distribution of employers and employees, by legal sector, 1991

Legal sector	Employers	Share (percentage)	Employees	Share (Percentage)	Employees per employer
Public	210	5.5	17 488	29.8	83
Parastatal	95	2.6	15 066	25.6	159
Mixed	45	1.2	3 803	6.5	84
Private	3 367	90.6	22 390	38.1	7
Total	3 717	100.0	58 747	100.0	16

Source: CNSS, *Rapport d'activité*, 1991.

Table VIII.4. Togo: distribution of employers and employees, by economic sector, 1991

Sector	Employers	Share (percentage)	Employees	Share (percentage)
Agriculture	108	2.9	4 298	7.3
Mining	2	0.1	3 106	5.3
Manufacturing	136	3.6	6 096	0.4
Construction	245	6.6	2 166	3.7
Utilities	33	0.9	2 397	4.1
Commerce	790	21.2	7 775	13.2
Transportation	118	3.2	4 458	7.6
Services	2 285	61.5	28 457	48.4
Total	3 717	100.0	58 747	100.0

Source: CNSS, *Rapport d'activité*, 1991.

On average, there were 16 employees per employer in 1991. Parastatal enterprises are the largest individual employers, private enterprises the smallest. The public and parastatal sectors account for over 55 per cent of the active contributors registered at CNSS. This explains why the restructuring of these sectors under the structural adjustment programmes caused workers much hardship and hurt the contributions paid to and benefits provided by CNSS.

The distribution of contributions of activity by economic sector indicates that 61 per cent of employers and 48 per cent of employees are in the service sector. The numbers on agriculture describe the modern sector only; agriculture in the informal sector accounts for 72 per cent of total employment.

172

Contributions are paid for by both the employee and the employer as social security taxes. It is the employee, however, who in the end bears the full burden of these taxes, although the part paid by the employer does not show on the employee's pay slip. The part paid by the employee is directly deducted from his salary by the employer.

2.2.2. Contribution rates

Contributions represent 20.5 per cent of the gross wage earnings of workers, and are distributed as follows:

(a)   12 per cent for family welfare (entirely paid for by the employer);

(b)   2 1/2 per cent for professional risks (entirely paid for by the employer);

(c)   6 per cent for old-age pensions (3.6 per cent paid for by the employer and 2.4 per cent by the employee).

The rate of contribution is the same for all employers irrespective of their size or the nature and sector of their activity. This is different from the policy followed in some neighbouring countries, such as Benin, Côte d'Ivoire and Senegal, where the rate of the contributions intended for professional risks coverage is determined according to the riskiness of the activities of each enterprise.

The application of a flat rate across the sectors is probably the easiest method of recovering contributions. It simplifies the procedures for CNSS, which therefore does not have to involve itself in complicated calculations of rates. It also saves CNSS possible disputes with contributors or employers about the rates that are applicable to them. However, this method poses some equity problem between high-risk and low-risk sectors.

As table VIII.5 shows, the contribution rate has evolved significantly since the beginning of the system in 1956, partly reflecting the evolution of the benefits provided by the system. The rate was quite low at the beginning of the regime, when only one category of benefit—family welfare—was provided. The rate increased progressively as other categories of benefit were provided, starting in 1964 with the addition of a professional risks branch.

The increase of the ceiling between 1956 and 1968 reflects the trends in real wage rates. It may also be warranted by the changes that took place in the political and administrative environment: the ceiling of 360,000 CFA francs per year was set four years before the country became independent. But most importantly, the raise and subsequent removal of the ceiling made the social security tax more progressive and probably more equitable.

The current rate of contribution of 20.5 per cent is close to the average rate applied in a few francophone countries of the region.

Table VIII.5. Togo: evolution of the rate of contribution since 1956

Period	Rate of contribution		Annual salary base ceiling[a] (CFA francs)
April 1956–March 1964	FW:	5.0	360 000
	Other:	0.2	
	Total:	5.2	
April 1964–June 1964	FW:	5.75	360 000
	Other:	0.25	
	Total:	6.0	
July 1964–June 1965	FW:	5.75	360 000
	PR:	2.50	
	Other:	0.25	
	Total:	8.5	
July 1965–June 1968	FW:	5.75	720 000
	PR:	2.5	
	Other:	0.25	
	Total:	8.5	
July 1968–December 1971	FW:	5.75	b
	PR:	2.5	
	OAP:	6.0	
	Other	0.25	
	Total:	14.5	
January 1972–December 1976	FW:	7.5	b
	PR:	2.5	
	OAP:	6.0	
	Other:	0.5	
	Total:	16.5	
Since January 1977	FW:	10.0	b
	PR:	2.5	
	OAP:	6.0	
	Other:	2.0	
	Total:	20.5	

Source: CNSS, Rapport d'activité and Bilan et comptes de résultat, various years.

Key: FW - Family welfare
PR - Professional risks
OAP - Old-age pension
a US$ 1.00 = CFAF 282.11 in 1991 (based on IMF, International Financial Statistics).
b No ceiling.

**Table VIII.6. Selected West African countries:
rate of contribution to social security, 1987
(Percentage of wages)**

	Benin	Burkina Faso	Côte d'Ivoire	Niger	Senegal	Togo
Contribution rate	21.2	23.0	14.5	17.0	25.0	20.5
Monthly ceiling (thousands of CFA francs)	none	200	none	250	60	none

Source: CNSS files.

Table VIII.7. Togo: social security benefits paid by CNSS, 1991

	Millions of CFA francs	Percentage
Family welfare	1 770.5	38.7
Child benefits	1 706.3	
Prenatal benefits	10.8	
Paternity benefits	7.6	
Maternity compensation	45.8	
Occupational safety	176.8	3.9
Disablement and survivor allowances	137.6	
Medical expenses	17.0	
Daily compensations	19.1	
Other	3.1	
Old Age	2 550.4	55.7
Old-age pension	1 764.3	
Disablement pension	79.2	
Widow's pension	171.4	
Orphan's pension	60.4	
Other	475.1	
Total	4 577.0	100.0

Source: CNSS, *Rapport d'activité*, 1991.

Interestingly, as is shown in table VIII.6, Senegal's system seems to be the least progressive of the group, with the highest contribution rate, of 25 per cent, and the lowest ceiling, of 720,000 CFA francs per annum. Côte d'Ivoire's system presents opposite features, with the lowest contribution rate and no ceiling.

175

2.3. *Social security benefits*

The social security regime offers three main categories of benefits to its contributors and their families: family welfare benefits, benefits to the victims of occupational accidents or diseases, and old-age benefits. In 1991, the social security benefits paid by CNSS totalled 4,577 millions CFA francs (about US$ 16 million). Table VIII.7 shows that old-age and family welfare programmes combined accounted for nearly 95 per cent of the benefits paid by CNSS during that year.

Family welfare benefits are various forms of supplements to the income of the family of the contributor. They consist mainly of child benefits, which represent over 96 per cent of the total. Child benefits are independent of contributions; they are paid quarterly at the rate of 1,250 CFA francs per child and per month, for a maximum of six children (up to 18 years of age) per contributor, subject to the condition that the contributor must be employed for at least 120 hours or 18 days per month during the period for which the benefits are supposed to be paid. The age limit is raised to 18 if the child is engaged in apprenticeship and to 21 if he or she is pursuing any type of formal education.

Occupational safety benefits cover occupational diseases and industrial accidents (accidents in the workplace and those that occur when the worker is traveling between his home and his workplace). Often, about 2 per cent of the population insured have been victims of industrial injuries, mostly in the industrial, transportation, utilities and construction sectors (table VIII.8). Over 60 per cent of the victims come from these four sectors, which employ fewer than one third of the contributors (table VIII.4). The benefits paid consist mainly of disability and survivor allowances and residually of medical expenses and daily compensation to make up for loss of income due to stoppage of activity.

Table VIII.8. Togo: professional risk victims, by economic sector, 1991

	Number	Percentage
Industrial	401	30.4
Utilities	182	13.8
Transportation	150	10.6
Construction	76	5.8
Commerce	302	22.8
Public administration	165	12.5
Other	56	4.2
Total	1 322	100

Source: CNSS.

Part of the social security contributions paid by people during their working life is intended to provide for their needs during their retirement or during the periods that they have any sort of disability. In 1991, 8,775 retired people were insured by the social security regime. This number equalled 5.7 per cent of the total population insured by CNSS, and 15 per cent of those in activity. These low ratios are due to the facts that (a) the population is young and life expectancy is low—54 years—and (b) employment in the sector covered by the social security regime has grown quite rapidly between the beginning of the regime in 1956 and the late 1970s. Thus, contributors reaching retirement age will remain in relatively small numbers for another decade or so. The population of retired contributors will continue to grow fast, however, probably at the yearly rate of 12 per cent that was recorded on average between 1983 and 1991. Old-age pensions represent over 70 per cent of old-age benefits (see table VIII.7). The other types of benefit are disability, widow's and orphan's pensions.

2.4. Remarks on the social security regime

The remarks set out below concern mainly (a) social security coverage and the equity issues that it raises, and (b) the management of the system.

2.4.1. Coverage

2.4.1.1. Population covered

The social security regime covers 2.7 per cent of the active population and retired salaried workers, who represent an equally small percentage of the population of this age group. Overall, about 360,000 people—less than 10 per cent of the population—benefit in one way or another from this social insurance system. Although there are possibilities of voluntary subscription to the system, such possibilities are open only to those whose employment contract is governed by the National Labour Code.

The system does nothing for those who have lost their employment. CNSS does keep their registration under the inactive category, but this does not entitle them to any immediate social benefit; evidently, one of the major weaknesses of the current regime is that it does not have any unemployment compensation scheme.

For a better coverage of the population, the system should be extended to independent workers and some carefully targeted informal-sector employees.

177

2.4.1.2.   Efficiency of the tax system

Contributions represent 20.5 per cent of the gross earnings of the employees insured. Although the burden of this tax is shifted forward to the employee, the employer also suffers a loss of labour employment and a consequent loss of output. Social security taxes, therefore, face the usual efficiency problems faced by other tax systems. In the case studied here, the problem arises also because it is a proportional tax, not a lump-sum tax that may transcend efficiency problems.

2.4.1.3.   Equity issues

Equity issues can be discussed with respect to (a) the contributions paid or the equivalent social security tax levied (directly or indirectly) on the contributor's wage income, (b) the benefits received by the contributor and/or his/her family, (c) how contributors as a group are treated by CNSS, and (d) how contributors from different economic sectors are treated.

Contributions

Contributions are proportional taxes that, by definition, are not very equitable. The system was even less equitable when a ceiling was put on the contributions paid by people of high income. But if one considers that paying for social security tax is saving for old age, the equity issue regarding the proportionality of the tax breaks down. The issues arises, however, in different terms when it comes to using the tax revenue to finance social welfare and other forms of social transfers. Indeed, it makes sense to have the wealthy make a greater effort for the financing of social welfare programmes.

Benefits

Even if the social security tax does not look equitable, the payment of some benefits is, in particular family welfare and occupational accident and disease benefits. For example, all types of family welfare benefits are independent of the level of the contribution made by beneficiaries. Likewise, the cost of medical expenses following an occupational accident or disease is independent of the wage rate of the victim. Thus, the payment of these particular types of social security benefits constitutes a form of transfer from the rich to the poor.

Comparison between contributions and benefits

The contributions that CNSS collects are greater by far than the benefits that it distributes. Often, overall benefits plus the administrative costs related to their payments represent less than half of the contributions. In 1991, benefits represented 37.5 per cent of the total financial revenues of CNSS, and non-old-age benefits payments represented 36 per cent of the related contributions. The surplus rate, therefore, is quite similar for the two categories of benefits, old-age benefits on the one hand and other social benefits on the other.

For the purpose of this type of analysis, it is important to draw a distinction between old-age benefits and other types of benefits, because, regarding the former type of benefits, there is a lag between the time that contributions are paid and the time that benefits are enjoyed. It can be expected that at least part of the contributions intended for old-age benefits should be invested to earn additional revenues. Thus, the revenues from the different types of investment made by CNSS with its surplus funds should be intended to support primarily old-age benefits programmes.

CNSS runs surpluses that it invests in various types of assets. Such a situation is due to the fact that the population is young and the proportion of the retired population is very low. CNSS should thus take advantage of this situation and accumulate assets in order to be able to face the more complicated situation that may arise as the system matures. None the less, given the extent of the surplus, CNSS may consider increasing the scope or the size of the benefits currently paid. One way of doing this would be to expand the regime and include new types of benefits, such as unemployment compensation and the provision of low-cost housing accommodations for workers and low-income groups, especially in urban areas.

Taking account of the differences between sectors

As was pointed out in subsection 1.3.2 and shown in tables VIII.3 and VIII.8 above, four sectors—industry, transportation, utilities and construction—which employ less than one third of the contributors account for more than 60 per cent of the professional risks. On the other hand, the contribution rates for the provision of all social security benefits are the same for all sectors. Such a situation poses an equity problem, because there is a transfer of net benefits from low-risk sectors to high-risk sectors. Some neighbouring countries, such as Benin, Côte d'Ivoire and Senegal, try to remedy this problem by setting contribution rates for professional risks according to the riskiness of each enterprise.

2.4.2. *Management of the social security system*

The system is quite solvent, and CNSS has always run operating surpluses that it invests in various types of assets, including bank deposits, bonds, stocks and real estate. In 1991, CNSS held 37 billion CFA francs of deposits—about US$ 131 million—in different local banks, as well as stocks and bonds of a total value of 15 billion CFA francs. Interest earnings on bank deposits amounted to 3.8 billion CFA francs (table VIII.9). In the early 1970s, CNSS started investing

179

Table VIII.9. Togo: financial situation of CNSS in 1991[a]
(Millions of CFA francs)

A. Revenues	
Contributions	7 900.0
Revenue from financial investments	3 942.0
of which interest on bank deposits	3 807.0
Revenue from real estate investments	366.2
Total	12 208.2

B. Expenditures	
Social security benefit payments	4 577.0
Administrative expenditures	1 709.8
Total	6 286.8

C. Financial investments	
Loans to the Government	13 830.425
Stocks	1 729.220
Bank deposits	36 604.423
Total	52 164.068

Source: CNSS, Rapport d'activité and Bilan et compte de résultat, various years.

[a] No data is available on the value of the real estate assets of CNSS.

heavily in real estate; it has built residential complexes with a total of 611 houses in Lomé and Kara. Earnings from the sale or the rental of these houses reached 469.5 million CFA francs in 1990. As table VIII.9 shows, resources devoted to the payment of benefits represent 37 per cent of total revenues of CNSS and 8.8 per cent of the total non–real estate assets of CNSS (12.5 per cent of liquid assets, i.e., bank deposits).

To manage the system well, CNSS must use the necessary means to have its partners comply with the rules. For example, it fines employers who do not pay their contributions on time. Fines vary from 5 to 8 per cent of the contributions due, depending on the length and the nature of the delay. Revenue from fines is insignificant, however: about 100 million CFA francs a year.

Overall, the system is managed quite satisfactorily by CNSS: its full autonomy is an important factor contributing to its good management.

3.   THE SOCIAL PROTECTION REGIME FOR CIVIL SERVANTS

The civil service is not governed by the National Labour Code, so that civil servants do not qualify for normal social security protec-

180

tion. There is, therefore, a special social protection regime for civil servants and the military. This regime, which covers a total of 32,000 contributors, 4,000 pensioners and their dependants, is managed by the Treasury and the *Caisse de Retraites du Togo* (CRT).

3.1. Sources of finance for the regime

The regime is financed almost entirely by contributions from civil servants and the State. The contribution is mandatory, and equals 27 per cent of the gross salary of each contributor, 7 per cent paid for by the contributor and 20 per cent by the State. The mechanism for the payment of the contribution is similar to the one used by CNSS in the case of the social security regime. Other sources of revenue are:

(a) Earnings on the financial assets held by CRT;

(b) Pension contributions by civil servants on secondment abroad;

(c) Subsidies from the Government;

(d) Gifts.

However, the revenues from these sources are negligible. Unlike CNSS, CRT does not receive much revenue from investments, since 85 per cent of its assets are interest-free loans to the Government and the remaining 15 per cent are bank deposits. Total revenues for CRT amounted to 5.7 billion CFA francs in 1991.

3.2. Benefits provided

The social protection benefits provided for civil servants and the military are in general similar to the ones provided by CNSS to wage-earners. The present system differs from CNSS in the way that the benefits are paid. Family welfare and occupational injury benefits are incorporated into the salary and paid directly to the contributor by the Treasury. Old-age schemes are managed by the CRT, which is a pension fund.

As the social security system, the social protection system provides the following types of benefit:

(a) Family welfare;

(b) Health insurance;

(c) Protection against occupational accidents and diseases;

(d) Maternity insurance;

(e) Old-age benefits;

(f) Housing benefits.

Regarding old-age schemes, it can be mentioned that, in 1991, CRT paid 3.8 billion CFA francs in benefits, while its revenue amounted to 5.7 billion CFA francs. These schemes cover a total of 7,000 people, 4,000 pensioners and 3,000 eligible beneficiaries.

3.3. *Management of the system*

The special social protection regime for civil servants is managed by the Treasury and CRT. Prior to 1986, CRT was simply a department of the Ministry of Finance. Its financial management was entrusted to the Directorate of Finance of the Ministry, and its funds were kept in a special account at the Public Treasury. In 1986, CRT became a Directorate of its own, thus independent from the Directorate of Finance. In November 1991, however, it gained full administrative and financial autonomy.

Because of its former relations with the Treasury, CRT holds a debt of 25 billion CFA francs on the State. Part of this debt may not be easy to recover in the short run, given the difficult financial situation of the Government. Since the Government is considered solvent in the long run, the current debt may not pose any serious liquidity problem to CRT in the future. The only other assets that CRT holds are bank deposits of a total value of 4.3 million francs. The ideal would be for CRT to invest its funds wisely now in order not to have problems paying pensions later. Bank deposits do not earn much interest, but they are safer and liquid.

4. CONCLUDING NOTE ON SOCIAL PROTECTION IN TOGO

Formal social protection is institutionalized in Togo through the social security regime and the special social protection regime for civil servants. Wage earners, civil servants and their employers are the ones who pay, but are also the primary direct beneficiaries; the families or dependants of the contributors are indirect beneficiaries.

Those who benefit from one type or another of formal social security scheme make up less than 5 per cent of the population, thus constituting a kind of privileged group compared to those who are left out by the system. This raises an equity problem of its own, because there are many people among those who are left out who would like to participate in the system but simply do not find the opportunity to do so.

On the other hand, the scope of protection is limited to basic social security schemes, leaving out broader social assistance programmes, such as unemployment benefits, poverty alleviation and protection against natural disasters.

Given the socio-economic situation of the country, it is difficult to increase significantly the coverage and the scope of the protection system. Such difficulties remind us that the formal social security model of developed countries cannot be applied to the Togolese context without modification. The traditional or informal model remains relevant in such a context. It should probably be transformed and better adapted to the current socio-economic situation of the country. Similarly, government social programmes—health care, education and employment—will continue to play an important role in social protection. Given the reduction in the resources available for such programmes, the Government faces the challenge to be more imaginative and efficient in the allocation of those resources.

REFERENCES

Assih Sizing, Eyana (1987). Les cotisations: principale source de financement de la Caisse Nationale de Sécurité Sociale du Togo. DESS research paper. Université du Maine, France.
Bongo, Kouma (1994). Les problèmes actuels de la Caisse de Retraites du Togo. Research paper. Lomé: Ecole nationale d'administration.
Caisse Nationale de Sécurité Sociale (various years). Rapport d'activité. Lomé.
_____ (various years). Bilan et compte de résultat. Lomé.
Gbadago, Alowonou K. (1985). Le rôle de la Caisse Nationale de Sécurité Sociale dans le processus de développement du Togo. Research paper. Lomé, FASEG, Université du Bénin.
Gruat, Jean-Victor (1990). Social security schemes in Africa: current trends and problems. International Labour Review, No. 129. pp. 405-422.
Guhan, S. (1994). Social security options for developing countries. International Labour Review, No. 133, pp. 35-53.
International Labour Office (1991). Colloque international sur l'avenir de la sécurité sociale dans les pays industrialisés. Proceedings. Geneva.
Kagbara, Bassabi (1971). La sécurité au Togo et l'économie nationale. CESSS research paper. Paris.
_____ (1977). La planification de la sécurité en Afrique. Doctoral thesis. Univer- isté de Paris-Panthéon-Sorbonne.
Kpetemey, Koffi M. (1987). Les ressources de la Caisse Nationale de Sécurité Sociale comme appui à la politique de développement du Togo. Research paper. Lomé: FASEG, Université du Bénin.
Mamadou, Gambo (1993). La gestion du fonds national de retraites du Niger. Research paper. Lomé: École nationale d'administration.
Murray, Matthew N., and Donna S. Bueckman (1992). Social insurance in develop- ing countries: are there net benefits to programme participation? Journal of Developing Areas, No. 36, pp. 193-212.
République Togolaise (1973). Ordonnance No. 39/73 instituant un code de sécurité sociale. Lomé.

183

Chapter IX

URBAN AND RURAL PENSION INSURANCE IN CHINA

Hou Wenruo *

1. INTRODUCTION

The Chinese economy has been growing rapidly. Real gross national product (GNP) growth, accompanied by an accelerated growth of industrial output, has recorded a rate higher than 10 per cent per annum over the last decade. Foreign trade and investment are increasing rapidly, especially in the coastal cities of Guangzhou, Snenzhen and Shangai and in the provinces of Guangdong, Fujian and Jiangsu. Nevertheless, primary-sector activities still account for close to one third of output and two thirds of employment, whereas manufacturing accounts for close to one half of output but less than one quarter of employment. Despite the adoption of market-friendly reforms, the State sector still accounts for nearly two thirds of industrial output, and the improvement of the efficiency of public production is still a concern. Furthermore, power shortages represent a major constraint on further industrial development, in spite of large energy reserves.

The country is still poor and developing, with a per capita gross domestic product (GDP) estimated at about $300 in 1990. The population growth rate has been reduced to almost one half of what was recorded in the late 1970s, but the peak effect of the 1962-1975 baby boom has yet to be seen. The total labour force is close to 600 million, and registered unemployment is very low. But according to sampling surveys, hidden unemployment may be higher than 200 million, so that the unemployment problem is in fact very serious.

The improvement in standards of living since 1980 has been significant, especially in urban areas. There has been a virtual elimination of urban poverty and a huge reduction of absolute poverty in rural areas which is now restricted to the resource-constrained remote upland areas, according to the World Bank (1990).

---

*Professor, Labour and Personnel College, China Renmin University, Beijing. This paper is an abridgement by the editor of the author's original paper, the full text of which is available upon request.

In many cities, housing is of poor quality and in short supply, but the number of hospital beds and of medical doctors nearly doubled between 1970 and 1989. There are still nearly 200 million adult illiterates or semi-illiterates—about the same number as the total student population, including adult students enrolled in education. The enrolment rate of primary-school children is nearly 100 per cent, and close to 80 per cent of primary-school graduates continue their study in junior secondary schools.

These indicators suggest a rapidly growing developing country with a greater supply of public goods in the social sphere—such as health and education—than its per capita income would suggest. The supply of social security follows the same pattern, but it is the variety of arrangements available that is stressed in the present paper.

This variety is apparent not only as regards urban and rural pension insurance but also as regards health insurance, work- related accident insurance and unemployment insurance. After a description in section 2 of how the social security system was established in China, sections 3 and 4 deal with the variety of urban and rural pension insurance schemes, respectively. Other social security arrangements are dealt with in Wenruo (1994). Section 5 concludes the paper.

2. HOW SOCIAL SECURITY WAS INTRODUCED IN CHINA

The social security system was created and began to operate during 1951-1952, shortly after the founding of the People's Republic of China. For employees in urban enterprises, the emphasis of social security was placed on social insurance, and a national insurance scheme was implemented. That is to say: (a) individuals did not have to pay anything; (b) all insurance funds came from the State budget; and (c) the rate of insurance benefits was unitary.

Enterprises paid 3 per cent of the total wage bill on a monthly basis to the trade union exercising the functions of social insurance agency at the time, thus contributing to social insurance funds for all enterprises in the country. But 70 per cent of those contributions were retained in the enterprises themselves to be used as payment of subsidies for old age, maternity, sickness and unemployment of employees and survivors of the deceased. The remaining 30 per cent of the contributions were handed over to the All-China Federation of Trade Unions. Any insufficiency of funds—to cover outlays by the enterprises—was submitted to the local trade union for compensation, while any surplus was handed over to the local trade union. In turn, the Federation would extend resources to local trade unions, if necessary, or collect their surpluses when they occurred. In this way, there was quite a large sum of funds to be used for regulation in the whole country, according to the principle of mutual aid inherent in social insurance. Since there were no private enterprises after 1956, all insurance funds had to come from the State and managers of State-owned enterprises were merely acting on behalf of the State.

The Great Leap Forward in 1958 claimed to have eliminated the 4 million remaining unemployed in urban areas of old China, and unemployment insurance was therefore cancelled: the Government denied the existence of unemployment. Since China had destroyed capitalism, it was argued, unemployment, as a hallmark of capitalism, naturally no longer existed. For farmers in rural areas, accounting for 80 per cent of the total population, the emphasis of social security was placed on social relief, a most inadequate security measure. Indeed, farmers in rural areas still mainly relied on family protection to tide them over all kinds of risks, just as they had done in the years before the founding of new China.

For servicemen, the emphasis of social security was placed on social care, which included regular support to army personnel and various forms of preferential treatment. Social welfare at that time also included free college education, free medical care and free housing— for those who qualified. Farmers in rural areas, however, accounting for the vast majority of the population, were not entitled to such welfare benefits. Their only recourse was to try to send their children to school and get themselves a job in enterprises or government agencies.

In 1965, the Cultural Revolution broke out and brought about almost total economic collapse; the catastrophe lasted until the downfall of the so-called Gang of Four in 1976. The Cultural Revolution caused the most serious damage to social security. In February 1969, the Ministry of Finance issued a paper entitled "Views on the reform of some financial schemes in State-owned enterprises" in which it was stipulated that all State-owned enterprises should stop drawing trade union expenses and labour insurance funds, and pensions for retired employees and long-time disease sufferers and other labour expenses should be paid from non-business expenditures.

As a result:

(a) Enterprises no longer contributed social insurance premiums, there were no longer unified social insurance funds in the country, and the national regulation of social insurance funds was totally eliminated;

(b) Enterprises collected insurance premiums and paid insurance benefits all by themselves. The burden of the former unified national social insurance scheme for the whole country was shifted to "enterprise insurance", and pensions for maternity, sickness, employment injury, old age and even the death of employees were totally paid from the profits of State-owned enterprises by the enterprises themselves. Old enterprises with a high proportion of retired employees suffered greatly, and some of them were even unable to pay pension benefits for several months. Newly established enterprises, with a high proportion of young employees, could afford generous welfare benefits.

The outcome of those changes is still being felt today. Currently, there is no single authoritative agency to exercise overall leadership and management of social security activities. Various departments under the State Council are each in charge of certain aspects of social security (see table IX.1). Social security management can currently be described as follows:

(a) *Rural areas*: social care, social relief, welfare for farmers and pension insurance are the responsibility of the Ministry of Civil Affairs and its subordinate agencies. The Ministry has also been responsible for social care and social relief in urban areas since the first years after the founding of the People's Republic of China, with no change. Pension insurance in rural areas was assigned to the charge of the Ministry of Civil Affairs in the 1990s. Pension benefits, however, are available primarily to employees in township enterprises. Township enterprises in China are considered to be the key to absorbing the surplus labour force in rural areas, promoting industrialization in the countryside and improving the living standards of the rural population. Nearly 100 million farmers have become employees of township enterprises;

(b) *Urban areas*: social insurance and social welfare, including pension insurance, health insurance, maternity insurance, employment injury insurance and unemployment insurance, are all the responsibility of the Ministry of Labour. That constitutes the bulk of social

Table IX.1. China: management of social security

Ministry	Benefits
Civil affairs	Social care Social relief in both urban and rural areas Welfare in rural areas Social insurance in rural areas Welfare for employees in urban enterprises Pension insurance in urban enterprises
Labour	Sickness insurance and maternity insurance Employment injury insurance in urban enterprises Unemployment insurance in urban enterprises
Health	Health insurance for public servants
Personnel	Welfare for public servants Employment injury insurance and maternity Insurance for public servants Pensions insurance for public servants Unemployment insurance for public servants

187

security in China in terms of coverage: about 500 to 600 million employees in both State and non-State enterprises and their dependants are covered. The Ministry of Labour has assigned its Social Insurance Department to take charge of pertinent policies, laws and regulations. The Social Insurance Management Bureau is responsible for the collection, management and administration of social insurance funds. On the other hand, all matters related to unemployment insurance—from policies, laws and regulations to the establishment and manipulation of insurance funds—are the responsibility of the Department of Human Resources Development;

(c) *Civil servants*: pension insurance, unemployment insurance, maternity insurance and employment injury insurance and welfare for civil servants are the responsibility of the Ministry of Personnel. Since the 1980s, the Ministry of Personnel has been responsible for the personnel management affairs of civil servants for such matters as recruitment, transfer, reward and punishment, training and promotion, just as the Ministry of Labour is responsible for the personnel management of employees in urban enterprises. Social insurance and welfare for employees in urban enterprises and civil servants are, therefore, assigned to the charge of two separate ministries in China. Furthermore, health insurance for civil servants is the responsibility of a third ministry, the Ministry of Health.

In addition to the ministries and agencies mentioned above, the State Planning Commission, the State Commission for Restructuring the Economic System, the Ministry of Finance and the All-China Federation of Trade Unions all exercise policy influence on social security matters.

3. URBAN PENSION INSURANCE

In 1978, China set out on the road of reform. Initial reforms were also made to the social security system, with emphasis on pension insurance for employees in urban enterprises.

Owing to factors that were compromising the stability of enterprise insurance, such as the rapid ageing of the population, the increasing number of retired employees and the low rate of pension benefits, the Government decided to implement local insurance schemes for pension insurance in urban enterprises. Local insurance schemes were to have unified regulation at the level of provinces, autonomous regions and municipalities directly under the Government, and they actually represented the first step to restore a unified national insurance scheme.

It was stipulated that enterprises could fix the rate of insurance premiums by themselves according to their past experience, and all enterprises in each locality should contribute on a compulsory basis to form the social pension insurance funds of that locality. The pension insurance premium had an average rate of 17 per cent in 1988, ranging from 10 per cent in Shaanxi to 23 per cent in Shanghai. The contribution rate in Beijing was 14 per cent.

With the establishment of local pension insurance funds, a new situation emerged in which pension benefits could be regulated among all State-owned enterprises within a given locality. No enterprises would suffer from their inability to pay pension benefits. Some enterprises suffering losses were unable to pay wages to active employees, but their retired employees could still get the full amount of pension benefits from social insurance agencies on schedule. That was also an encouragement and incentive to active employees. Furthermore, the local insurance rescued some enterprises and enabled them to rally their forces again.

In 1986, the Government of China began to implement the labour contract system, and issued the Interim Provisions on the Implementation of the Labour Contract System in State-owned Enterprises. As a result, pension insurance premiums began to be collected from contract workers. It was stipulated in the provisions that contract workers had to contribute pension insurance premiums on a monthly basis at a rate of 3 per cent of their standard wage. Without a doubt, this was a major advance in the development of social insurance. The long-established practice of labourers themselves not having to contribute any insurance premium was changed, and workers began to develop a sense of self-protection. Sources of funds were also expanded, and a precedent was set for other employees to contribute insurance premiums in the near future. But the number of employees who actually make contributions has been very limited, and has not yet reached one fifth of employees in State-owned enterprises. Estimates for 1990 show that the number of contract workers in State-owned enterprises was 13.52 million, accounting for only 13.1 per cent of the total number of employees in State-owned enterprises in that year. In addition, the total amount of insurance premiums collected has also been limited. The rate of insurance premiums is 3 per cent on paper only: the actual rate of insurance premiums has been only 1.5 to 1.7 per cent. The structure of the total wage for employees in State-owned enterprises is such that the total wage includes basic wage, post wage, supplementary wage, welfare expenses, bonuses, allowances and over-time wage. The standard wage, however, is composed of basic wage and post wage only; its share of the total wage fell from over 85 per cent in 1978 to about 55 per cent in 1990.

Unfortunately, shortly after pension insurance funds for urban enterprises were established based on contributions of contract workers and enterprises in 1986, inflation rose from 6 per cent to close to 20 per cent in 1988 and in 1989. In the meantime, the interest rate paid on deposits remained at 5 per cent in 1986 and 1987, and rose to 11 per cent in 1989 for one-year deposits. The rate for eight-year deposits, the longest maturity, was 7.2 per cent in 1986 and 1987, and rose to 17.6 per cent in 1989. This led to a severe depreciation of insurance funds.

In the 1980s, the retirement age of some employees was increased. For employees in State-owned enterprises and public servants in State organs, the retirement age was 60 for males and 55 for females at the beginning of the 1950s, which was appropriate for a population that was relatively young at the time. In 1983, it was decided that the retirement age of professionals and managers could reasonably be extended to facilitate production and management.

In addition, it was argued at that time that since the average life expectancy of the Chinese population had increased and had already reached 69 in the late 1980s, the retirement of all employees should be extended. This appeared reasonable from a theoretical point of view, since health conditions and life expectancy had indeed improved greatly compared with the early 1950s. However, as sampling surveys showed, a 150-to-200-million-strong labour force in rural areas was experiencing hidden unemployment, and 20 to 30 million employees in urban areas were actually unemployed even though they held a post.

There were nearly a million young people in urban areas each year waiting for jobs; the employment problem was very serious. If retirement was postponed to an older age, it would only aggravate the problem of labour-force surplus. It was decided, therefore, to maintain the status quo and extend the retirement of only a small number of the most needed personnel to a higher age to ensure that the urgent needs of economic reform and economic take-off were met.

In the 1990s, the Government officially announced that it would discard the planned economy and establish a market economy. The transformation called for in-depth reforms to be carried out to the social security system to suit the needs of the new market economy. Since the beginning of the 1990s, an entirely new contributory pension insurance scheme has been established.

In 1991, the State Council issued the Decision of the State Council on the Reform of the Pension Insurance Scheme for Employees in Enterprises, and assigned the Ministry of Labour to draw up a proposal and organize its implementation. In its proposal, the Ministry of Labour stipulated that all urban enterprises, including State-owned enterprises and private enterprises, should participate in the contributory pension insurance scheme on a compulsory basis. It was further stipulated in the scheme that:

(a) Pension insurance funds should be established. The funds would be composed of contributions made by employees and enterprises, subsidies from the State and profits gained by social insurance agencies. Employees would contribute at the rate of 2 to 3 per cent of their wages. Subsidies from the State would include pre-tax payment of insurance premiums, tax exemption on social insurance funds and on the returns on these funds and necessary financial grants. Profits reported by social insurance agencies indicate that positive returns have been achieved by investing social insurance funds.[1]

(b) Pension benefits should follow a multi-tier scheme, consisting of basic pension benefits, supplementary pension benefits provided by enterprises and pension benefits deposited by employees, in conformity with international practice.

The Municipality of Shanghai also proposed a pension insurance scheme for enterprise employees. Considerable attention is now being paid to the Shanghai scheme by the Government, which sees it as a model for the reform of pension insurance.

The Shanghai scheme is set out in detail in "Measures of pension insurance for urban employees of Shanghai Municipality" a document promulgated as resolution No. 63 by the Municipal Government of Shanghai on 27 April 1994, and scheduled to be implemented from 1 June 1994. In brief, the contents of the Shanghai scheme include the following:

(a) Coverage extension: all enterprises, government organs and institutions located in Shanghai Municipality, regardless of their subordination and ownership, as well as their active employees and retirees, should participate in the pension insurance scheme on a compulsory basis;

(b) Establishment of special pension funds: funds would be formed with resources to be collected through the following four channels:

(i) Contributions by enterprises, at a rate of 25.5 per cent of the previous month's total wage bill of all active employees;

(ii) Contributions made by employees, at a rate of the previous year's average monthly wage of employees, with an upper limit of 200 per cent of the previous year's average monthly wage of active employees in the whole municipality and a minimum contribution equal to 60 per cent of that average wage;

(iii) Subsidies from the local government, such as pre-tax withdrawals of insurance premiums, tax exemptions for the running costs drawn of social insurance agencies and profits gained from the investment of pension funds and their accrued interest, and allocations of the State budget to cover the payment of pension benefits in case of insufficiency of pension funds;

---

[1]According to available data, in the period from 1987 to the first half of 1993, the accumulated reserves of pension insurance funds in State-owned enterprises increased by a factor of 10.1.

(iv)   Revenue from the operations of social insurance agencies, including overdue fines, penalties, accrued interest on deposits, and returns from investment of pension funds;

(c)   Establishment of individual pension accounts: social insurance agencies should establish individual pension accounts and issue a pension handbook for active employees. The entries in individual pension accounts would include:

(i)   Contributions of employees themselves, that is, 3 per cent of their own wage;

(ii)   The share of the total contributions of enterprises, that is, 8 per cent of wages;

(iii)   A proportion of the previous year's average monthly wage of active employees in the whole municipality, that is, 5 per cent, also funded by contributions of enterprises.

As is evident, entries in the individual pension account amount to 16 per cent of wages and far exceed the 3 per cent contributed by employees themselves.

It is also defined in the scheme that the rate of interest on deposits in the individual pension account should not be lower than that accruing on one-year fixed deposits of residents in the same period of time.

Two accounts are in fact established after collection of insurance premiums: one is the individual pension account, as specified above, the other is the social mutual-aid account. A measure of combination of individual deposit and social mutual aid is thus achieved.

The Shanghai scheme also calls for the establishment of a multi-tier pension scheme on a gradual basis. Besides basic pension benefits, enterprises that have the economic capacity should set up supplementary pension benefits for their employees, and employees are encouraged to establish deposit pension benefits for themselves.

In addition, different methods have been introduced for calculating pension benefits for young, middle-aged and old employees: for employees who retire during the period 1994-1996, the traditional method will still apply, and in addition to the benefits to which they are entitled, another 11 to 16 per cent of the accumulated amount of contributions made by employees themselves is to be added to their pension benefits on the basis of service years. For employees who joined the enterprise before 1994 and retire after 1996, pension benefits will be the amount of funds in the individual pension account multiplied by a given coefficient to assess the total amount of contributions in the entire contributory career, divided by 120 months (10 years). For new employees who commenced work after June 1994, pension benefits will be the amount accumulated in the individual pension account divided by 120 months. It is also specified in the Shanghai scheme that the amount in the individual pension account should be earmarked for the sole purpose of payment of pension benefits. In case of death, payment can be made to the employee's legal heir, but the amount of benefit extended is limited to the balance of contributions made by the employee himself in his individual pension account.

Finally, the Shanghai scheme also establishes mechanisms for annual adjustment to pension benefits, based on fluctuations in the consumer price index of the Shanghai Municipality. In addition, retirees can receive subsistence allowances, and the scheme provides for special subsistence allowances to be granted to retirees who face extreme difficulty.

The Shanghai scheme and the scheme of the Ministry of Labour share some common features: (a) the partial funding method; (b) the establishment of special pension funds through tripartite contributions of the State, enterprises and employees; (c) a multi-tier pension scheme; (d) emphasis on the importance of employees' contribution; and (e) introduction of some indexation of pension funds. All five features are obviously the results of the work done on the reform of pension insurance in China. They tally fully with the market economy and comply with current international practice.

The Government has attached great importance to the individual pension account. First, the individual pension account has a strong incentive mechanism built in. It can motivate the initiative and consciousness of labourers to participate in social insurance. Second, the total take-home pay of employees may not be reduced at the enterprise's discretion and the individual pension account may provide a mechanism by means of which employees can monitor enterprises. Third, individual pension accounts offer greater flexibility of operation, since funds can be inherited or transferred with the movement of labourers.

4.   FAMILY PROTECTION AND SOCIAL SECURITY IN RURAL AREAS

Until the beginning of the 1990s, farmers in vast rural areas of China got protection for their livelihood from three channels: family protection, social security and commercial insurance against natural calamities or other risks causing loss of working capacity. Of the three, family protection holds the leading position, which is a quite different situation from that in urban areas, where social security is of the first importance.

The Cultural Revolution broke out in the 1960s. After the loss of control of means of production, the aged also lost their respect as parents. In the 1980s, the household union responsibility system was practised. Land was allocated to rural households for long-term use, and was even allowed to be given to their children. Households whose

193

Table IX.2. Survey on the support given to the aged, conducted in Tongren Village, Taoyuan County, Hunan Province, in 1990

Age of the people surveyed	Number of people	Supported by community [a]	Supported by children [a]	Relying on their own spouse [a]	Supported by labour [a]
60-64	52	43.40	15.07	41.51	0.00
65-69	34	60.61	6.03	30.30	3.03
70-74	21	95.24	0.00	0.00	4.76
75-79	15	86.66	0.00	6.67	6.67
80-89	7	100.00	0.00	0.00	0.00
Total (60-89)	129	63.78	7.87	25.98	2.36

Source: A Community Analysis of the Developing Trend of Family Structure in Rural Areas (China Population Press, 1993).
[a] Percentage.

members were tied together by blood relationship once again became the basic unit of production and operation. Family protection once again became a most important umbrella for the aged in rural areas. The Chinese Academy of Social Sciences conducted a sampling survey in 1987 on people aged over 60. According to the data collected by the survey, those relying on support of their families accounted for 67.8 per cent of the total aged population surveyed, which suggests that the aged in rural areas today still mainly rely on family protection. Some Chinese scholars conducted a sampling survey in 1990 on the support given to 127 aged people in Tongren Village, Taoyuan County, Hunan Province, and they arrived at a similar conclusion; table IX.2 shows the results of their survey.

Since the 1980s, the Government has revised some existing laws and issued new ones, making family protection compulsory. The revised version of the Constitution of the People's Republic of China states that children who have come of age have the duty to support and assist their parents. The revised version of the Marriage Law of the People's Republic of China stipulates that in case children fail to perform this duty, parents having no working ability or living in difficult conditions have the right to demand that their children provide them with protection expenses. The newly issued Heritage Law of the People's Republic of China makes the support of aged parents an important criterion for the exercise of inheritance rights. Besides the revision and issuance of those laws, the Government has also adopted a number of effective measures to encourage the support of the aged by family protection in rural areas, such as:

(*a*) Undertaking new activities to show respect for the aged, on such themes as "Models of respect for the aged", "Civilized families" and the "Festival of respect for the aged";

(*b*) Strengthening the moral education of middle-school and primary-school pupils;

(*c*) Formulating and issuing local regulations on the protection of rights and interests of the aged. Until the beginning of 1993, 23 provinces, autonomous regions and municipalities directly under the Government had formulated regulations on protection of rights and interests of the aged. Some of the regulations stipulated that children who have come of age, no matter whether they live together with their parents or not, have to perform the family duty of protecting the life of their parents;

(*d*) Offering favours and rewards for activities conducive to family protection;

(*e*) Making preparations for the formulation of the Law of the Old People.

Due to the enforcement of the measures described above, about 80 per cent of the aged in rural areas are supported and protected by their families, and only 4 per cent of the aged are still neglected by their children. To further consolidate family protection, a project entitled Agreement on family protection of the aged has been universally implemented in rural families in China since 1985. Children sign with the village notary an agreement in which obligations, forms and rates concerning the support of the aged are specified. The fulfilment of this family duty is thus under the supervision of the community.

It is possible to say that until the present, traditional forms of support for the aged and the values behind them have not been much affected by social changes. Most people in rural areas still take it as their bounden duty to support their parents in order to enable them to live happily with all the family members. Most of the aged people in rural areas think that living together with their children is the best way to spend their remaining lifetime.

The Government has assigned the Ministry of Civil Affairs to take charge of the management of social security in rural areas. Different focal points are fixed in activities of social security conducted by departments of civil affairs in different rural areas.

The focal points in poor rural areas are assigned to practice social relief and disaster relief. Social relief generally refers to assistance to farmers in areas where the average annual per capita net income is equal to or less than approximately 30 United States dollars. Most farmers are located in remote areas that are subject to natural disasters or that are not favourable to agriculture. As of 1991, there were 74.87 million poor people in rural areas of China, as shown in table IX.3.

Table IX.3. China: poor population in rural areas, 1980-1991
(Millions)

	1980	1985	1987	1988	1989	1990	1991
Total rural population	795.65	807.59	816.26	823.65	831.64	841.42	852.80
Poor population	651.64	305.50	222.55	155.26	128.41	72.28	74.87
Extremely poor population	450.34	120.20	67.26	43.98	38.09	17.00	23.28

Source: China Statistical Yearbook 1992 and 1990 Census data.

Since the 1980s, the Government has greatly intensified its support for the poor in rural areas. The State Council Leading Group for Economic Development in Poor Areas was set up in 1986, and was renamed the State Council Leading Group for Support and Development in Poor Areas in 1993. Financial departments at various levels are instructed to make sound arrangements of the funds to be used for support of the poor, to give consideration to poor rural families and individuals in assessing agricultural taxes and to offer assistance to the poor.

Focal points in average less poor rural areas are mandated to carry out mass activities financed by local welfare reserve funds, to rely on the contributions of farmers themselves to help poor families and individuals, and at the same time to establish and develop welfare enterprises and undertakings mainly employing poor farmers and disabled persons. They are also mandated to set up institutional homes to take in the orphaned, widowed, disabled and aged who do not have any family members to look after them.

Finally, focal points in the relatively better off rural areas are mandated actively to guide farmers in conducting undertakings related to social security, such as pension and medical care, with the community (township or town) as the basic unit.

In 1986, the Government assigned the Ministry of Civil Affairs to conduct experiments on social insurance in rural areas. The experiments on pension insurance were launched by the Ministry of Civil Affairs in 1991. Several factors underline the need to introduce pension insurance in the rural areas: (a) the aged in rural areas are now the poorest population group; (b) the concept of raising children to secure protection in old age is the major obstacle to the smooth implementation of family planning; (c) population ageing will be faster and more serious in rural areas than in urban areas; and (d) family size is being reduced.

China has selected a number of relatively well-to-do rural areas—defined as those having an average annual per capita net income exceeding 134 United States dollars—as experiment areas for the introduction of its pension insurance scheme. The households in such areas accounted for about one third of the total households in rural areas in 1991, approximately 275 million people; they are mostly suburban outskirts of large or medium-sized cities and coastal rural areas. Experiments on pension insurance have been conducted mainly among employees of township enterprises in these areas. As of 1992, the number of counties conducting experiments reached 720.

There have been long discussions about what funding method should be adopted for pension insurance in rural areas. In autumn 1994, it was finally decided that a method of combining contributions with subsidies should be adopted. Farmers are required to contribute on a monthly basis, and collectives offer the necessary subsidies to form pension insurance funds. The funds are divided into individual accounts and collective accounts. The accumulated amount in individual accounts is used by individuals for their retirement. The amount in collective accounts is used, among other things, to assist low-income retirees.

5. CONCLUSIONS

What emerges from the foregoing analysis and is confirmed by studies of other social security arrangements carried out by the author is that the variety of arrangements does mitigate the negative financial consequences of a universal system, but only at the cost of greatly reduced social protection. Even though the determinants of the viability of the Chinese system — which remains essentially a pay-as-you-go system — do include the rate of economic growth, the fact that growth has been very robust does not eliminate concerns brought about by other factors, such as demography, system dependency ratio, wage replacement rate etc.

It may be said that pension reform is at a crossroads in China, as indicated by a recent report by the World Bank (1994). An important observation regarding the Chinese case and noted in the Bank report deserves to be mentioned here: the one-child policy and the impressive improvements in health care are leading to a rapid ageing of China's population. Indeed, the old-age dependency ratio is expected to rise from the current level of one sixth to a level of one half in the year 2030. There is undoubtedly a pressing need for continuing and moving ahead with the reform of the present system. Any reform, however, will have to take into account the peculiarities of the Chinese system, some of which were discussed above, namely:

(a) Informal systems prevail in rural areas, where only 1 in 20 persons receives a formal pension;

(b) Urban workers have pensions based on a pay-as-you-go system at the enterprise level, which restricts mobility;

(c)   Wage replacement rates are 75 per cent of the average urban wage, but pensions are not indexed;

(d)   Pensions are tied to wages earned during the last year of work, evasion is high and costs are soaring;

(e)   Pension-pooling arrangements among enterprises exist in more than 2100 cites and counties;

(f)   There have been successful programmes to help the needy old.

Because of the high rate of growth, a move to a fully funded system could be contemplated, perhaps with a centralized fund management as exists in Singapore. A tax framework for voluntary employer-sponsored plans is also called for. The contributory pension programme for rural workers is small and will take time to reach most rural areas.

In any event, it would seem that the current variety of arrangements is a feature that any reform of the social security system in China should preserve if the system is to be sustained.

REFERENCES

China Statistical Yearbook. Beijing. Various issues.
China Labour Yearbook 1990 (1991). Beijing: China Labour Press.
China's Population: Problems and Prospects (1991). Beijing: New World Press.
Chow, Nelson W. S. (1988). T*he Administration and Financing of Social Security in China*. Hong Kong: Centre for Asian Studies of the University of Hong Kong.
International Labour Office (1984). *Introduction to Social Security*. Geneva.
The Labour Law of the People's Republic of China (1994). Beijing: China Labour Press.
Reform of Labour, Wage and Social Insurance 1991 (1992). Beijing: China Labour Press.
Reform of Labour, Wage and Social Insurance 1992 (1993). Beijing: China Labour Press.
Wenruo, Hou (1993). *Theory and Practice of Social Security*. Beijing: China Labour Press.
_____ (1994). *Contemporary Social Security System of China*. Beijing: China Economic Press.
_____ (1995). The variety of social security arrangements in China. Paper presented at a social security seminar, Nova University, Lisbon.
World Bank (1990). *China: Reforming Social Security in a Socialist Economy*. Washington, D.C.
_____ (1994). *Averting the Old Age Crisis*. Washington, D.C.

ANNEX

List of participants at a seminar on Sustaining Social Security organized by the Department of Economic and Social Information and Policy Analysis of the United Nations Secretariat and the Universidade Nova De Lisboa
(Lisbon, 26-28 April 1995)

Maria Auguzstinovics
Professor
Budapest University of Economics

Jorge Braga de Macedo
Associate Professor
Universidade Nova de Lisboa

René Cortázar
Research Economist
Corporación de Investigaciones Económicas para América Latina
Santiago

Ana Luiza Cortez
Economic Affairs Officer
Microeconomic and Social Analysis Division
Department for Economic and Social Information and Policy Analysis
United Nations Secretariat

Kodjo Evlo
Senior Lecturer
Université du Bénin
Lomé

Colin Gillion
Director, Social Security Department
International Labour Office
Geneva

Jean de Kervasdoué
Président Directeur Général, Compagnie Française de Gestion de Santé
Boulogne-Billancourt
France

Ian Kinniburgh
Chief, Office of the Under-Secretary-General
Department for Economic and Social Information and Policy Analysis
United Nations Secretariat

Diogo de Lucena
Professor
Universidade Nova de Lisboa

Po-Hi Pak
Director
Korea Institute for Social Information and Research
Seoul

Valentin Shetnin
Professor
Diplomatic Academy
Moscow

Lars Söderström
Professor of Economics
University of Göteborg

Geedreck Uswatte-Aratchi
Chief, Development Analysis Branch
Microeconomic and Social Analysis Division
Department for Economic and Social Information and Policy Analysis
United Nations Secretariat

Hou Wenruo
Director, Social Security Institute
Professor, Labour and Personnel College
People's University of China
Beijing